INSIGHT
GUIDES

Rajasthan

Edited by Samuel Israel and Toby Sinclair
Executive Editor: Bikram Grewal
Directed and Designed by Hans Höfer

APA
PUBLICATIONS

RaJasthan

First Edition (2nd Reprint)
© **1991 APA PUBLICATIONS (HK) LTD**
All Rights Reserved
Printed in Singapore by Höfer Press Pte. Ltd

ABOUT THIS BOOK

as an expert on tourism, Hans Höfer was convinced that, rich as Rajasthan was in places of tourist interest, only a fraction of its potential had been presented to the foreign tourist, and it was necessary to help the traveler break out of the routine of the commercialized conducted tour.

The editorial team consisting of **Samuel Israel** and **Bikram Grewal**, was joined by **Toby Sinclair**, a travel, wildlife and adventure tourism specialist. In addition to his editorial contribution, Sinclair has written several of the aritcles, contributed photograhs and the Travel Tips section at the end of this volume.

Aditya Patankar who was commissioned to take a number of photographs for this guide, has been a chronic traveler since his youth. His photographs have appeared in a number of Indian publications and in 1984, he was commissioned to do the photography for *Lives of Indian Princes* by Charles Allen.

Writers of varied backgrounds have contributed to this volume. Some were chosen for their knowledge and experience, and others for their close physical and emotional links with the places they write about.

Dr. Kamala Seshan, geographer on the staff of the National Council of Educational Research and Training, New Delhi, introduces the reader to the varied landscape of what some might think is a drab, desert land, with no typography to speak of. Her description of the land's often harsh and seemingly unfavorable geography is the background in which the ways of life of its people have evolved and can be understood – including, in seeming paradox, their colorful lifestyle, art, dance and drama.

Professor Harbans Mukhia, as a specialist in medieval Indian history at Delhi's Jawaharlal Nehru University, is right in his element when drawing together the dominant traits and complexities of the history of a region which till recently, was split into a score and more princely states, a region where war had been endemic for a thousand years.

Rajasthan *today*, on the other hand, has, very appropriately, been covered by a senior political journalist based in Jaipur – **Milap Chand Dandia**. Dandia represents *The Telegraph*, a Calcutta daily, and *Sunday*, a leading national political weekly belonging to the same group. He is editor and publisher of a year-book on Rajasthan, the first handy reference volume on the state.

P.C. Mathur of the Department of Political Science, University of Rajasthan, is the author of numerous reserch papers and the book *Social Basis of Indian Politics*. His survey of the varied groups who, with the minority Rajputs, constitute the population of Rajasthan, goes beyond its bare demography into the area of socio-political roles and interactions.

Jyoti Jafa, a former member of the Indian Foreign Service, is a freelance writer on political, travel and cutural themes, She has also written novels, screenplays for major U.S. networks, and commentaries for documentary films. Born a Rathor – a member of the ruling family of the former Bikaner State – her knowlege of Bikaner and its neighborhood is personal and intimate.

Jaipur and Jodhpur (and their environs) have been covered by British travel writer **Louise Nicholson**, author of the popular *India in Luxury*. A student of history and art, Nicholson's first visit to India was on her honeymoon. Her experience as a leader of

Israel   *Grewal*   *Sinclair*   *Seshan*   *Mukhia*

British and American tourist groups in India makes her contributions to this guide eminently practial ones.

Shail Mayaram, a political scientist, writes for the press on history, women's issues, wildlife and environment, and cultural subjects. She is the convenor of the Alwar Regional Chapter of the Indian National Trust for Art and Cultural Heritage (INTACH), which makes her an authoritative writer on this city and its surroundings.

As co-authors of *Rajasthan, The Painted Walls of Shekhavati*, **Francis Wacziarg** and **Aman Nath** were obvious choices for the article on Shekhavati. They have spent years studying the area, its history and the way of life of its people.

Shalini Saran is a freelance writer/photographer on places of historical interest, peoples, crafts, and lifestyles. Her writings and photographs have been published widely in travel and art magazines.

For Kota, again, the writer is one born and bred in the tradition of the erstwhile princely state. **M.K. Brijraj Singh** of the former ruling family, for some time a member of parliament, is a wildlife conservatinist and photographer. He writes on the basis of close knowledge of and identification with his subject. As head of the Brijraj Bhawan Palace Hotel, Kota, he has a professional interest in the tourist atttraction of the Kota area which he brings fully to bear in his contribution. Brijraj Singh is deeply interested in and knowlegeable concerning art and his work. *The Kingdom that was Kotah* has been described as "a positive contribution to Indian art history".

Indi Rana who contributes on Mewar, is active in a number of fields, from planning, writing, designing and producing books for children, to research on and design of aids in developmental communication at all levels.

Uma Anand brings years of experience to her contributions to *Rajasthan* – experience as an editor, broadcaster, actress, commentator, newspaper reporter, journalist, writer of books for children and the Indian Tourist Development Corporation's *Guide to Rajasthan*. For the past 15 years, she has also edited *Sangeek Natak*, Journal of the Performing Arts of the Indian Sangeek Natak (music and theater) Akademie, New Delhi.

Dr. Geeti Sen who contributes on Rajput painting, is an art historian who has made a special study of the Indian "miniature" tradition. Dr. Sen is currently Associated Professor in the School of Art and Aesthetics, Jawaharlal Nehru University, New Delhi.

The famed crafts of Rajasthan are competently covered by **Laila Tyabji**, a designer specializing in textiles and handicrafts, who is also active in graphic and theater set design and exhibition displays. She is currently consultant on Indian Crafts for the Metropolitan Museum of Art, New York.

There are many others to whom thanks are due for assistance in the course of preparation for this guide. **Surit Mitra** of Dass Media Pte. Ltd.; **Dr. Sarah Isreal**, **Dr. Shobita Punja** and **Jessy Mathew**.

Others who helped in various ways too numerous to mention are **Elizabeth Abraham, Bhim Singh, Divyabhanusing, Kesri Singh** of Mandawa Castle, **Ashish Madan Shgun Mohan**, of Special Expeditions, **Tripti Pandey, Naomi Medows, Manju Patankar**, the staff of **Rajasthan Tours, Lakshmi Sinclair, Oliver Sinclair**, and **Maharaj** and **Rani Sultan Singh**.

–Apa Publications

Mathur   *Jafa*   *Nicholson*   *Mayaram*   *Rana*

CONTENTS

MAPS

TRAVEL TIPS

PALACES, FORTS, PEOPLE

Rajasthan is sometimes presented as an enormous site on which forts, palaces and gardens, the relics of an erstwhile princely order have been frozen for the benefit of posterity and the tourist—as if in a mammoth open-air museum. A museum which offers not only the sights but, also for a price, living experience of some of the splendor and way of life of royalty—staying in their palaces-turned-hotels and even traveling as they did, till as recently as the 1930s, in special personal trains and coaches, the royal "saloon."

Rajasthan is all this and much, much more—a mosaic of landscape and terrain, each of singular beauty, whether it is the dunes of the desert, or the craggy, forested hills on which the formidable Ranthambore fortress perches, in the midst of what is today one of India's best wildlife parks, or the lake-studded environs of Udaipur.

The people of Rajasthan are perhaps the most colorful in a land of color—their history, religion, music and dance, arts and crafts remain vibrantly alive and active—and are presented here in all their variety and ways.

As one of the contributors to this volume puts it, Rajasthan is very much part of progressive, developing, modernizing India, but nowhere else in the country does the long, continuous past so pervasively press on the present as it does in modern Rajasthan. This, perhaps, is the secret of its charm.

THE LANDSCAPE

Rajasthan is separated from the Ganga basin by the watershed of the Aravalli mountains which bend from the northeast to the southwest because of a deep fault which displaced these mountains some 765 miles (1,225 km) in the central portion to 190 miles (300 km) in its eastern portion near Delhi.

The typical topographical regions into which Rajasthan's 132,152 sq. miles (342,274 sq. km) can be divided are the northeastern hill tract, the Vindhyan plateau extensions in the southeast, the basins of the Chappan and Banas, the Aravalli backbone, the Shekhavati uplands in the northwest and the Luni basin of the southwest, merging into the large area on the west—the desert which occupies some 82,000 sq. miles (213,000 sq. km).

Travel across this varied landscape usually begins from the east since the gateway to Rajasthan is from Delhi which lies in the Jaipur-Delhi saddle between Rajasthan and the Ganga plain.

Entering here, from Delhi, one encounters the northeastern hilly tract. Some 2,200 feet (670 m) high, the hills near Alwar are a lofty threshold to the plains below. Here the Aravallis have elevated plains and high valleys between quartzite ridges.

The northeastern hilly tracts open out into the eastern plains of the Banas and Chappan rivers which lie between the highland plateau of the Hardoti on the east and the Aravalli range and Bhorat plateau on the west.

Known as the Mewar plains to the north and the Chappan plains to the east, this stretch from Jaipur, through Tonk and Bhilwara, up to Udaipur is of hard rock, usually speckled granite. The rocks here have been cut and carried away for ages for carvings, and the silver, lead and zinc deposits from Zawar for making the beautiful jewelry worn here. The Banas and Chappan rivers flow east from the Aravalli watershed and their western tributaries flow from the Vindhyan plateau.

Farther south is the tribal belt along the Mahi river's tributaries. A land of hills and deep valleys, an area which is deeply eroded and hence so different from the gneissic plain of Mewar. Here separate hillocks stand on a rough uneven land covered with scanty forests of sal.

East of these plains, almost shielding Rajasthan from southern India stand the sentinels—the Vindhya ranges, known here as the (Haraouti) Hardoti plateau. This area is drained by the river Chambal. Southwards, a sharp scarp overlooks the Bundelkhand area of Madhya Pradesh. Formed by the bending of the Aravallis by a mighty thrust from the southern plateau is this *pathar* or stony upland of the Kota-Bundi area near Banswara and Pratapgarh. It is here that the Deccan lava lands meets the folded Aravalli ranges, connecting the peninsula to the mainland.

West of the plains of the Chappan and Banas are the Aravalli hills where the massive quartzites mix with metamorphic rocks of an earlier period to produce a stepped arrangement of the landscape, like a hand fan, from the Bhorat plateau near Udaipur, 4,000 feet (1,225 m) high till the northeastern highlands.

The southern hilly region of Rajasthan has conical hills, rugged slopes and sheer vertical scarps, and on the plains are hummocky dunes with exposed, now smooth, sides of granite rock.

The areas near Ajmer have extensions of the Aravallis and granites of every hue are found here. Looking back from here to the Banas-Chappan plains through the pass, which is the passage to the east of Rajasthan, rising on each side of the pass are peaks of reddish granite on blue micaceous slate. Beyond here is a quick ascent through prickly-pear country across to the desert plains.

West of the Aravallis, before entering the Marusthali, or the great desert, is the desert margin. The plains of the river Luni, the Shekhavati region, and, in the north, the saddle between Jaipur and Jodhpur, with the Ghaggar plain, is a desert land with several salt lakes.

The Shekhavati area, because of the low broken hills of the Aravallis in the north, affords a doorway into the desert. The wind gaps here invite the dusts of the desert eastwards, even into the plains of the Banas river. This lake country has the Sambhar, Didwani and Degana lakes which collect the rare rain water in the monsoons and, in the dry weather, become mere muddy pools.

South of here the land has many dry rivers, the largest being the Luni, which gets its waters from the tiny rivulets that run off the Aravalli hills. This river rises at the Ana Sagar at Pushkar near Ajmer and with its few tributaries flows into a briny swamp in the Rann of Kutch. A river in the desert bringing sweet water to the driest parts of Rajasthan, the Luni has thick deposits of sand in its channel and the water courses become a mere trickle in summer. The land has steep slopes and large areas of open alluvial plains. Between the river courses are uplands of hard granite and rhyolite. The thick deposits of sand make the area seem like a floating carpet with many

even seams of lignite and coal are seen. These were formed only 60 million years ago. This explains why the desert in India is so different from the other great deserts of the world, in that it was a flourishing principality.

The land is neither barren nor uninhabited; it is covered with bushes and shrubs and even small trees. It is a great sandy tract with no streams and few rocks that protrude above the lower land now covered with sand, seeming to be immobile sand dunes. The grasses on these dunes

bumps.

Rajasthan's Marusthali is a unique desert. The evidence of fossils of plants found in the rocks of Jaisalmer and Barmer and the now stone forests of what were once trees, of the Barmer sandstone, tell of the time when the sea covered this land.

The limestone of Jaisalmer has many fossils which have left their mark on dark colored limestones. The jasper rock found here was much used in the floral decorations of the Mughals. South, in Palana,

Preceding pages: Maharaja of Pratapgarh's sword; a day's work; Pushkar Fair; Pushkar Lake; watchful eyes; young girl, traffic policeman. Above, camel herd.

grow in clumps, indicating the availability of water just beneath the sandy soil. This desert is a rearing ground for camels, buffaloes and cows which are known for their strength and size. They are bred mainly in the Rathi and Tharparkar areas. These areas of Rajasthan, a desert in the heart of India, supported a mixture of kingdoms and tribal settlements, each with a distinctive personality. The differences in the landscape, the variety of minerals, of trees, and the isolation of one part of this desert from the others accounts for the singularity even in the crafts from wood carvings to fine embroidery on camel leather, from silver filigree to groundglass *meenakari* jewelry.

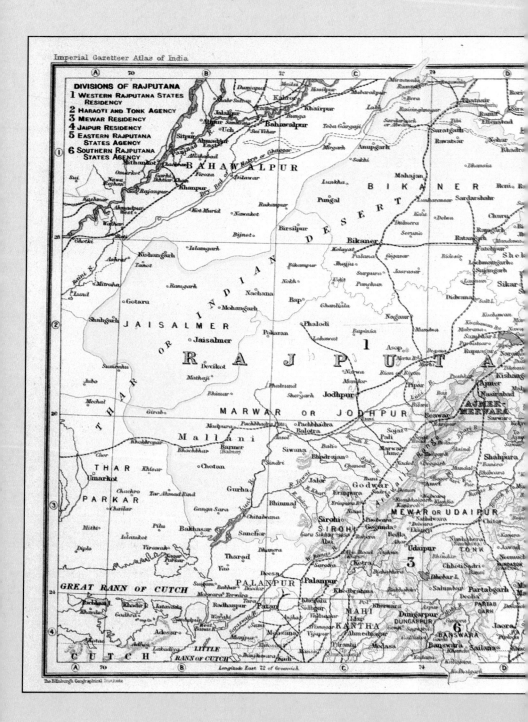

DIVISIONS OF RAJPUTANA
1 WESTERN RAJPUTANA STATES
  RESIDENCY
2 HAROTI AND TONK AGENCY
3 MEWAR RESIDENCY
4 JAIPUR RESIDENCY
5 EASTERN RAJPUTANA
  STATES AGENCY
6 SOUTHERN RAJPUTANA
  STATES AGENCY

Plate **36**.

Ajmer, previously the seat of a Mughal governor, became the base of a British resident.

Rajasthan lies between 22° and 30° north latitude and 69° and 78° east longitude, in the track of the Arabian Sea branch of the south-west monsoon. The Aravallis and, in the south-east, the plateau of Hardoti being the only highlands, they channel the monsoons coming from Kathiawar and stop the drier eastern flow, creating a desert in the west.

The area of Malwa, a tableland extending up to the Vindhyas, is covered with green forests on black lava country because of the rain from the monsoons. West of the Aravallis, beyond the desert margin, where the Luni flows over sandy channels, is the land of saline lakes in the north and dunes in the southwest. Here the summers are hot and with the slightest showers the white salt encrusted saline marshes become muddy.

The winters that follow the monsoons are coldest at about 54°F (12°C) in the northeastern hill tract and the Shekhavati and Ghaggar plains. Most of the desert, the Banas basin and across the Vindhyan plateau is warmer, about 57°F (14°C) and southern Rajasthan, which is most of the Bhorat plateau and the lava plains, is above 61°F (16°C).

The wetter parts east and south-east of the Aravallis have taller trees than the drier west. The south and eastern parts between 885 feet (270 m) and 2,530 feet (770 m) has the axlewood (*Anogeissus Pendula*), dhokra and dhak (*Butea monosperma*) forests.

The Banas basin and northwards to the northeastern hilly tracts have mesquite or **salai** (*Boswellia serrata*) forests. The wetter regions with red and yellow alluvial soils support this tall tree which is used for making packing-cases.

Traveling westwards across the Shekhavati and the Godwar tract, the rainfall decreases and so do the khejra (*prosopis*) forests. Grasses which are tall and yellow fill the patches between the amla trees (*Emblica officinalis*) with their yellow blossoms. This land with the pipal (*Ficus religiosa*) marks a boundary with the desert. Deserts, though thought to be treeless, here have a wide variety of trees, the most common being the babul (*Acacia nilotica*) and the khejra, often found cracking the hard rock surface.

In these deserts, in the heat of summer and in the cold of winter, the air is dry and, in the early mornings, in the midst of the desert plain, one can see phantom towers and arches, groves and domes, reflected on the glowing surface of the plains which vanish with the onset of the afternoon.

HISTORY WRAPPED IN LEGEND'S COLORS

Rajasthan is a land where life in all its aspects comes emblazoned in the brightest of colors. When the sun sets, the desert sands aflame every dawn and dusk, the camel rider derives all the hues of his headgear from it and the desert woman fashions her garment in imitation of nature's primordial color scheme. The desert-dweller's emotions too are fashioned in similar basic natural colors: superhuman valor, inviolable sanctity of the pledged word, an overwhelming presence of the sense of honor in life's every deed, including cheerful courting of death in its defense. It is these attitudes that have made Rajasthan a land where each historical episode is so wrapped in legend that any attempt to segregate the two takes away some part of the truth from each; for the legends too are often no less of historical occurrences than the stuff which mundane history recounts.

Geographically, Rajasthan comprises two distinct regions divided by the Aravalli range running southwest to northeast, its last low ridge spilling into Delhi. Marwar, Jaisalmer and Bikaner are situated in the western and northern parts which are marked by aridity of shifting sandhills, the major portion of the Thar desert. The other side of the divide boasts of dense forests and fertile irrigated valleys which support the historic cities of Udaipur and Jaipur.

Even western and northern Rajasthan were not always desert. Evidence suggests that elephants had once made this part of the land their habitat; surely then it must have abounded in dense forests where elephants feel most at home. It is in a relatively recent geological time-scale, over the past three to four millennia, that ecological changes have replaced forests with sand-dunes and the elephant with the camel.

In the historical time-scale, civilization came to Rajasthan before the rest of India. If Harappa culture (2500 B.C. – 1700 B.C.) is the general starting point of the evolution of Indian civilization, Rajasthan takes precedence, for some of its pre-Harappa locales, such as Kalibangan, bear evidence of fully-developed plowed agriculture and therefore of sedentary, organized society.

Preceding pages: Shiv and Parvati (shown as a Rajput princess) on a Shekhavati window shutter. Left, Terra-cotta bangle and C.3000 B.C. pottery shards at Kalibangan near Ganganagar.

There are, too, several sites of the Harappa period in Rajasthan pointing to the integration of the region with that impressive stage of human civilization in this part of the world.

The history of early Rajasthan is frequently the history of tribal republics or at best oligarchical socio-political systems. Often at war with one another and with neighboring kingdoms, tribal organizations were to give way to the process of internal stratification as well as the impact of external aggression during the centuries immediately preceding and succeeding the birth of Christ. Nor could the region remain immune to the influence of the rise and fall of vast empires in north India. Thus, even if Rajasthan was not integrated with the Gupta empire of the 4th and 5th century A.D., it still bore a subordinate status to the empire.

Warrior Clans: The most spectacular development in Rajasthan's history was to take place from about the sixth and seventh centuries, when some new warrior clans were formed. These, the Rajputs as they came to be called, were to dominate the history of the region as that of many other parts of the country for centuries to come. Their origin, whether indigenous or foreign, has long aroused heated controversy among historians. National pride no doubt played a part in influencing those who insisted that they were wholly Indian. However, more recently, the general consensus is that the Rajput clans owe their origin to both indigenous and foreign sources. Among the former were some groups then having low social status but possessed of the skills and determination of warriors. In the given social set-up the two were mutually incompatible: no one too low in the social hierarchy could be allowed to take up the profession of a higher caste, especially the honorable profession of arms. The conflict was resolved through a mythical purification by fire ritual which enabled the warriors to abandon their old low status and assume one that corresponded to their profession. To further reinforce their new-found glory, they were assigned mythical descent from the sun and the moon.

Also purified were descendants of foreign invaders, such as the Huns, who had stayed behind and were indigenized. They too were given the caste status of a warrior. Thus were Rajput clans formed, originating in diverse sources but evolving into relatively homogeneous social, if not political, groups. In calling themselves Rajputs (corruption of *rajputras*, sons of princes), they segregated themselves from the rest of society by their social status, profession and the code of honor.

The polities that the Rajputs established comprised two levels. At the lower level were the subject people, paying revenue to the rulers and enjoying their protection. At the higher level, political power in all its ramifications was shared by a kind of large kin group in which the Rajputs of a particular clan were entitled to conventional, if unequal, shares within the territo-

ry of that clan. The term they used for this collective sharing of power was "brotherhood." However, the clan did not forever remain a homogeneous unit; often there were conflicts within the "brotherhood" leading to splits which in turn established new "brotherhoods" seeking either to wrest territories from their erstwhile cousins or conquering new lands. The Rajputs, never exceeding seven to eight percent of Rajasthan's population, remained the ruling class *par excellence* for centuries.

As the Rajput clans evolved, they divided up a great deal of Rajasthan and the neighboring regions among themselves. By about the 12th century some of the leading houses of Rajput rulers had fairly long

traditions of chivalry behind them. The house of the Chauhans, ruling from Ajmer, was the foremost among them, though several others at Ranthambore, Chittor, etc. also counted for a great deal. Needless to say, in situations of constant warfare and intrigue, the relative importance of these houses kept changing over the centuries.

Muslim Invaders: Prithviraj Chauhan of Ajmer was the first great Rajput ruler to come into conflict with Muslim invaders from Central Asia towards the end of the 12th century. In the first battle between them, the Rajput chief inflicted a humiliating defeat on his adversary, Muhammad Ghori. Ghori, described by an eminent Indian historian as "a hero of three stupendous defeats," possessed one cardinal

quality: he never allowed himself to be crushed by a reverse on the field of battle. Thus, as the Chauhan warrior had begun to imagine that the last had been seen of Ghori on Indian soil, the Turk reappeared on the field of the earlier battle to avenge his defeat, in fact as much as in spirit.

Prithviraj Chauhan's defeat in 1191 is the subject of an immortal epic composed two centuries later. The poet, exempt from restrictive demands of the historian's discipline, wove a beautiful story around the grand event, a story that has all the elements of medieval drama-chivalry, treachery, war, sex and, of course, nemesis. In this epic, Prithviraj is left alone in the field of battle, his fellow Rajputs keeping aloof. History, however, records that several of the Rajput houses in the Chauhan neighborhood did come to his aid, though one Rajput ruler, Jai Chand, whose daughter Prithviraj is supposed to have kidnapped, much to her delight, continued to watch from the sidelines. He too was to lose to Ghori a little later. In folklore, Jai Chand has become the archetype of a traitor, much as Judas has in Christianity.

Prithviraj Chauhan's defeat gave the Turks from Turkistan in Central Asia a foothold in India, a foothold that was to expand into a vast empire which lasted well over five-and-a-half centuries. Ghori had ruled over his Indian territories from Ghazni in Afghanistan, capital of his impressive empire that included territories in almost all directions. In 1206, Ghori died and his viceroy in India, one of his thousand slaves, whom he fondly used to refer to as his thousand sons, became an independent ruler. Thus was established the Delhi Sultanate, the empire that ruled from Delhi, which lasted 320 years, giving way in 1526 to another invader from Central Asia, Babur, founder of the Mughal empire.

The Delhi Sultanate and the Rajput States: With the establishment of the Delhi Sultanate, the history of the Rajput states of Rajasthan became inseparably intertwined with it. For over 350 years, relations between them were characterized by incessant conflict.

The Turks who had migrated to India from Central Asian regions via Afghanistan and had established their kingdom here had initially adopted a two-pronged strategy. They had incorporated into their state structure the established administrative machinery as well as the existing administrative personnel at the village level. Thus, in the vast countryside, the administrative system remained in the hands of the Hindus. At the higher echelons of this administrative system, and especially in the towns, the new rulers helped themselves to positions of power. At the same time, in the first flush of victory, the Turks showed extreme reluctance to share political power even with fellow Muslims who happened to be non-Turks. However, acute tensions generated by keeping the power base extremely narrow led to a situation in which, a century after the establishment of the

Sultanate, the floodgates were thrown open, the old policy given up, and entry into the highest offices was permitted to persons without respectable lineage. This newfound generosity of the rulers to men of mean social order left one 14th century aristocratic historian aghast, for he could not reconcile himself to the fact that among those elevated to high offices before his own eyes were "a singer, a washerman . . . and all those rogues."

However, the Rajputs comprised a rival ruling class with an even longer tradition than that of the Turks of the exercise of power and the use of arms. Their territories, individually or even collectively, were not very large compared to the Sultanate; their resources were not as large either, but their determination was, for it was based above all on their sense of honor that brooked no surrender to anyone. Conflict between the Rajput states and the Sultans of Delhi was therefore hardly avoidable.

Conflict was unavoidable for another reason too. Starting with the region around Delhi as its nucleus, the Delhi Sultanate, right from its inception, was on an expansion spree made possible by a centrally controlled, highly organized and efficient army, and a nobility that had often to fend for itself. Within a half-century of the Sultanate's inception, most of north and east India had been brought under its dominance. Further expansion was possible only southward and westward.

The west beckoned the sultans for another reason, for it was here that the enormously rich region of Gujarat was located. The very fertile soil of Gujarat was particularly conducive to the cultivation of a very valuable crop, namely cotton. Besides, the port town of Cambay opened India to the sea trade with West Asia. But the route from the northern plains, the heartland of the Delhi Sultanate, to Gujarat lay via Rajasthan. To secure this route permanently, the sultans had to conquer Rajasthan.

Many were the battles fought between several sultans and rulers of Rajput houses. In a couple of them, the sultans suffered defeats; in most cases they inflicted defeats on the Rajputs.

However, power was so divided between the two sides that, if the Rajputs failed to throw the sultans out of India, the sultans failed to crush individual Rajput houses, even if they defeated them in battles. Thus it was that for over 350 years the two remained locked in conflict without either side obtaining a decisive advantage

Left, Prithviraj Chauhan and Princess Sangukta, Alwar Museum. Right, hallucinating opium addicts pursuing imaginary rat, Mehrangarh Museum, Jodhpur.

over the other.

Three and a half centuries was by any standards a long enough stretch of time for realization to dawn that a lasting solution to the problem had to be found outside the battlefield—through mutual accommodation. The initiative in working out such a political solution was taken by the Mughal emperor Akbar who ruled over most of India from 1556 to 1605.

Akbar and the Rajputs: Akbar had inherited from his dashing grandfather, Babur, an admirable cultured bearing and a breadth of vision that treated religious and other diversity with tolerance and understanding. From his somewhat mediocre father, Humayun, Akbar, at the age of 13, inherited a tiny piece of territory as his "empire"; a half century later he bequeathed on his son Jahangir the Mughal empire that spanned the land from Kabul in Afghanistan in the west to Bengal in the east and Kashmir in the north to the northern parts of south India. Perhaps more important than the vast territory was an administrative structure and a set of strategic policies that gave the Mughal empire an unexcelled grandeur and a long term stability that made it the longest-lasting empire in Indian history.

Akbar's tolerance of religious diversity was translated from a personal attitude to a state policy. He achieved this by, on the one hand, reducing every single group, including his own kinsmen, in the higher echelons of the ruling class to a small minority, and, on the other, by incorporating ever newer local elements at those levels. With each group being a small minority, none would be in a position to dictate to the rest. Mutual tolerance thus got rooted in the day-to-day functioning of the imperial polity.

Among the new elements invited by Akbar into the high precincts of the imperial nobility were the Rajputs. The emperor realized that nothing could lend the nascent empire a firmer rooting in the soil than the support of the local ruling class; he would not have been unaware of the fact that a clash of arms with that class could only prove futile. Perhaps on an experimental basis, he sought an alliance with what was then a minor Rajput house situated at Amber (or Amer), near Jaipur, by proposing marriage to a princess of the family and offering high positions in the imperial hierarchy to some of the princes.

Akbar was willing to accommodate the many susceptibilities of the Rajputs: although they had to surrender their kingdom to the empire, in return for which they would obtain often disproportionately high positions and incomes, he would refrain from depriving them of the ancestral capital of the kingdom, on which they tended to stake a great deal of prestige. And the princess who became Akbar's queen did not have to give up her religion and convert to Islam. In fact, Hindu temples were constructed within the palace precincts to facilitate worship by the princesses in their own tradition.

Man Singh–Rajput Prince, Mughal Noble: Among the most illustrious sons of the house of Amber was Man Singh, whose father's sister was the first Rajput princess to become Akbar's queen. Man Singh was to become the most trusted of Akbar's nobles, fighting battles on his behalf in almost every corner of the fast-expanding empire. Mainly thanks to his loyalty to the empire and his capable generalship, the Amber house acquired a lustre that still lends the family a halo in the region. The descendants of the ruling family at Jaipur trace their lineage to him, though the city of Jaipur was founded by another eminent son of the family, Raja Jai Singh, in the first half of the 18th century.

Encouraged by the early success of a new policy towards the Rajputs, Akbar extended it to several other Rajput houses, entering into matrimonial alliances with them and elevating them to high positions. The Rajputs, who had until then been a provincial ruling class, came to be integrated with a larger imperial ruling class; on the other hand they gave the empire support, in place of earlier hostility. Within this broad framework of alliance, Akbar was willing to accommodate predilections of individual Rajput houses. Thus when the ruler of Ranthambhore made it a condition that no princess of the family would be demanded in marriage by the emperor, the latter found the condition perfectly reasonable. However, defiance of imperial authority by a Rajput house was something he was unwilling to brook and he was prepared to go to any lengths to enforce obedience.

Valiant Chittor: The most glowing case of such defiance was that of Rana Pratap Singh of Chittor, where a ruler with relatively small resources stood up to an enormously superior imperial power with super-human determination. He and his family, including very young children, often had to starve for days and sleep on straw spread out on the ground under the open sky; but the more they suffered, the more their will was steeled. Even in a region where war was the chief preoccupation of the rulers and the code of chivalry the sole guiding spirit, Chittor's case stands out to inspire awe in the heart of admirer and critic alike. Indeed Chittor's extremely colorful story goes back long into the past, far beyond Rana Pratap's time, and is therefore worth narrating in some detail.

The rulers of the Mewar region of Rajasthan, with Chittor as its capital, claimed descent from the Sun, following the ritual purification of which we have spoken earlier. The state of Mewar came under the dominance of the Rajputs sometime early in the eighth century. The history of the next six centuries is filled with some pleasant and other unpleasant events in

in a mirror, to guard her chastity from being defiled by his direct carnal glance. Alauddin laid an ambush and was able to get hold of Padmini's husband whom he promised to release in exchange for her. Seeing no way out, the condition was agreed to and Padmini set out in a veiled palanquin accompanied by "maids" in seven hundred similarly veiled palanquins. In reality the "maids" were some of the bravest Rajput men. At an opportune moment they threw the veils away and pounced on Alauddin's men, putting them to flight and rescuing their master, Padmini's husband.

Alauddin, however, was not one to forget the slight. He attacked the fort again with a massive force. The defenders soon real-

which some capable and other not-so-capable rulers were involved.

At the beginning of the 14th century the reigning Sultan of Delhi, Alauddin Khalji, besieged Chittor, apparently to seize the superlatively beautiful queen, Padmini, the lotus-faced, word of whose beauty had reached his ears. Not coming near success, he professed a desire to retire from Chittor if only he were allowed a glimpse of the queen. The Rajputs took the sultan at his word but agreed to let him look at her only

Above, unusual sight of three princesses and a prince playing polo. Mehrangarh Museum, Jodhpur.

ized the hopelessness of their situation. Any other group of warriors would have sued for peace; but in the Rajput code of honor there was nothing more disreputable than shying away from battle, no matter what the situation. Thus they decided on a ritual that has marked the end of many a desperate battle in Rajasthan's history: *Johar*. Whenever Rajput warriors realized the inevitability of defeat, they prepared to join battle and perish fighting, to the last man. Since concern for the chastity of their womenfolk was an inseparable part of their code of honor, the women would dress themselves in all their finery and sacrifice themselves in a huge fire so that their men would not have them on their minds while fighting.

their last battle. This was the *johar* which led to the destruction of Padmini and Rattan Singh, her husband, and the defeat of Chittor, though the kingdom was to become independent again in a short while.

The story, even on the face of it, has clear marks of a legend. It is of course true that Sultan Alauddin Khalji conquered Chittor early in the 14th century; the performance of *johar* is also a fact in Chittor's history as in the history of several other princely states of Rajasthan. It is difficult, however, to vouch for the historical existence of Padmini; at any rate, Alauddin Khalji, who was one of the greatest conquerors in the history of medieval India, giving himself the title of the second Alexander, was not known to be moved by feminine beauty in and Rana Pratap Singh.

Kumbha, who ruled for a half century between 1419 and 1468 was a capable and ambitious warrior who in 1440 defeated the combined forces of the powerful rulers of Gujarat and Malwa (now in Madhya Pradesh). The Victory Tower at Chittor was built by him in celebration of his feat. At a slightly later stage, Kumbha and his erstwhile adversary, Mahmud Khalji, ruler of Malwa joined hands against the imperial forces and crushed them in battle. But then the imperial forces by this time had retained nothing of their grandeur or strength and therefore defeating them was not a real feat.

Rana Kumbha is entitled to considerable fame on another count too, on account of

his desire for the territorial expansion of his empire. Indeed, the story of Padmini and Khalji was the creation of a mid-16th-century poet. Ever since this work of poetry was composed in the popular language of the region, the story has become so much a part of folklore that its historicity seems to have become an irrelevant issue.

Three Who Ruled Chittor: But the subsequent history of Chittor, in many ways far more romantic than the story of Padmini and Alauddin, is nonetheless more firmly grounded in historical fact.

The 15th and 16th centuries saw Mewar scale high peaks of glory in war under the generalship and determination of three eminent rulers: Rana Kumbha, Rana Sanga one of his wives, Mira Bai, herself a Rajput princess of some stature. Mira Bai is one of the most eminent of medieval Indian poets who devoted herself to the love and worship of Krishna, one of the two chief deities of the Hindus. In singing of her love for krishna, which incresingly filled her entire being, she caused considerable scandal in contemporary society where upper class women were required to lead a completely secluded life under the protection of their husbands and where value placed on sexual chastity was so high that it was unthinkable for a woman to express desire for the company of a man other than her husband, even if this other man were a god!

Rana Kumbha had defeated several of his adversaries, strengthened his kingdom militarily by building as many as 32 new forts to bring the total in the kingdom to 84, and erected some grand temples in his half-century-long reign. The reign was terminated in 1468 with his assassination by none other than his son, known to history by the epithet "the assassin."

Over the next couple of generations, Chittor's royal chronicle is marked by filial discord. There was, however, a code of honor that governed even this discord. Prithviraj, one of three brothers and a claimant to the throne, was in perpetual conflict with his uncle, Surajmal, and they had fought battles with each other. After one hard day's fight, the nephew visited his uncle's camp where he was cordially received and offered dinner. While taking leave, Prithviraj expressed the hope that the final battle between them might be fought the next morning. "Yes, my child," replied the uncle, "come early tomorrow."

In terms of material prosperity as well as political stability, Mewar reached its zenith in the first quarter of the 16th century during the reign of Rana Sanga who ruled from 1508 to 1527. Sanga was frequently at war with his near and distant neighbors, including the Delhi Sultanate. Among the prizes of war he was prone to displaying, with some well-earned pride, were the loss of one eye, an arm and 80 wounds all over his person. However, within the boundaries of his kingdom, Sanga proved an able administrator who felt concerned at the need to provide security and prosperity to his subjects.

In 1526 Babur had fought the first major battle with the Sultan of Delhi, Ibrahim Lodi, and defeated him. Thus Mughal rule in India began. However, 1527 was to be the truly decisive year, in Babur's Indian enterprise. In that year the Mughal forces came face to face with those of Rana Sanga who stood at the head of an immense army to which most Rajput princes, tributaries of the Rana, had sent levies. Confronted by such a formidable force, and the awesome reputation of the Rana as a warrior, Babur was utterly unsure of the outcome of the impending battle. He resorted to various tantrums, like taking a holy oath never to touch liquor again (an oath he soon forgot), and holding forth on the virtues of being a

soldier to his army, he joined battle with some nervousness. However, the vast mass of Rana Sanga's army ultimately proved a handicap in the face of Babur's agile and much better equipped soldiers, and his far superior tactics. In a pithy statement, Babur was to sum up his observation of the Rajput war psychology. "The Rajputs," he remarked, "know how to die in a battle but not how to win it."

In the long chain of outstanding warriors whose exploits fill the chronicles of Mewar state, there were occasional weak links too. Among them was Udai Singh, after whom the city of Udaipur is named. But, of course, the same Udai Singh was to father Rana Pratap who, even in his political failure to defend his territory against the

imperial onslaught, has filled every little vacant space in the land of Mewar with memories of superhuman achievements of the unbending spirit of defiance.

In 1567, when Akbar laid seige to Chittor, Udai Singh was its ruler. Defenses began to break one after another. It was this desperation that created two of the immortal heroes in Mewar's history, both still in their teens. Their names: Jaimal and Phatta. Phatta's father, ruler of a small state in Rajasthan, had taken on himself the charge of defending one side of the fort and had fallen in the effort. Phatta's mother, witnessing her husband's death, commanded her son to assume charge and, lest his young heart demur, she armed herself and her son's young bride and plunged into the battle. Phatta followed the two women. On seeing Akbar's cannon balls knocking holes in the fort wall, Phatta placed himself in one of them in a vain attempt to prevent the wall from crumbling. It did not take Akbar's guns long to blow him to smithereens. Jaimal too died a reckless death at Akbar's own hands. The two names became hallowed in folk memory in Rajasthan; Akbar too acknowledged the bravery of his foes by erecting statues of them at the gates of the imperial fort at Agra.

Akbar had conquered Chittor; but he had not defeated Rana Pratap. Pratap succeeded to the titles of his house in 1572. The thought of recovering Chittor became obsessive, though he lacked the material

several encounters Pratap had with the Mughal army, the most celebrated one at Haldighati (the Yellow Valley) in 1576, had another great Rajput warrior, Man Singh, at the head of the Mughal force. Pratap lost this battle, as he did several others.

The Mughals kept pursuing Pratap through the varied landscape of Rajasthan; and Pratap kept eluding or fighting them. He had taken a vow never to sleep on a proper bed, nor live in a mansion, nor eat off metal utensils until Chittor had been recovered. The thought of doing this through a political compromise with Akbar repelled him. He did not succeed in his life's mission, but his last wish, expressed as he lay dying in the wilds in 1597, was that no mansion ever be built nor any creature

resources to do so. He was able to inspire fierce loyalty among his followers, even when they were not Rajputs. The Bhil tribe of Rajasthan, aboriginal inhabitants of the region, whose chief had been treacherously murdered by the founder of the Mewar state, nonetheless stuck to Pratap through all his travails. Bhamashah, a great merchant of the region, placed all his enormous wealth at Pratap's disposal in his fight against the Mughals. And of course Rajput leaders, like the sons of Jaimal and Phatta, fought by his side in his quarter-century-long struggle which brought him, his family and his partisans untold privation. The severity of the situation also led some Rajput princes to desert him. Among the

comfort be provided to his successors until they had Chittor back in their hands.

Treachery Too: If Rana Pratap is an extreme example of the Rajputs' fierce dedication to honor, there were others who were far more down-to-earth in their pursuit of personal ambition and did not allow any scruple to interfere with it. Thus, early in the 14th century Hammira, ruler of Ranthambore, was deserted by the chief commander of his army, who joined forces with his enemy, Alauddin Khalji, at a time when Khalji had laid siege to his fort. Some of the other Rajput generals too defected to the opposite side at that critical juncture. On the other hand, some Muslim soldiers, fighting on Hammira's side stuck with him to the end. One of them, wounded in the battle and captured alive, was asked by Khalji what he would do if his wounds were healed by the sultan's doctors. His reply was unhesitating: he would try to slay Khalji and place the dead Rajput's son on the throne. The sultan had him trampled to death under an elephant's feet, but gave him an honorable burial. Hammira's betrayers were trampled to death too by the Sultan's orders, for he never rewarded treachery which he had himself engineered.

Even Rana Pratap failed to command the unreserved loyalty of all his followers; among those who could not stand the enormous strain of his unrelenting struggle against the Mughals was his own brother who went over to Akbar; in return he was given the title of Rana and the capital of Mewar.

Barring Rana Pratap, Akbar had been able to come to terms with almost all Rajput rulers who were enlisted as high officials of the empire and many of whom gave their daughters in marriage to the emperor and his princes. Henceforth, alliance with the Rajputs was to become one of the cornerstones of imperial polity. Rajputs became, in the words of a Mughal historian, "at once the props and the ornaments of the (Mughal) throne."

Decline: Henceforth, while an individual Mughal emperor might be more inclined towards one rather than another Rajput house, and might bestow some extra favors on it, the imperial polity always functioned with the support of the Rajputs as a whole. There was an eruption of considerable tension between the empire and one eminent Rajput house in the last quarter of the 17th century. The last of the "great Mughals," Aurangzeb, plagued by one crisis after another, had sought respite from his troubles by accommodating the newly emerging Maratha troublemakers, led by their great leader, Shivaji, at the expense of the Rajputs. This was openly resented by the Jodhpur ruler, but the rest of the Rajputs continued to side with the Mughal empire.

So strong had the interdependence between the Mughal empire and the Rajputs become that Rajput strength, which had stubbornly defied the Delhi Sultans for three-and-a-half long centuries, declined with the decline of the empire in the 18th century. As in the case of the empire's other former as well as existing territories, the subjects and lands of the Rajputs were plundered at will by the rising new power, the Marathas. Several Rajput rulers secured their territories against such plunder by paying large sums in annual ransom to them.

Gone also were the rainbow colors of chivalry which had lent so much charm to the everyday life of Rajput ruling families. Once the overarching Mughal suzerainty was withdrawn, subterranean clan and family tensions rose to the surface within each kingdom and, of course, between them. These were routine, petty tensions, devoid of the grandeur that had marked the relationship between the Rajput states and the great empires of the Sultans of Delhi and the Mughals. Bit by bit, some Rajput states—among them Mewar with its glorious history of defiance of imperial might for over three centuries—were reduced to a situation where they became protectorates first of the Marathas and later of the British power in India. Mewar paid six million rupees to the Marathas for protection and Marwar a similar amount.

Enter the British: The British, along with several European traders, had come to India in the early 17th century, attracted by the fame of Indian cotton and silk textiles and indigo. Their trading interests had expanded over the centuries; with that had grown their attempts to get a foothold in the faction-ridden polity. They had brought with them gold and silver to pay for the goods purchased here; but their own value in the local factional policies was enhanced as they brought into the field the most advanced firearms of the time and superior military organization. They were in great demand in the various states that had emerged following the disintegration of the Mughal empire.

In the ensuing free-for-all, the British and the French were the chief competitors for establishing their hold over the whole of India; in the end, the British emerged the victors though the French and the Portuguese continued to hold on to bits of Indian territory.

The British started on their path of conquest from around the mid-18th century in Bengal; by the end of the century, their presence could also be felt far away in the west and the south.

Out in the west, the British initially let the Marathas plunder the Rajput states by assuming a posture of strict neutrality in the mutual relations of Indian states. This, of necessity, made the Rajputs turn to them for protection. The British too did not

Left, the Maharawal Udai Singhji of Durgapur sitting in durbar during the festival of Gangar. Wall paintings from the Juna Mahal Palace, Dungarpur.

desire the annihilation of the Rajput states at Maratha's hands, for it was clear to them that, along with them, the Marathas were to be the chief contenders for imperial status in India and it would therefore be politic to preserve a force essentially hostile to the Marathas. The preservation was achieved through a series of treaties between the British Indian Government and various Rajput states. Through them, each side was obliged to treat the friends and enemies of the other as its own friends and enemies, and to render assistance to each other in the event of a threat to either side's security.

Unequal Treaties: The conclusion of a treaty did not fully assure assistance in meeting external threats, for often a treaty was violated on one flimsy pretext or

The pretentiousness of this claim was recognized even by Lord Hastings, Governor-General of India, in 1814: "In our treaties with them (the princes) we recognize them as independent sovereigns. Then we send a Resident to their courts. Instead of acting in the character of an ambassador, he assumes the functions of a director; interferes in all their private concerns; countenances refractory subjects against them; and makes the most ostentatious exhibition of his authority..."

By the second decade of the 19th century the British had buried the Maratha pretensions to imperial status forever, in turn firmly establishing their own claim to it. Thus, although the chief trouble-makers, as far as the Rajput states were concerned, had

another by either side if compliance did not suit it. But, on the whole, the treaties were far more advantageous to the British than to the Indian states. Following these alliances, the British authority in the states came to be represented by Residents—one in each major state. The Resident would soon emerge as the real center of power in the state, freely interfering with the internal administration and justifying it with the claim that a properly administered people would secure the prince against any internal disturbance or external threat. "The exclusive aim of our interference," wrote one such Resident, "was the welfare of the Rajput princes and the tranquility of their country."

by and large been silenced, the states were no longer in a position to snap their ties with the mighty new power. Indeed, in a pathetic sight, at an assembly of the princes at Ajmer in 1832, they complained against each other to the British Governor-General and each pleaded for his personal intervention to sort out their petty disputes. They even sought his protection against robbers operating in their own territories.

Even as the British Residents interfered with the internal affairs of the states, the Imperial Government wisely refrained from depriving any Rajput ruler or his successor of his throne or his title, unlike in some other states in north and central India where such deprivation had taken place on a considerable scale. The wisdom of this policy was demonstrated in 1857 when almost all the Rajput princes came rushing to the aid of the beleaguered British, and greeted the crushing of the great rebellion of that historic year in India with unconcealed glee.

Not all of Rajasthan was, however, on the side of the British in that fateful year. As in the core of the rebellious territory, intermediate levels of landed aristocracy combined with the civilian population to participate in the uprising in Rajasthan and, for a brief while, met with impressive successes. Often, the common soldiers sent to suppress the rebels expressed their solidarity with them by downing their guns, though their active participation in the uprising

tration, justice, education, etc. came to be introduced in Rajasthan as in the rest of the country. Initially some of these met with resistance, but this was followed by slow acceptance.

Towards the end of the 19th century and the beginning of the 20th, a kind of ferment was agitating the minds of the educated Indian elite, and the ferment was percolating down to the mass of the people. Its main thrust was one of hostility to British rule, initially moderate but growing intense with the passage of time. The Governors-General realized that the princes might prove their chief bastion of support in the face of growing popular agitation. In 1903 Lord Curzon organized the Delhi Durbar, an assembly of princes at Delhi organized

remained rather marginal.

Immediately following the rebellion of 1857, the princes were engulfed in a sort of euphoria, for Queen Victoria as she declared herself Empress of India, had assured the princes that the earlier reckless policy of depriving them of their thrones was being given up for good. The declaration was reassuring even in Rajasthan where the former policy had hardly ever been implemented. However, gradually, various British institutions of adminis-

Left, Maharawal Udai Singhji of Dungapur in conversation with General Sir David Ochterlony; first British Resident of Rajputana, Juna Mahal Palace, Dungarpur. Above, wall painting.

to gauge the extent of support for the British Government; the response should have pleased him. Most princes demonstrated an almost excessive eagerness to attend and reiterate their loyalty to their imperial masters.

The Princes and the Nationalist Movement: In 1905 Curzon partitioned Bengal into two provinces, professedly for reasons of administrative convenience, but actually to separate the Muslim-dominated east Bengal from Hindu-dominated west Bengal in the hope of creating dissensions between them. This single act electrified the mass of the people in Bengal and galvanized it into a most uncompromising hostility to the Government. The effect of the agitation naturally spilled over into the entire sub-continent. In Rajasthan, the princes, more loyal to Britain than the British themselves, took several steps to prevent the spread of the agitation (termed "sedition" by them) to Rajasthan: severe restrictions were placed on the press as far as the news of any agitation anywhere was concerned. All the restrictions notwithstanding, Rajasthan did not remain untouched by some of the revolutionary activity that had engulfed much of India at this time.

The outbreak of the First World War witnessed the princes in Rajasthan similarly eager to demonstrate their loyalty to Britain. "What orders has my King for me and my troops?" asked one prince.

The character of India's freedom move-between the two sides. "The Chamber will be a means by which the bonds of mutual understanding will be strengthened and the growing identity of interests between the Indian States and the rest of the Empire will be fostered and developed," declared the Duke of Connaught as he inaugurated the Chamber at Delhi. He referred to the princes fondly as "the pillars of the Empire." The Chamber was thus visualized as a bulwark against popular agitation.

The rest of the story of Rajasthan conforms closely to the story of the freedom movement in India as a whole. The combined force of the British Government and the Indian princes failed to thwart the tidal surge of the people's movement everywhere demanding independence. The movement

ment began to change considerably after the peace treaty of 1919. While British imperialism remained the chief target of hostility, especially in the territories directly under British administration, attention also began to be directed towards the problems of the subjects of the princely states. Consequently, agitations were launched to secure redress of their grievances. Clearly the agitations in the princely states were double-edged: they were directed both against the Indian princes and their British masters.

This necessarily threw the two even closer into each other's arms. A Chamber of Princes was established with the professed objective of achieving closer cooperation found various manifestations: sometimes depending solely on non-violence under the leadership of Gandhi; at other times taking to revolutionary violence and paying for it with life itself. When independence came to India, all the different strands of the movement found their fulfilment.

In Independent India: Aug 15, 1947 brought to India both independence and partition of the country into India and Pakistan. The princes had been given the option of either merging with India or Pakistan or retaining their autonomy. Since the partition had taken place on the basis of the Hindu-Muslim divide, it would have been unthinkable for the Hindu princes of Rajasthan to throw in their lot with Pakistan. Long history and common religious identity with the rest of India made it inevitable that they should merge with India. The new Government of independent India made it attractive to the princes to opt for India by providing them with a generous Privy Purse and several other privileges; on the other hand it was made clear to them that the Indian Government did not quite like the idea of several independent states scattered all over its conventionally bounded territory. Rajasthan princes were quick to grasp the messages and one by one came over to merge with India. They enjoyed the Privy Purse and other privileges until 1970 when Indira Gandhi abolished them through an Act of Parliament in a bid to appeal to

Art and Commerce: In two other spheres of human activity, the cultural and the economic, Rajasthan has made impressive contributions. In the late medieval era, during the 18th and early 19th centuries, a specific Rajasthan school of painting branched out of the parent Mughal school and earned considerable recognition for itself. The chief center of the Rajasthan school was at Bundi.

In the economy, the term "Marwari" (from Marwar, around Jodhpur) has come to signify a trader *par excellence*. The Marwaris had spread themselves out from west to east as carriers of trade from the 17th century onwards and by the 18th century had established themselves well enough to be the chief bankers and money-

populist sentiment on the eve of elections.

Although Rajasthan has, with the rest of India, changed a great deal over the past four decades, almost every Rajasthani citizen will enthusiastically recite the history, often generously mixed with a great deal of charming fantasy, of almost every fort, palace or former ruling family from its beginning to the present day, to any willing listener. Nothing brings a brighter gleam to a Rajasthani's eye than telling stories to a captive audience.

Left, the infant Maharaja of Jaisalmer surrounded by his courtiers. Above, Maharaja Col. Sawai Bhawani Singhji of Jaipur receiving *nazar* **on his birthday in the Zenana Deodi.**

lenders to provincial governments such as the one in Bengal. The tradition continues to this day, though of course their business now includes industrial manufacture.

While the Marwaris have taken to modern commercial activity with great zeal, their social and family life remains steeped in tradition. The sense of family solidarity remains extremely strong with them and their children's marriages are mostly arranged by the parents. It is still rare to come across a non-vegetarian Marwari. The Marwaris represent an outstanding case where old social traditions and social structures can successfully be merged with modern technology and business practice.

RAJASTHAN TODAY

Rajasthan is a recent addition to the political map of India. Prior to March 31, 1949, when 22 princely states were merged into one single administrative unit, the area used to be identified as Rajputana—the land of the Rajputs or rajas. Each state was ruled by a prince, one of whose ancestors had entered into a subordinate treaty relationship with the British Crown. The princes governed their subjects through *jaghirdars* (land-holding nobility). With the end of British rule in the Indian subcontinent on August 15, 1947, the British government relinquished its paramountcy over the princely Indian states, leaving them technically free of all central control since there had been no formal transfer of paramountcy to the successor governments of India and Pakistan. This posed great danger to India's national integrity, already sorely damaged by partition. Efforts were therefore made to get the princes to accept the suzerainty of the Government of independent India as they had that of the British Government of India.

The task was a formidable one, as most of the princes were reluctant to accept any arrangement that curtailed or deprived them of their privileges and denied them absolute power over their territories and subjects, and they strived hard to retain them. The then Maharaja of Jodhpur even went to the extent of thinking in terms of signing a treaty with Pakistan. But this came to light and was effectively stalled before any damage could be done. However, under the strong, dynamic and far-sighted leadership of the then Indian Home Minister, Sardar Vallabhbhai Patel, the seemingly impossible task was accomplished peacefully. Rajputana's princes accepted the sovereignty of the Government of India. They even agreed to surrender their rights to rule their individual states, paving the way for their integration into a single administrative unit. In lieu of this, the princes were granted certain privileges and a fixed annual privy purse in cash.

Creation of a State: Rajasthan, as a single, unified administrative unit, was created in stages. The first step in this direction was

the formation of the Matsya Union, integrating the princely states of Alwar, Bharatpur, Dholpur and Karauli. Within a week of this, on March 25, 1948, another merger took place forming the Rajasthan Union, unifying the states of Banswara, Bundi, Dungarpur, Jhalawar, Kishangarh, Shahpura and Tonk. Three days later the Maharana of Mewar also agreed to merge Mewar State into the Rajasthan Union, which was renamed the United State of Rajasthan. The process of merger and unification of the princely states of Rajpu-

tana was completed on March 30, 1949, with the rulers of all the remaining states of the region, including the princes of Jaipur, Jodhpur, Jaisalmer, Bikaner and Kota, signing the instrument of integration. With this, a new unified state, the United State of Greater Rajasthan, was formed, comprising the area of these states, the Matsya Union and the United State of Rajasthan. The Maharana of Mewar was appointed Maharajpramukh and the Maharaja of Jaipur Rajpramukh of the United State of Greater Rajasthan.

A single administrative unit for the whole of the geographical area of Rajputana, however, came into existence only on November 1, 1956, when the centrally

Preceding pages: family transport. Left, Rajasthan villages are now electrified. Above, the Shriram Fertilizer Plant, Kota.

administered state of Ajmer was also merged with the United State of Greater Rajasthan. After this merger, the state was renamed Rajasthan. Simultaneously, the offices of the Maharajpramukh and Rajpramukh were abolished and, as for the other states of the Indian Union, a governor was appointed in Rajasthan also. After about a decade, the privileges and privy purses granted to the ex-rulers and their families were withdrawn by amending the constitution.

The Days of the Jaghirdars: Under British protection, many princes and their *jaghirdars* had severely oppressed their people. Civil liberties and other elementary human rights were denied them. The will of the rulers was law. In some cases, even the

the public was in many cases limited to collection of land revenue with little concern for welfare activities. As a result, Rajasthan, which was once the home of a flourishing and prosperous civilization, gradually became the most economically backward part of the country.

There were, of course, some honorable exceptions both among individual princes and states. For example, in Bikaner and Jaipur, some attention was paid to the people's welfare. In the late 1940s, these princely states, and some others, made a move towards providing some form of civil rights by inducting public representatives into their governments. However, full democracy in Rajasthan dawned only in 1952, when, for the first time, a Vidhan

possession of a typewriter was considered a crime. The farmers were entirely at the mercy of the *jaghirdars* or rajas who enjoyed unlimited and unchallenged authority and power. People in authority often treated the common people as slaves. Wearing one's shoes in the presence of a *jaghirdar* was prohibited, and at the time of the death of the raja or *jaghirdar*, all the people in the state or *jaghir* were compulsorily clean-shaved head and face.

Before the advent of British rule, the princes and *jaghirdars* had spent most of their time on wars, personal feuds and palace conspiracies, and during British rule, indulging in personal whims, luxuries and extravaganzas. Their relationship with

Sabha (Legislative Assembly) was constituted on the basis of universal adult franchise.

Princely Influence: Many of the ex-rulers and *jaghirdars* found it difficult to reconcile themselves to their changed status. Some, under the leadership of the ruling Maharaja of Jodhpur, made a bid to regain power collectively through the ballot box in the elections to the first Vidhan Sabha. The fact that groups opposed to the Indian National Congress, (despite the poor past record of a number of princes) were able to capture 78 of the 160 seats, was a measure of the influence of the princes and *jaghirdars* even after they had ceased to exercise ruling powers. Some of this influence is to be attributed, no doubt, to fear of economic and other powers of reward and reprisal still meted out by the princes and *jaghirdars*. But for the premature death of the Maharaja of Jodhpur in an air crash, before the newly elected Vidhan Sabha could assemble, the formation of a government by the Congress party in Rajasthan would have been extremely difficult. With the untimely removal of the leader around whom the opposition to the Congress party could have rallied, the alliance of ex-princes and their supporters fell apart and Rajasthan's first democratically elected government was formed by the Congress party.

Some ex-princes continued to retain and even enhanced their popularity amongst potential electoral threat to the nationally dominant Congress party. However, despite the hard reality of the persisting influence of members of many an ex-royal family, barring a brief interregnum of less than three years, when the Janata Party came to power on a near all-India scale in 1977, the state has been under Congress party rule ever since 1952.

As the years went by, the ex-princes adjusted themselves to the new situation and their new circumstances. The services of some of them were utilized by the Government of India on diplomatic assignments; the younger generation competed with other young Indians for higher government services and executive and managerial positions in commerce and industry.

the people in their states.

When Maharani (now Rajmata or Queen Mother) Gayatri Devi of Jaipur entered politics and contested the Lok Sabha (Parliamentary) election from the Jaipur constituency in 1962, she smashed all electoral records by winning the largest-ever lead over her nearest, Congress party, rival. She even rose to the position of Vice-President of the right-wing Swatantra Party at the national level.

The ex-princes in Rajasthan thus posed a

Left and above, the conversion of royal residences into hotels has created an infrastructure for tourism and brought employment to many areas.ʼ

Many of Rajasthan's ex-princes turned to business and some even converted their palaces into luxury hotels. The Rambagh Palace Hotel, Jaipur, the Lake Palace Hotel, Udaipur, the Umaid Bhawan Palace Hotel, Jodhpur, and the Lalgarh Palace Hotel, Bikaner, are all former palaces of *maharajas*. These palace hotels now attract tourists from all over the world.

Though the princely order came to an end in 1949, the *jaghirdari* system persisted for quite some time. After Rajasthan's first elected government came to power in 1952, steps were initiated to free the peasants from the clutches of the *jaghirdars*. A law abolishing *jaghirs* was enacted and far-reaching land reforms were gradually introduced. To further strengthen the democratic system, the administration of the local affairs of the villages was handed over to elected *panchayats* (village councils) in 1959.

Then and Now: At the time of the formation of Rajasthan the state had a population of 15.2 million. Only 8.95 percent of the people were literate. Facilities for education were meager. The first university of the state was set up in 1947, the year of Indian Independence. The only medical college of the state had only just started. Medical facilities were available at only the capital towns of eight erstwhile states. Piped water supply was available in only five towns, and wells or village tanks were the only source of drinking water elsewhere. In the arid

low level of development was discernible in almost every sphere of public life.

The scene has since changed considerably. The state's annual budget of expenditure which was Rs 172.3 million ($14.33 million) in 1951–52, went up to Rs 25 billion ($2.08 billion) in 1986–87. The state's first five year plan (1951–56) had an outlay of Rs 675 million ($56.25 million). The outlay for the seventh five-year plan (1986) has risen to Rs 30 billion ($2.5 billion). A sum of Rs 11.12 billion ($926.7 million) was spent on the power sector till the end of the sixth five-year plan (1985). As a result, from the corridors of royal palaces, electricity has even reached small hamlets. The power availability in the state has now gone up to over 1800 MW. The farmers

region, at many places, the water table for tube wells was as low as one hundred meters. Even today, in many villages, at least one member of the family spends her/his whole working life in meeting the family's water needs. Major irrigation schemes, except for the Ganga Canal in Bikaner, were conspicuous by their absence. Only an area of a little more than 740,000 acres (300,000 hectares) was irrigated. Electricity was then a luxury used only to illuminate royal palaces. At the time of the formation of Rajasthan, total power generation in the state was only 8 MW. Only a couple of big industrial units existed and the total number of registered small-scale units was unbelievably low at 16. The

irrigate their fields from electrically energized wells and drawing water with the help of bullocks for agricultural purposes is fast becoming a thing of the past. Over 24,000 villages in the state now have piped water supply.

Many major irrigation projects like those on the Chambal in Kota, the Mahi in Banswara and the Indira Gandhi Nahar (canal) were launched and commissioned after the formation of Rajasthan. Irrigation facilities are now available for an area of over 9.88 million acres (4 million hectares). This has given a big boost to agricultural activity in this once desert state of India.

The waters of the Himalaya, carried to Rajasthan by the Indira Gandhi Nahar have lent an entirely new look to the topography of the northwestern part of Rajasthan. The resounding silence of the shifting sand dunes has been largely replaced by the murmur of water flowing in the canals irrigating paddy fields or fruit orchards. In 1951, total foodgrain production in the state was 3.9 million tonnes; only 149,000 bales of cotton were grown; oilseeds production was less than 200,000 tonnes. With the creation of additional irrigation facilities and adoption of modern farm practices by the farmers, foodgrain production has now risen beyond 10 million tonnes per annum. Oilseeds and cotton production has also shot up to 80,000 tonnes and 600,000 bales respectively. However, despite this progress, the state is still largely dependent on the mercy of the Rain God for a good crop. The monsoon has been behaving in a most erratic manner for the last few years, resulting in recurring droughts which have severely handicapped further progress.

Industrial Development: The industrial scene too has witnessed a rapid transformation. Over the years more than 175 industrial areas have been developed and almost every part of the state is now humming with one industrial activity or another. Today the number of registered small-scale industries in the state is more than 125,000. Over 200 large and medium-sized industries are in production. According to a rough estimate, about Rs. 20 billion ($1.7 million) stands invested in the industrial sector in the state. During the last 35 years, the state has become a major producer of synthetic yarn, cement, zinc, copper, trucks, tractors, scooters, tyre cords, tyres and tubes, railway wagons, ball-bearings, water and power meters, automobile parts, instrumentations, electrical equipment, and electronic goods like copper foils, copper-clad laminates, television sets, picture tubes, milk testers, wireless equipment, etc.

Education: Educational facilities, which were earlier limited to major towns, have now reached many villages. The state today has five universities, five medical colleges, five engineering colleges, a number of *ayurvedic* (Indian system of medicine) colleges, a National Institute of Ayurvedic Research, a large number of industrial training centers and colleges of general education. The literacy rate has also gone

The daily passenger train from Nawalgarh to Jaipur serves as a convenient milk run for local farmers.

up to 24.1 percent. Medical facilities have been expanded.

Development has thus been substantial, but its impact has been greatly neutralized by the great increase in population.

The Indira Gandhi Nahar: When the idea of quenching the thirst of the great Thar Desert with the waters of the Himalayas was mooted, most people did not take it seriously. They dismissed it as an engineer's day-dream which would never come true. But what was considered impossible yesterday, is a reality today. Himalayan water is now flowing among the sand dunes of Thar through the Indira Gandhi Nahar (IGN).

Of the various projects initiated after the formation of Rajasthan, the Rajasthan Canal Project (it was renamed after the death of Prime Minister Mrs Indira Gandhi), was the most ambitious. It was scheduled to be implemented in two stages. In the first stage, a network of canals to irrigate sandy lands in the districts of Ganganagar and Bikaner were excavated and pressed into service, providing irrigation facilities to about 1.73 million acres (70,000 hectares) in Ganganagar and Bikaner. With the completion of work on the main canal, Himalayan waters reached Mohangarh in Jaisalmer district on January 1, 1987.

The topography and economy of areas under the command of canals so far constructed have undergone a tremendous transformation. Land which did not grow even a blade of grass earlier, today produces wheat, paddy, groundnut, cotton, sugarcane, oil-seeds, pulses and other commercial crops in abundance. Ganganagar district, which was once dependent on others for its food requirements, has now become the granary of Rajasthan.

For the people in the northwestern parts of the state, the advent of the IGN signified the virtual reappearance of the fabled Saraswati which once flowed here. Some call it *Maru Ganga*, the Ganga of the desert. The 403-mile (649-km)-long IGN has the capacity to carry 18,500 cusecs of water. It takes off from the Harika Barrage in Punjab. Passing through the states of Punjab and Haryana, the first 127 miles (204 km) of the canal serve as a feeder. The rest of its 276 miles (445 km) run almost parallel to the Pakistan border through the districts of Ganganagar and Bikaner to Mohangarh in Jaisalmer. A revised plan proposes to extend the canal to Gadra Road in Barmer district, extending the length of the canal by 84 miles (135 km).

THE PEOPLE OF RAJASTHAN

The Rajasthanis are a sturdy, cheerful lot, despite their ecological adversities and their long feudal history which, while it made Rajasthan a fascinating land of palaces and forts, left it with very low agricultural productivity and a near-total absence of modern industry till a few decades ago. Nevertheless no visitor to Rajasthan will fail to notice the extremely good physique of the average Rajasthani male and the (often veiled) beauty and colorful dress of the women, who seem to counter the dullness of the round-the-clock drudgery of their daily routine not only by the brightness of their garments but also in their music and dance and in the murals they paint on their walls.

It is not uncommon for large tracts of Rajasthan to face water, food and fodder scarcity for several consecutive years; even in years of normal rainfall, in many villages, women daily trudge several miles to fetch a head-load of water; yet the people have managed to evolve lifestyles which vibrate with hope, faith and cheerfulness.

Scattered Population: The ecological adversities responsible for continuous agricultural scarcities kept Rajasthan's population in check till the early 1920s but, since India became an independent country in 1947, the growth rate of Rajasthan's population has taken demographers as well as policy-makers by surprise. During the decade 1971-81, Jaipur, Rajasthan's capital and premier city, recorded the second-highest growth-rate amongst all urban centers in India, while Rajasthan's total population grew by 32.36 percent against the all-India average of 24.75 percent. Some districts of Rajasthan recorded even higher growth-rates, setting off alarm bells in many a corridor of power; but to those familiar with Rajasthan the growth-rates are not so menacing because the absolute population totals in these sprawling arid and semi-arid regions are still small and, given appropriate development investments in irrigation, agriculture and other infrastructural facilities, there is considerable scope for sustenance of much larger populations in most parts in Rajasthan.

Preceding pages: turbans provide insulation from the desert heat; a perfect Rajput beauty. Left, village elder. Above, shepherd boy.

According to the 1981 census, Rajasthan had a population of 34.1 million (up from 25.76 million in 1971 and 20.16 million in 1961), which constituted nearly five percent of the country's total population of 683 million. But Rajasthan occupies nearly 10 percent of India's total area, giving a very low spatial density of 100 persons per square kilometer with some districts having startlingly low densities—Jaisalmer six, Bikaner 31, and Barmer 39, for example. The people of Rajasthan thus inhabit a sparsely populated space, a factor which

shapes not only politico-administrative policies but also the rhythm of socio-cultural life, based as it is on long-distance communication and periodic congregations of people belonging to several villages. The latter gatherings have a ritual significance as well as great social salience, which extends even into the economic sphere as the people of rural Rajasthan are virtually forced by territorial ecology to make the bulk of their purchases at colorful fairs and *hats* (periodic, usually weekly, markets) organized at frequencies regulated by seasonal necessities. The fairs are usually also endowed with socio-religious significance.

The people of Rajasthan, then, occupy a large territory characterized by several techno-ecologic handicaps which have resulted in the persistence of substantial socio-economic backwardness reflected in the low per capita annual income in 1980–81 in Rajasthan (Rs 1,227) as compared to the all-India average (Rs 1,608). On the other hand, against the all-India average of 48.13 percent, only 33.76 percent of the people of Rajasthan are estimated to be living below the "poverty line" as defined by the Planning Commission. This is not a mere statistic; even a casual visitor to the villages and hamlets of Rajasthan will not have his sensibilities wounded by the sights and smells so characteristic of dire poverty and low levels of nutritional intake. Their staple foods, *jowar* and *bajra*, compare favorably with rice and wheat in nutritional

context of the internecine and external armed warfare its princes indulged in for nearly 10 centuries; it also makes Rajasthan a traveler's delight as in practically all its regions one can find urban amenities for rest and recreation, with as many as 10 cities (Jaipur, Jodhpur, Ajmer, Kota, Bikaner, Udaipur, Alwar, Bhilwara, Ganganagar and Bharatpur) topping the 100,000 mark in 1981.

However much one might admire the Rajasthani's will to overcome physiographic and techno-ecologic handicaps, one cannot close one's eyes to the region's abysmally low level of literacy (24.05 percent against 36.17 percent for the country as a whole in 1981). The rural female literacy rate for Rajasthan as a whole is as

value even though they are regarded as "coarse grains" by the sophisticated.

True, the people are still handicapped by low levels of per capita availability of social overheads like health care and education, as well as economic overheads (e.g. railways, roads, and electricity), but the material base of Rajasthan's economy is rich enough to enable the people to develop and sustain a life characterized by cultural creativity and mass participation in leisure festivities as any visitor to Jaipur can note while witnessing *teej* and *gangaur* processions in the heart of one of the 12 of India's million-plus cities. The durable nature of urbanization sustained by the people of Rajasthan is, indeed, remarkable in the

low as 5.41 percent; in touristically important districts like Jaisalmer and Barmer it is virtually non-existent (1.64 and 1.68 percent respectively). These low literacy levels are reflected in such social customs as child marriage and *sati* which persistent legislative and executive efforts have failed to eradicate. A newspaper report in 1986 estimated the number of child marriages in Rajasthan annually at 50,000. While this appears to be a substantial overestimate, there is no doubt that many are still "married" in their infancy with some marriages even being aranged, on a mutual-exchange basis, by potential parents while the partners are still in their mother's womb. Similarly, occasional cases of *sati* even now occur every year in Rajasthan and newly built magnificent memorials devoted to such *satis* are a common sight even though the government is committed to ending the practice.

Warrior-caste: Turning from the macro-structural to the micro-structural dimensions of the social system of Rajasthan, one cannot but begin by noting that the Rajputs constitute the social fulcrum of community life in Rajasthan. Some observers of the Indian social scene might be inclined to use the past tense in the previous sentence, but many a social scientist would agree with the thesis that a past stretching over nearly a thousand years cannot be expected to just vanish without traceable remnants and residues, short of a violent revolutionary

Indian Union and the gradual de-recognition of their special privileges and prerogatives, culminating in the dramatic abolition in 1970 of the privy purses of the ex-rulers of what the British called the Native States of India.

Who are the Rajputs? The available historical records do not appear to be sufficient to pierce the veil of romantic mythology which ascribes their origins to the *Agni-kula* ceremony performed by Brahmin priests at Mount Abu, which is the highest point along the Aravalli range of mountains in Rajasthan. Be that as it may, it appears safe to conclude that this consecration story only epitomizes the actual political role of the Rajputs in this part of India, namely, consolidating autonomous

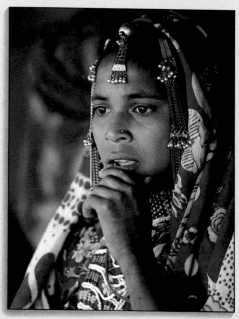

upheaval of a type which India's power-elite have been consciously trying to avoid, let alone advocating or advancing the cause of sudden and total social change. Although the Rajputs never constituted more than a tenth of the total population, they have commanded the heights of the polity and the society in Rajasthan for nearly a thousand years. The glorious innings of this brave and chivalrous warrior-caste is now coming to an end with the accession of the territories over which they ruled to the

Tribal and nomadic women are known for their love of silver jewelry.

princely states amidst the emergence of chaotic conditions in the wake of the decline of empires like that of Harsha in the sixth century and, later, fiercely resisting invasions and encroachments over their territories, by the Muslim (and Mughal) armies from within and without present-day India.

The political role of the Rajput rulers of the princely states of Rajasthan is borne out by the fact that, amongst the 22 princely states and chiefdoms which were merged into Rajasthan in a multi-phase consolidation between 1947 and 1950, as many as 19 had Rajput rulers. The more prominent among these were Bikaner, Jaipur, Jodhpur, Kota and Udaipur—the order is alphabetical because, even in modern Rajasthan, any other rank-ordering of these princely states is bound to arouse acrimonious debate. Super-sensitivities on this score have split the people's political psychology into a whole spectrum of hues, even though the economic and ecologic gradations between, say, Bikaner and Jodhpur, or between Udaipur and Kota, are minimal and are gradually becoming irrelevant with the growth and development of modern technologies of communication and transport.

Thanks to their glorious traditions which have nurtured deeply imprinted cultural patterns into the psyche of even non-Rajputs, ranging from Brahmin priests to Marwari traders and Adivasi tribes like the Meenas, the Rajputs of Rajasthan continue

lieu of their commitment to perform military service at the command of the *durbar*, the ruler. The Rajput *jaghirdars* were not, however, mere land-grantees of the *durbars*; all of them claimed kinship with the rulers whose ancestors their forefathers had helped in their territorial conquests and political consolidation.

The Rajputs of Rajasthan, thus, constituted a warrior aristocracy divided into a number of prominent clans, each of which regarded a princely state as its traditional patrimony, whose ruler was the social head of the clan besides being the political ruler. The princely state of Jaipur was thus ruled by the *Kachchwaha* Rajputs, the *Rathors* ruled in Jodhpur and Bikaner, the *Hadas* in Kota, and the *Sisodias* in Mewar

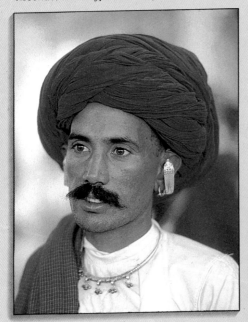 

to command the political support of a large section of the electorate on the occasion of elections to the legislative assemblies even though their traditional sources of material luxuries are vanishing. (There are, to be sure, people styling themselves "Rajputs" Rajasthan-based Rajputs they are, with some honorable exceptions, somehow different.)

The entire Rajput community of Rajasthan was, in fact, accustomed to a military existence. Their personal and family expenditure was met of out of the tax and non-tax revenues they were able to collect from the cultivators and other rural producers from the villages assigned to them as *jaghir*, in

(Udaipur).

For nearly a thousand years, these Rajput clans ruled, and virtually every generation of each Rajput family lost one or more members in armed warfare. Sometimes entire families perished at one stroke, men donning saffron robes and rushing out to meet attacking armies which enjoyed overwhelming superiority, and women performing *johar* by entering mass funeral pyres whose flames spurred on their menfolk to lay down their lives in defense of their land.

The advent of *Pax Britannica* in the early years of the 19th century signaled the virtual end of the Rajputs' fighting days, while the growing sophistication and technological modernization of warfare made their traditional attitudes redundant. True, most Rajputs had acquired some *jaghirdari* rights but, in actual practice, very few had bothered to learn the tricks of either estate administration or assets management which modern tax laws and commercial prudence demand. For nearly 150 years after the princely states signed "Treaties of Friendship" with the British, the Rajput *durbars* and *jaghirdars* were able to maintain a life of sumptuous luxury and ostentatious consumption, but their growing family budgets gradually became imbalanced as their subjects became increasingly conscious of their rights and refused to pay excessive taxes and non-tax levies. The spread of modern concepts of statutory

which only a few have tried to overcome by converting their palatial assets into modern hotels and motels. The long-term success of this strategy is still open to doubt, as very few Rajputs seem to possess the skills necessary for sound management of men, money and materials.

Priests and Scholars: Like the Rajputs, the Brahmins also constitute less than a tenth of the total population of Rajasthan but, unlike in most of the rest of India, they do not occupy the top rungs of the socio-political and socio-economic ladder although they do enjoy the ritual esteem which the Hindus traditionally accord to Brahmins as priests and scholars. In fact, if we are allowed to coin a phrase, Hinduism in Rajasthan has a distinctive profile which

taxation and separation of a ruler's personal income from public treasury receipts were climaxed by the statutory abolition of *jaghirdari* (1954) and princely privy purses (1970). True, some far-sighted Rajput *jaghirdars* and *durbars* did manage to play their cards well and were able to retain substantial land and other properties under their personal possession, but India's socialistic legislations are gnawing away at even such assets. These developments have placed the Rajput nobility in an economic crunch

Different styles of turban indicate the class, caste and region of the wearer.

can be described as "Rajput Hinduism" in contrast to the "Brahminical Hinduism" prevalent in other parts of India. This makes the people of Rajasthan much more heterodox as far as the classical norms and forms of Hinduism are concerned. On the one hand, this heterodoxy allowed the rural people to sustain many of their folk traditions woven round local deities and personages like *Pabuji*, *Ramdeoji*, *Tejaji*, *Gogaji* and *Jambhoji*, while, on the other hand, it enabled the princes to maintain cordiality towards Islam and its followers within their territories, even while indulging in virtually non-stop warfare against Muslim rulers over several centuries.

The Brahmins' failure to dominate the

courts of Rajput princes thus imparted a secular flavor to the social life of the people. At the time of India's partition in 1947, Muslims remained unmolested in Rajasthan. More recently, in November 1984, following Mrs Gandhi's assassination, not a single Sikh was killed in Rajasthan, even as anti-Sikh passions were raging in adjacent areas.

At the apex of Rajasthan's social pyramid, unlike the situation in most other parts of India, not only do two castes, the Rajputs and the Brahmins, vie for top honors, but these two groups have also to reckon with people belonging to several social strata who also enjoy elite status. In the economic sphere, the Marwaris of Rajasthan are well-known all over India for

even the economic handicaps of poverty and near-total ignorance of the tricks of the trade of commerce. Outside the Muslim-majority state of Jammu & Kashmir, Rajasthan was the first in the Indian Union to have a Muslim Chief Minister, while the Rajasthan unit of the erstwhile Jan Sangh, an all-India political party which was usually considered to be Hindu-oriented, had the distinction of being the first party in the state to field a Muslim for the state legislative elections.

As in other parts of India, Rajasthan's Muslims are mainly concentrated in the cities and bigger towns where their skills as artisans in dyeing, bangle-making, paper-making, etc. are in great demand. Nevertheless, a large number of Muslims also live

their trading skills, but what strikes a newcomer to Rajasthan even more forcefully is the fact that people belonging to such lowly castes as *Kayasthas* and *Charans* (traditionally a caste of minstrels) occupy prominent places in the public and private sectors while Jains (specially the Oswals amongst them) who constitute less than two percent of the total population, are conspicuous by their substantial presence in public service and education and also vie with the Marwaris in trade and other economic activities.

Muslims: Islam is the religion of about 10 percent of Rajasthan's population, and Muslims occupy a distinct place in its socio-political topography, overcoming

in the countryside, many forming distinct communities which are very nearly indistinguishable from the Hindus living in the same area, sharing with them as they do many life-cycle rituals and social customs. Many such communities (e.g. *Meos, Kayamkhanis* and *Cheetahs*) have been thus living in peaceful coexistence with their Hindu neighbors in several parts of Rajasthan for centuries. Of late, they have become the unwilling objects of a tug-of-war between Hindu revivalists and Muslim fundamentalists.

In southeast Rajasthan there is a subcommunity of Shi'ite Muslims, the Bohras, really an extension from the main homeland of the community in Gujarat. Like other Gujarati communities, the Bohras are a highly mercantile group doing extensive business in Bombay, Ahmedabad and Karachi (Pakistan) and numerous other centers in Western India. Though small in numbers, it is said that it was the electoral support of the Rajasthan Bohras that turned the balance in favor of former Chief Minister Mohan Lal Sukhadia and kept him in office for 17 years without a break.

Scheduled Tribes: According to the 1981 census, some 12.2 percent of Rajasthan's population belongs to the constitutional category of Scheduled Tribes. Discerning observers however feel that most Meenas, who constitute a sizable proportion of the total tribal population of 42 million, do not qualify on the basis of recorded history

percentage of Meenas were employed as watch-and-ward staff by the Jaipur *durbar* and his *jaghirdars*. Another significant chunk of Meenas became skilled agriculturists, cultivating substantial landholdings, thus making the entire Meena community rather well-off. However, they are taking maximum advantage of the special facilities available to Scheduled Tribes to improve their situation still further.

In contrast to the Meenas are the Bhils, the next largest Scheduled Tribe, most of whom live in the hilly forests of southwestern Rajasthan and, despite their high sociopolitical status on account of their military support to the Sisodia rulers of Mewar in general and Maharana Pratap in particular, even today eke out a miserable existence

as well as currently observable socioeconomic trends, to be included in a "Schedule" meant essentially, to identify groups requiring special assistance for their economic and educational development. Today's Meenas are, in fact, descendants of tribes which ruled over most of the later princely state of Jaipur before the Kachchwahas established their rule there nearly a thousand years ago. A Meena chief was always associated with the coronation ceremonies of Kachchwaha rulers and a sizable

bereft of the amenities of education, communications, transport and other benefits of economic modernization. So primitive is the Bhils' capacity to interact with the modernizing world and to assimilate the developmental benefits being directed at them under various plans and special subplans, that several well-meaning social activists advocate a policy of go-slow in the extension of techno-economic modernity to the Bhils of Dungarpur, Banswara, Udaipur and parts of Chittorgarh district.

The Bhils and Meenas account for roughly 50 and 40 percent of the total tribal population of Rajasthan. Of the rest, Garasias and Sahariyas constitute roughly three and one percent respectively. The tiny

Left, winowing *bajra*. Above, young city girls celebrating the Teej Festival.

63

community of Dangis are famous for their musical skills. The small tribe of Gaduliya Lohars have also become famous as no less a person than Jawaharlal Nehru took a personal interest in ensuring their settlement in fixed abodes and the abandonment of their nomadic life, whose beginnings their oral traditions ascribe to the days of the sack of the proud fort of Chittorgarh at the hands of Akbar nearly five hundred years ago.

While members of all these Scheduled Tribes, with the partial exception of the Bhils, are highly "visible" on the social scene in Rajasthan, systematic documentation of their customs, kinship-patterns and cultural beliefs has yet to be undertaken. They do not now suffer from any social

state, Chamars constituting 45 percent of the total.

Chamars are the traditional leatherworkers of India and suffer because of orthodox Hindu notions concerning purity and pollution but nevertheless occupy a higher social rank than Meghwals and Balais (who constitute roughly nine percent each of the total) whose traditional occupation involves the handling of animal carcasses and hides and skins.

All Scheduled Castes are, of course, ex-"untouchables" and still suffer several social disabilities in rural Rajasthan, but the deprivations inflicted on them are much less severe than those suffered by corresponding castes in, say, the neighboring ex-British-Indian territories of Uttar

stigma on account of their tribal way of life, except those tribes to which the British administrators applied the designation "criminal" or "notified." Although such appellations have been done away with in free India, yet, today, it is considered unsafe (even by police personnel) to go to villages where such Scheduled Tribes predominate.

Scheduled Castes: The Scheduled Caste population of Rajasthan (17 percent of the total) is larger than that of the Scheduled Tribes (12 percent). The categorization again is on the basis of backwardness and the need for special assistance and consideration. Rajasthan's Scheduled Caste population is scattered throughout the

Pradesh, Bihar and Madhya Pradesh, not to mention the southern states where even their shadow was regarded as polluting. The same observation applies to the Bhangis, the traditionally hereditary community of scavengers, who are, primarily, residents of towns and cities where the purity-pollution norms are bound to be more relaxed. Besides these major Scheduled Castes, Rajasthan is well known for such communities as Madaris, Naths, Bazigars and Bhands whose dance, dramatic and acrobatic performances still entertain the people.

A Pastoral People: Despite ecological limitations, agriculture and animal husbandry constitute the primary occupation of the bulk of the people of Rajasthan, with livestock management having been refined into a productive art to suit the arid and semi-arid lands. Rajasthan's geomorphological handicaps and hazards have, indeed, made its agriculturists more hardworking and the minimal vegetation has been skillfully exploited to sustain large herds of sheep, goats and camels. In conditions of low rainfall and high levels of evaporation and transpiration of moisture, the people of Rajasthan have evolved varieties of cattle, amongst the best in the country, well adapted to these conditions. In recent years, these ecologically-adapted packages of agriculture and animal husbandry are being threatened by new policies of agricultural development which have little relevance to the ecological specificities of

their sheep along circulatory migratory networks each year. The non-nomadic livestock farmers produce a great quantity of milk which is collected by public sector dairies for pasteurization and consumption as far away as Delhi.

Rajasthan produces nearly 40 percent of India's wool and a large number of people in rural Rajasthan are engaged in sheep husbandry. The introduction of modern technologies of agricultural production and inputs like irrigation and tractors, coupled with the absence of wool processing facilities in Rajasthan, is indeed, endangering their economic future but, as of today, they are amongst the most colorful and cheerful people in the rural areas of Rajasthan where large (and growing) communities of animal

Rajasthan. The farmers are, no doubt, taking full advantage of the new inputs—irrigation, improved seeds, agro-machinery and credit—but their traditional ecology-specific life-styles are being modified without taking due account of the possible long-term impact of current changes.

These eco-developmental considerations are crucial to understanding the way of life of the pastoral people of Rajasthan who can be seen even in neighboring states herding

Left, a traditional royal wedding. Above, village labor being transported to work.

farmers have adapted themselves to a waterless ecologic regime.

Hardy Farmers: Despite all appearances to the contrary, the soil of Rajasthan does support a substantial agricultural population who harvest adequate yields of protein-rich crops like *jowar* and *bajra*. With the advent of modern inputs, agricultural castes like the **Jats** have been able to achieve an economic momentum which may eventually make Rajasthan an important granary for wheat and rice; it may even steal a march over the rest of India in production of cash-crops like sugarcane and cotton.

Ethnologists and historians are still not clear about the origins of the Jats who excel at agriculture, not only in the water-rich regions of Punjab and Haryana, but even the arid Thar desert in Rajasthan. There is some ground to believe that the Jats were the anterior rulers of modern Churu and its adjacent areas before the Rajput state of Bikaner subdued them.

The princely states of Bharatpur and Dholpur also had Jat rulers, but their history dates back only to the late-17th century, when the Jat rulers of Bharatpur mauled even Mughal armies and carried away valuable booty from Delhi and Agra which is on display in the famous palaces of Deeg. In more recent times, however, the Jats have been known mainly for their farming skills which have been enhanced in the wake of the tenurial reforms enacted in

post-1947 Rajasthan—the abolition of the *jaghirdari* system and conferment of inheritable property rights upon the lands previously husbanded by them as tenants-at-will. The Jats are now one of the most conspicuous upwardly mobile communities in Rajasthan. They constitute a tenth of the total population, but they are limited to only some 10 districts, and this, coupled with their growing achievement-consciousness as far as politico-economic modernity is concerned, has made the Jats one of the most "visible" communities on the socio-political map of Rajasthan, despite their long history of economic backwardness and exploitation at the hands of *jaghirdars* and their petty revenue-collection functionar-

ies. Visitors to Rajasthan are likely to hear a lot about Jats as a community of the future who are bound to make optimum use of the seeds of development being sown in the rural soil under various plan programs.

Conservationists: Another rural community of Rajasthan which deserves a special mention on the basis of its currently relevant traditions is that of Bishnois, who have shot into international prominence on account of their conservationist religious beliefs which forbid the wanton taking of animal and vegetable life. As far back as in the 16th century, the Bishnois were known to have resisted royal edicts ordering the felling of trees by literally wrapping their bodies around them, and even today it is impossible for poachers or others to kill any animal for pleasure in any village where a substantial number of Bishnois live. The environment protectionist beliefs of the Bishnois are rooted in the religious teachings of their spiritual mentor, Jambhoji, and are currently the focus of attention of all policy-makers concerned with development as they constitute an indigenous model of an attitude which they would like to promote in order to minimize the hazards to the environment of technological advancement.

The people of Rajasthan are people with a long, continuous past which dominates the present in a way it does in no other part of India. The glorious innings of the Rajput polity characterized by constant warfare ended nearly 200 years ago, but the people of Rajasthan are still steeped in its social psychology, even though several plans for their techno-economic development have been implemented since 1947.

Though Rajasthan is an integral part of the Republic of India, the socio-cultural life of its people is still characterized by distinctive life-styles, even as they are being enveloped by all-India patterns of politico-economic modernization. No visitor to Rajasthan can fail to feel the distinctiveness of the people there, and many may readily ascribe it to the long "feudal" history, which some may even characterize as "medieval." Such catch-all labels, derived from the history of Western Europe, do not do full justice to these people who are amongst the most hospitable and chivalrous in the world. Rajasthan is backward in techno-economic terms, but after struggling for ecological and political survival for centuries, they have learnt, adapting a wall-slogan at Jaipur's Medical College cricket field, to not only add years to one's life but also life to one's years.

MARWARIS—MERCANTILE COMMUNITY

The Marwaris are Rajasthanis both by origin and orientation. Although their business operations are spread all over India, they take special care to maintain a social base at their "home" villages. They are traders *par excellence*, and in the last five or six decades have established substantial industrial empires also.

For reasons not yet adequately fathomed, either by historians of Mughal India or by historians of British India, Rajasthani businessmen began to migrate and establish trading outposts outside Rajasthan. Some of these operations commenced as early as the 16th century, when Marwari businessmen accompanied the princes of Jaipur, Jodhpur and Bikaner who were appointed governors of far-flung provinces in eastern and northwestern India by successive Mughal emperors. The Marwari emigration from Rajasthan, however, acquired more impressive volume only in the late 18th century with the business "presence" of Marwaris in such metropolises as Calcutta being felt only as recently as the late 19th century.

From small beginnings, the Marwaris built a strong tradition of trading and business management which involved indigenous but nonetheless sophisticated techniques of accountancy, cash and credit conveyancing, and economic intelligence. Cultural and community linkages provided a social fence for protecting this stock of economic skills. During the troubled decades of the 18th and 19th centuries before *Pax Britannica* was firmly established all over India, the Marwaris were able to sustain an all-India economic network mainly because of their social cohesion, which was periodically renewed at family reunions at their original villages where they continued to maintain ready-to-use residences.

As their home-bases were situated in the princely states of Rajasthan, most Marwari businessmen were hardly in a position to participate actively in India's freedom struggle (which was aimed, primarily, at freedom from *British* rule) but many Marwari businessmen maintained close personal links with the leaders of the Indian National Congress and even provided liberal financial support to its campaigners.

Over the centuries, the Marwaris had acquired considerable skills in judging the political moods of rulers and, no doubt, they deploy these skills even in today's India which is committed to the nourishment of a public sector.

According to the Monopolies Inquiry Commission Report (1964), 17 Marwari Industrial Houses had assets worth Rs 7.5

billion out of a total of Rs 19.6 billion owned by 37 large Industrial Houses.

The commanding position of the Marwaris in the Indian economy as a whole derives from their control of the sinews of trade, finance, commerce and marketing—irrespective of whether the goods being traded are manufactured in the public sector or private sector or whether they originate from India's organized corporate sector or the vast unorganized sector. In this last sector, the Marwaris' all-pervading presence can be seen in their indirect control of credit and direct communal linkages amongst the village traders and moneylenders, and their co-castemen operating from the bigger cities.

Left, Bhil tribesman takes aim, Banswara. Above, the late G.D. Birla, the foremost Marwari industrialist, in London.

RELIGION, MYTH & FOLKLORE

Religion in Rajasthan ranges from pure nature worship to the most esoteric and abstract thought. Most Rajasthanis are either Hindus, Jains or animists, but there is also a substantial Muslim population besides Christians.

Hinduism: The wealthy Indo-Gangetic region attracted foreign invaders, who brought their religions to India. Around the third millennium B.C., the Aryan conquerors worshiped deities like Surya (sun), Indra (rain), Varun (water), and Marut (wind), personifying nature's forces. In the course of time they absorbed the Indus Valley gods. Hinduism thus developed from this mixture of Dravidian and Aryan beliefs. The central Hindu belief is that every living thing is a manifestation of the One, Unchangeable, Absolute and Impersonal Being, Brahman.

In the Hindu pantheon, the Supreme Being has three manifestations: *Brahma* the Creator, *Vishnu* the Preserver, and *Shiva* the Destroyer. Brahma, the Creator, has four heads, each of which rules a quarter of the universe.

Vishnu, Preserver of the world, is a popular aspect of the Hindu trinity who incarnates on earth whenever mankind is in trouble. He is depicted as a divinely handsome warrior wearing a crown and holding the Sudarshan Chakra (a deadly, divine discus), a conch shell, a long mace, and a lotus flower. It is Vishnu's duty to protect the weak, remove suffering, and punish evil-doers. So far, Vishnu is believed to have incarnated ten times in a rather Darwinian sequence—as a fish, a tortoise, a boar, a lion, a horse, and a dwarf. The Buddha is believed to be his latest incarnation. The most popular of his incarnations are Rama and Krishna, heroes of the Aryan epics, the *Ramayana* and *Mahabharata*, respectively.

The Hindu epics are based on historical legends, myths, and folklore. The *Ramayana* tells the story of King Dashrath's eldest son Rama, his exile due to his stepmother Kaikeyi who wanted the throne of Ayodhya for her own son, Bharat; the abduction of Rama's beautiful wife Sita by

Lanka's king, Ravana; and Sita's rescue after a long war. Rama is the embodiment of all the qualities of the perfect son, husband, brother, and king. His faithful wife, Sita, is the traditional role model for all Indian women. His brother Lakshmana is the perfect, self-sacrificing younger brother. The fearless monkey god, Hanuman, who helped Rama recover Sita from Ravana, is the perfect devotee, venerated throughout Rajasthan. Hanuman's statue guards the entrance to forts and villages, and people ask him to protect them from evil spirits, black magic, and powerful enemies.

The dark-skinned Krishna is the hero of the *Mahabharata*. A handsome, playful pastoral god, Krishna charmed all creation with his magic flute. As a cowherd he danced with his beloved Radha, and all the milkmaids round Brindavan. As Lord of Dwarka, Krishna helped the Pandavas, his friends, in their just war against their wicked cousins, the Kauravas, who had usurped their kingdom and dishonored their shared wife, Draupadi. The *Bhagvadgita* (often referred to as just the Gita) consists of Krishna's eve of battle counsel to Arjuna, the Pandava prince, torn by doubts about the morality of fighting and killing his own kith and kin, however evil they might be.

This scripture, just a small part of the *Mahabharata*, is one of the most basic to Hinduism. The core of its teachings is that each individual must perform his/her duty without concern for the outcome because God himself is the doer, the deed, and outcome. Everything flows from God, and lapses back to God. The path to *moksha*, *nirvana*, or merger with the infinite, lies for different people through *karma* (action), *bhakti* (devotion), or *gnyan* (knowledge), according to his/her nature and abilities.

Shiva, the Destroyer, often symbolized by the Shivalinga (phallus), is depicted in sculpture and painting as Mahadeo, the Great God, with a third eye, through whose matted hair the sacred Ganga flows gently to earth, having spent its destructive momentum in Shiva's locks; as Pashupati Nath, protector of animals, he is depicted garlanded with snakes, wearing a tigerskin, holding a *trishul* (trident), a drum, and ritual fire in three of his hands, with the fourth raised in blessing. Shiva is also

Preceding pages: a young Nautch girl strikes a pose in Phool Mahal, Mehrangarh Fort, Jodhpur. Left, Tejaji, a tribal deity; painted terra-cotta plate, Molela, near Nathdwara.

71

depicted as the detached yogi *par excellence*, meditating in the Himalaya. He is also portrayed as the Cosmic Dancer, Nataraj, from whom the universal life force flows, and into whom it lapses. In his destructive aspect, Shiva is Maha Kaal, garlanded with human skulls. Shiva's mount, the bull Nandi, is also worshiped and a statue of Nandi is often seen in the courtyard of Shiva temples.

Shiva's consort, Parvati, takes many forms: the Mother Goddess who manifests whenever the gods of mankind need her; the eternally faithful and happy wife, Gauri; the mighty ten-armed Durga, wielding awesome weapons; or Kali, the dark goddess of death. She is symbolized as the female *yoni* round the Shivalinga, which is

historical, mythological, and philosophical Sanskrit material written by Aryan sages, priests and poets and called the *Rig*, *Sama*, *Yajur*, and *Atharva* Veda. Additions called *Brahmanas* contain instruction, incantations, and sacrificial formulas or *mantras* for invoking the help of specific gods and goddesses for specific purposes. The *Upanishads*, which are complementary to the *Vedas*, provide the philosophical foundations of Hinduism. Among the ancient Hindu texts are also the *Puranas*, a miscellany of legend, myth and history.

Jainism: Mahavira was the founder of Jainism. Born in 599 B.C., Mahavira, like Gautama Buddha, renounced a throne and and left his family to preach the message of non-violence. He joined the Parasnath

worshiped as symbolic of creation's fountainhead.

The elephant-headed Ganesh, son of Shiva and Parvati, is the lord of wisdom and good fortune. A popular deity, he is invoked before starting a religious ceremony, wedding, or other function. He clears away obstacles, ensuring success and good luck. Images of Ganesh are installed over Hindu thresholds in Rajasthan; his shrines dot the countryside, and shopkeepers start the day's business after lighting a lamp and incense sticks before a Ganesh image.

The second major source of Hindu belief and observance is the *Vedas*, the oldest written religious texts in the world. They consist of four huge collections of religious,

monastic order, which followed the teachings of a succession of *tirthankaras*, ('perfect souls'). Mahavira who went about naked all the time, a sign of his detachment from worldly things, the triumph of mind over matter, became the 24th and last *tirthankara* of the Jains. To gain salvation or *nirvana* from the cycle of birth and death, the Jains practice the Triple Jewel: Right Belief, Right Conduct, Right Knowledge. Jain monks and nuns take five vows: to be non-violent, to be truthful, not to steal, not to become attached to possessions, and to be celibate (*brahmacharya*).

Mahavira starved himself to death at the age of 72. His teachings were spread by itinerant monks and nuns, who preached that all living things had a soul, and deserved equal respect with humans. His teachings were codified in the 3rd century B.C. A schism divided Jain monks into *Digambaras*, or "sky-clad," naked ascetics like Mahavira, and *Swetambaras*, who wore white robes. There is no fundamental difference between their respective doctrines, but the Digambaras are wandering ascetics, practicing severe penances, while the Swetambaras, are great scholars and teachers. Thanks to the Jain love of learning and their belief that it is a meritorious act to make a copy of a worthwhile manuscript, many ancient texts and literary works have been preserved in copies prepared by them.

The Jains do not worship a deity, because

include images of many Hindu deities.

Islam: Rajasthan has had a Muslim population from the time of the Ghori invasion in 1193.

A mystic Islamic group called *Sufis* became very popular in medieval India at the same time as its Hindu-oriented counterpart, the *Bhakti* (devotion to God) movement. Both were products of the unique interaction between Hinduism and Islam during the 14th and 15th centuries. One of the world's greatest Sufi shrines lies in Rajasthan. It is that of the Sufi saint, Khwaja Moinuddin Chishti (1142-1256 A.D.), a direct descendant of Prophet Muhammad's son-in-law, Ali. He came to Ajmer during the reign of Prithviraj Chauhan, who gifted the saint with the land on

they believe that the universe functions according to an eternal law of progress and decline.

Jains today are a prosperous commercial community, noted for their endowments for charitable institutions, hospitals, schools, colleges, animal shelters and veterinary hospitals. Jains are tolerent of all religions, and the magnificent Jain temples built by wealthy merchants between the 7th and 14th centuries A.D. at Abu, Ranakpur, Ossian, Jaisalmer, Bikaner and Chittor

Left, shrine of popular Hindu God Shiva. Above left, the Maharaja of Bikaner at Karni Mata Temple, Deshnok. Right, a pandit (priest) at the shrine of Baba Ram Dev, Pokhran.

which his shrine now stands. At the age of 114, the saint locked himself in his cell to pray. Six days later his disciples broke open the door and found the Khwaja Saheb dead. That is why his *urs* (feast) is celebrated for six days. His *dargah* (mausoleum) is the most popular Muslim pilgrimage center in the subcontinent. Hindus, Muslims, Sikhs, and Jains alike believe that this benevolent Sufi saint intercedes with God on behalf of his devotees.

Haminuddin Nagori was a disciple of Moinuddin Chishti. His tomb at Nagor, the Atarki Dargah, is also a pilgrimage center where many miracle cures are said to have occurred. Sayed Fakhruddin, a saint of the Ismaili Shias, has a shrine at Galiakot in tribal country. Several other Muslim *pirs* (saints) are venerated by people of all faiths seeking healing, freedom from the evil eye and evil spirits, or the birth of a much-longed-for child.

Local Cults and Deities: There are hundreds of simple animistic shrines in Rajasthan, dating back thousands of years. Stones resembling abstract sculptures are painted vermilion and covered with silver foil. The tribes and most villagers revere all nature. Snakes, cows, monkeys, and peacocks are considered sacred. There are sacred trees in every village and town, and sacred groves which cannot be cut down. Tree worship is one of the oldest human cults, and Hindus and Jains revere the *Kalpa Vriksha*, or Tree of Life, portrayed in mythological paintings

hide and watch her. But he broke his promise, and found her assuming the form of a tigress whenever she suckled their son. She returned to heaven, and Pabuji became a great warrior, who protected the oppressed, and broke caste barriers. He is invoked during times of misfortune and sickness by people who hold *jagrans* (night vigils), with Pabuji's *bhopas* (priests) singing his epic in their homes.

Gogaji was an 11th-century warrior. The story is that he was so true to his word that the Snake God gave him the power to heal snakebite victims. Revered by Hindus and Muslims (the latter call him Gogaji Jahir Pir), snakebite victims are carried to his shrine and kept awake by the beating of drums and gongs so that the poison cannot

and temple carvings. The peepul (*Ficus religiosa*) has been considered sacred since the protohistoric Harappan and Kalibangan period. The bo or banyan tree (*Ficus indica*), under which the Buddha attained enlightenment, is also considered sacred.

Rajasthan has five major folk gods: Pabuji, Gogaji, Mehaji, Harbhuji, and Ramdeo Baba. Belief in the supernatural power of these departed folk heroes to mediate in their devotees' lives has made them folk gods, and shrines dedicated to them are to be seen in every town and village.

Pabuji's mother was reputed to be a celestial nymph, who asked her husband, a 13th century Rathor chieftain, never to

take effect. Stone carvings of Gogaji on horseback always include snakes. Gogaji's chief *thaan* (shrine) is at Gogameda near Ganganagar, where a huge cattle fair is held every year.

Mehaji and his son Harbhu are deified as *bhomiyas* (braves) who died heroic deaths while protecting the village community, specially its cattle. Because the village economy in medieval Rajasthan was based on milk and milk products, Rajput feudal chiefs were expected to emulate Meha and Harbhu, and save cattle from raiders and predatory animals at all cost.

Ramdeo Baba, the legend goes, appeared miraculously in a cradle beside the newborn son of a hitherto childless Rajput couple. He became an invincible hero, devoting his life to the poor. His white horse, on which he covered vast distances to help needy people, is believed still to carry grain to drought-stricken areas if he is properly invoked.

The Bishnois are followers of Jambhoji, who made environment and wildlife protection a religion in the early 15th century. The Bishnoi cult spread from Bikaner to Jodhpur, and even today the most well-connected *shikaris* (hunters) dare not shoot game in Bishnoi territory, for Bishnois are ready to die for their beliefs. A great *shaka* (sacrifice) took place at Dhawa in the 19th century, when the Maharaja of Jodhpur ordered the chopping down of a forest which was a dacoit hideout. Hundreds of Bishnois gave their lives trying to save the trees by tying themselves to the trunks. Today, the Bishnois are a wealthy farming community of pure vegetarians, who are very orthodox about observing the 29 (*bish nao* in Hindi) principles laid down by their enlightened guru.

For Hindus in Rajasthan, the Mother Goddess (Mataji or Devi), the embodiment of *Shakti*, the Cosmic Life Force, is the most important deity—giver of wisdom, wealth, victory and peace.

The most famous Rajasthani incarnation of Devi is Karni Mata of Deshnok, who lived for 151 years. A *Charan* (bard) by birth, this 15th century miracle-worker could not revive the only son of a distraught Charan couple who came to her for help. Yama, the Lord of Death, told Karniji that the boy had already been reborn. So Karniji decreed that henceforth all dead Charans would be reborn only as sacred *kabas* (rats) in her temple, to escape Yama's clutches and reincarnate as humans at her command. She made a blind carpenter carve her image, which is enshrined at Deshnok near Bikaner. Her body is said to have disappeared into a dazzling orb of light in 1538 A.D., and, ever since, Karni Mata's temple has attracted worshipers.

In Rajasthan, certain *Sati Matas* are also worshiped. But all *satis* (women who immolate themselves on their husband's funeral pyre) are not deified. Rajput women who committed *sati* for political reasons (like Queen Padmini of Chittor), or as a result of a husband's death on the battlefield, are not folk goddesses. Only those *satis* are deified who were under no social compulsion to do so, but chose to burn alive with their dead husbands, and continue to manifest and perform miracles after their self-sacrifice.

Folklore: Each area of Rajasthan has its enduring myths and folklore, but the folklore motifs are universal. Social welfare measures are often promoted in the form of superstitions like not sitting or sleeping under a tree at night for fear of evil spirits—in reality the carbon dioxide the leaves respire at night. The epic of Heer-Ranjha is sung when there is a cattle epidemic, and several prohibitions are imposed on the entire village for 36 days. Cures in such cases have been recorded, but how they came about, no one can say. Customs that have proved beneficial have frozen as rituals or taboos. There is pragmatic value in a number of these beliefs, however illogical they may appear to be.

There is widespread belief in astrology, and the power of the nine planets, the gems and metals worn, celestial beings, demons, and departed souls of ancestors, on the life of every human being. A person's present status, looks, and luck are believed to be the outcome of his past *karma* (actions). But the intervention of supernatural forces can help anyone to overcome trouble and evolve spiritually.

Knowledgeable persons can forecast the weather and coming events by studying animal, bird and insect behavior. In Jaisalmer, Barmer, and Bikaner, villagers believe that water from a lake where wild animals drink should be given to a newborn infant for seven days, so that he becomes wise in the ways of nature, and understands bird and animal talk.

Folklore, myth, and Rajasthan's religious institutions, communicate something of this region's value system, and concept of the good life.

Religious tolerance is a striking feature of Rajasthan. The harsh climate and terrain make people tolerant of each other's beliefs, and at the same time impose discipline on public life. From the earliest times, Rajput kings claiming descent from the sun, moon, fire, and mythological heroes protected all their subjects, irrespective of caste or creed, and guaranteed them freedom of worship. They welcomed the saints and preachers of every faith, and gave donations to temples, mosques, and Jain monasteries. In that day and age, when Europe was torn apart by religious wars and the Inquisition, the people of Rajasthan lived in an environment that breathed tolerance and goodwill.

Muslim devotees carry a *chador* in procession during the *urs* celebrations of Hazrat Khwaja Muni-ud-din-Chishti, Ajmer.

All the regions of Rajasthan have their distinct folk entertainment. The hilly tracts of central and southern Rajasthan are rich in community entertainments because of the lifestyle of tribes like the Bhils, Meenas, Banjaras, Saharias and Garasias.

The harsh desert areas of western Rajasthan are scantily populated. People here have very little leisure for merrymaking. Therefore, in this region, entertainment is provided by professional performers like the Bhats, Dholis, Mirasis, Nats, Sargadas and Bhands. Eastern Rajasthan is fertile

heads and faces. The rhythm is very simple.

The *ger* dance is performed only during the Holi festival by men alone. The singers play huge *duffs* (tambourines) to accompany their singing. The dancers ring them in concentric circles, striking attitudes in keeping with the words of the song.

The *ger-ghoomer* of the Bhils is a colorful Holi dance, which attracts huge crowds of spectators. This is a combination of the *ger* and *ghoomer*. Men dance in the outer circle, striking sticks together to the rhythm of the drum beat. Women dance in the

and affluent, with plenty of patrons to sustain professional entertainers like the *Kathputli* (puppeteer) *Bhats, Kamads, Bhopas,* and *Kacchi Ghodi* dancers. A major school of the sophisticated classical *kathak* dance form originated in Jaipur.

The *ghoomer* is a community dance for women, which is performed on all ceremonial occasions, marriages and festivals. Each region and community has its own variation, which is performed to *ghoomer* songs particular to a family or an area. *Ghoomer* in Udaipur is danced with small sticks in the dancers' hands which are struck together to the rhythm. It can be danced in a circle by several women, in pairs, or individually, with veils covering

inner circle to start with. Everyone sings, and the men and women change circles with every change of rhythm.

Kacchi ghodi is a spectacular dance performed by three or four pairs of elaborately costumed men riding hobby-horses. The dancers holding naked swords move with gusto on the hobby-horses to the accompaniment of a big drum and fifes, while a singer narrates the exploits of the Bavaria bandits of Shekhavati, Robin Hoods whom this dance eulogizes.

The *fire dance* of the Sidh Naths of Bikaner—renowned for their *tantric* feats—is a thrilling experience. First a fire is prepared on raised ground in the form of a large platform of smoldering wood or charcoal. Big drums and pipes are played, and a special song begins with a low humming tune. Excitement rises, and the Sidh Nath men and boys jump on to the fire and dance on it as if the fire under their feet did not exist. The dance grows vigorous as the music reaches a crescendo.

The *drum dance* of Jalore is a professional folk dance performed at weddings. Five *dholis* play huge drums slung round their necks, while others beat large cymbals. A dancer holding a naked sword in his mouth, another twirling two painted sticks,

and a third with colorful scarves hanging from his wrists, perform a vigorous dance to an overpowering drumbeat.

The nomadic Banjaras (gypsies) used to be peddlers carting goods to remote villages till modern rail and road transport forced them out of business. Colorful and artistic, Banjaras have always been famous for their folk dances.

Kavelias (snake charmers) are another nomadic tribe famous for their skilful *been* (a musical instrument made out of dry

Left, Nautch girls, Jaisalmer. Above, Langa musicians playing the *murli* (a traditional flute) in Badnawa village, Barmer district.

gourd) playing, and hypnotic, rhythmic dances. They play special tunes for luring snakes, and have jealously guarded secret mystic spells and talismans for catching them to extract expensive snake venom, used in many medicines. Their popular dances are *indoni, panihari,* and *shankaria,* performed by Kalvelia· women wearing striking bead-embroidered veils, skirts, and blouses, and men in twisted red and white turbans.

The *terah taal* of Deedwana and Pokhran is a physical feat rather than a dance. The Kamads perform this dance in groups of two men and two women in honor of their deity, Ramdeoji. The men play the *choutara* (a four-stringed instrument) and sing, while the women play on tiny cymbals tied all over their bodies, striking intricate postures.

Kathputli or puppet shows are invariably performed at night by a highly skilled puppeteer and a female partner. The woman plays the drum, and sings the ballad to which the man makes his puppets act and dance. An interesting discussion goes on between the two, serving as a running commentary on the show. Puppet plays are based on popular legends.

Pabuji ki pad has more poetic than dramatic value, but it is very popular with those who worship Pabuji, a great 14th-century hero. Believers in Pabuji's mystic powers invite his *bhopas* (bards) to their homes in times of sickness and misfortune to sing this ballad at all-night vigils. Pabuji's *pad* (ballad) is sung before an open scroll, about 30 feet (10 m) long and about eight feet (2.5 m) high, depicting his life. The *bhopa* sings and plays the *ravan hatta* (a stringed instrument), while his wife sings and dances, holding an oil lamp to illuminate Pabuji's images on the scroll at appropriate points in the narrative.

Mand is sophisticated folk music centered on the romantic life-style of Rajasthan's rulers. The Mirasis are professional entertainers who sing *mand* songs on special occasions or at private gatherings, often accompanied by women dancers. The Langas and Manganiars of Jaisalmer render simple folk songs and ballads to the accompaniment of musical instruments.

Rajasthan has also developed several dance drama forms which are a great source of cultural and social education.

CRAFTS

Jaipur is a city built on a formalized, square grid but the chaos, color and spontaneous rhythm in its streets prevent one from perceiving it. Extensive areas of Rajasthan are monotone, beige-brown desert, but the dramatic spectacle and visual variety that pervade it make it one of the most vibrantly colorful of Indian states.

These paradoxes are seen again and again—a recurring motif reflected in its crafts.

It is one of the poorest and most backward parts of India, yet it houses the most opulent and richest treasures.

Its history is a long saga of blood feuds and violent battles, but the forbidding stone battlements of its forts shield mirrored rooms and marble carvings of incredible delicacy and grace.

It is a land whose social customs are still governed by primitive and reactionary attitudes to women, but where fierce, mustachioed men will melt the heart telling legends of tenderness and deathless love and the valor of women in war.

The same high-balconied prisons that prevented their women from venturing out into the outside world were marvels of exquisite ornamentation. The jeweled belts, bracelets and anklets that proclaimed them ornamental chattels were also rich symbols of love and pride.

Rajas who sacrificed wealth, power, territory, life itself, to withstand the Mughals, generation after generation, at the same time borrowed freely from Mughal art and esthetics, taking styles, symbols and techniques, often stealing craftsmen, and incorporating them into their own eclectic, rich tradition.

Some contrasts, however extreme, seem almost inevitable. It seems natural that a landscape so parched and brown should produce paintings bursting with vibrant flowers and foliage and running water; that people starved of natural color and beauty should almost obsessively decorate everything—be it a camel, a kitchen wall or a king's diadem; that warriors going into bloody battle should arm themselves with delicately decorated, jeweled shields and swords.

Other contradictions are more inexplicable, even sad ...Why should women of vigor, beauty and charm have spent their lives embroidering garments to embellish themselves, and sat, bejeweled and bedecked, in mirrored rooms reflecting only their own images, unseen by any male eye except their husband's?

Why should village women, even today, seemingly independent, harvesting the crop, or carrying pots of water many miles across the fields with that proud, lilting characteristic sway of skirt, still feel impelled to pull their veil, or *ghungat*, over their faces at the approach of a man? Even more strange, when that veil itself is a symbol of such bold sexual imagery; its bright red tie-dyed circle symbolizing the breaking of the maidenhead in the bridal bed.

Rajasthan and its crafts are a source of endless fascination—whether one approaches them for purely visual, esthetic pleasure or pauses to savor the underlying history, culture and symbolism.

Behind the main squares and streets of its cities, Jaiphur, Ajmer Udaipur, Jodhpur, and in every little village; in narrow lanes and little dark houses with steep winding stairs, craftsmen still live, practicing ancient arts, handed down generation by generation, from father to son, in a tradition passed on only by word of mouth and skill of hand. It is worth bypassing the big tourist souvenir emporia and seeing Ganpat Lal Parihar in Udaipur turn a gold-damascened dagger, or Munnalal Minakar in Jaipur delicately apply a luminous flake of translucent red enamel to a serpent-headed bracelet with jeweled eyes, or to see the devotion with which Dwarka Dass in Nathdwara depicts the yearning in Radha's eye as she looks at Krishna, in the miniature he (Dwarka Dass) is painting, symbolizing the eternal yearning of man for union with God.

Just as one's eye, dazzled by the color and pageantry of Jaipur streets, forgets the geometric symmetry of their right-angled layout, the richness and color of Rajasthani craft can lead one to forget the religious or cultural symbolism from which they derive their inspiration, but in India every color, shape and motif has a meaning. To ignore it is to miss much.

Preceding pages: traditional dance during the Holi festival, Kanasar, Barmer district. Left, a modern miniature painter from Udaipur still uses traditional methods.

The Indian stone-mason works his "frozen lace" filigree magic on the sandstone trellised balconies of Jaisalmer with four crude tools: a pointed punch or *tanki*, a cold chisel or *pahuri*, a *hatora* (hammer) and a *barma* (borer), but the disciplines with which he carves were laid down in the *Manasara* and *Shilpshastras*, Sanskrit texts on art and esthetics dating to pre-Christian times. For example, every pedestal should have 24 parts of which the plinth is five parts, the fillet one, the dado 12, next fillet one, patica four, and topmost fillet again one. Similarly, the height, width and diameter of every shaft, arch and building detail is strictly enjoined, handed down by precept and example. Within these formal principles individual creativity can run

striped version, done mostly in Udaipur; *chira*, when the stripes are of variegated colors; *chunari* is the dotted one; *ekdali* has small circles and squares; *tikhunti, chaubandi, satbandi*, have groups of three, four, and seven dots respectively; in *dhannak* the designs form flowering circles; in *jaaldar* and *beldar*, the dots form diagonal or flowering patterns; *shikari* is a design with human, tiger, horse and elephant figures. Patterns may be simple or complex, the technique is the same: the cloth is bleached and washed repeatedly to remove all starch and chemicals, and the design block-printed on with washable *geru* (earth color). The village women then take over, their left hand thumb and little finger nail specially kept long for this purpose. They push and

riot. One generation finding inspiration in flowing arabesques of peacocks and poppy flowers, another in severe Mughal-inspired geometric squares and stars.

If color is an essential adjunct to Rajput life, it is the dyer and the printer who supply it. Each town and village has some distinctive skill. In Alwar a few families still exist who can perform the apparently miraculous feat of dyeing one side of a sari red and the reverse of it green, without any overlapping of color! In Kota they dye the warp one color and the weft another to create a shot effect. All over Rajasthan the *bandhani*, tie-dyed sari, veil and turban reign supreme. Different designs have different names. *Laheria* is the diagonal-

pinch the fabric up into small points which they tie with two or three twists of thread. When dyed the knotted parts remain uncolored. The more intricate *bandhanis* are tied and dyed several times, separately for each color, starting with the lightest one.

Weaving of all kinds is practiced as a cottage industry. Men and women, and often their children, steal a few hours from the fields to sit down at the pit loom in their courtyard and weave a few inches of a *durry* (cotton carpet), a goat-hair blanket or intricately patterned camel bag. Camels, peacocks, eight-pointed stars or the triangles of a tented settlement are familiar stylized motifs. The fine self-checked cotton saris of Kota are famous and Jaipur makes beautiful woolen, knotted carpets in the Mughal tradition.

Block printing, too, is a traditional art of Rajasthan, and towns like Sanganer and Bagru have been devoted exclusively to this occupation since medieval times; their products going as far afield as China, Europe and the Middle East. Incongruous though it may seem, Jane Austen's gently nurtured heroines' sprigged muslins were almost certainly block-printed in Sanganer by some fiery, crimson-turbaned and ear-ringed Rajput male—his views on the role of women perhaps not all that different from theirs! The towns of Sanganer, Barmer and Bagru between them produce about 275,000 yards (250,000 m) of printed fabric a day all printed by hand with carved wooden blocks also made locally. Sanganer specializes in delicate floral sprigs, Barmer in red and indigo geometric *ajraks*, Bagru in brick and black, linear and zigzag stripes. The motifs and layouts are delicate and subtle; the colors are spectacular. Stunning, unusual combinations of scarlet and shocking pink, purple and orange, turquoise and parrot green, saffron and crimson, often shot with gold and silver, and set with shining mirrors, are worn by men and women alike, as turbans, flared skirts, veils or saris.

Till recently the dyes were vegetable and earth colors extracted from flowers, bark, roots and minerals: jasmine, saffron and myrobalan producing oranges and yellows; mulberry bark and the kirmiz insect, reds and purples; indigo and pistachio galls, blues and greens; sulfate of iron, black. The ingenuity of the Indian dyer had no bounds, with over 250 different shades in common use in the mid-19th century and, we are told, a very successful green being extracted from the soaked green baize exported from England for billiard tables!

Woven, dyed and block-printed, the fabric is then further embellished by embroidery. Though Rajasthani women, curiously enough, seldom stitch their own clothes, depending on the local tailor to do this, they do embroider them. Skirts, bodices and veils, as well as coverlets and decorative pieces for their homes, are covered with beautiful, often ad-lib designs of dancing figures and flowers, peacocks, the tree of life and the *mandala* (a circular religious motif). The Barmer region is

Left, the intricate and laborious craft of block printing continues to thrive in Sanganer.

known for its flat, geometric, surface satin-stitch motifs, other areas use chain and herringbone stitch, and worn fabric is excitingly recycled into stunning patchwork quilts, cushions and shoulder bags.

Clothes—their color, design and cut, may express your personality, and tell people which village and caste you come from, but it is jewelry in which you invest your wealth. In the Rajasthan villages it is silver. Huge, heavy chunks of it round your ankles, round your waist, round your neck and round your wrists, dangling in rings from your ears, nose and hair, in chains of buttons down your *kurta* or *choli* front. The beautiful, ornate designs of tribal Indian jewelry have now become a fashion craze among the urban elite, and can be bought everywhere. Silver is too soft to be durable on its own and is generally mixed with copper before being worked. The silver in the shops ranges from 65 to 90 percent silver content, and prices vary accordingly. Of course, every jeweler will assure you his silver has 95 percent purity. Pure silver has a coarse, dull sound when struck, unlike the shrill, vibrating sound of other metals. Apart from jewelry, Rajasthani silver-smiths make beautiful boxes, trays, small statues of Krishna and Ganesh, and ornamental *objets d'art*—birds, horses and elephants, enameled as well as plain.

The aristocracy and the well-to-do did not wear silver. *Kundan* and enamel jewelry inlaid with precious stones was a speciality of Rajasthan, particularly of Jaipur. Rajasthan is rich in precious and semi-precious stones. Emerald, garnet, agate, amethyst, topaz and lapiz lazuli are all found locally. Other stones came from further afield as the fame of the Jaipur jewelers and gem-cutters spread. Men as well as women wore elaborate jewelry, and the hilts and scabbards of swords and daggers, goblets and condiment boxes were all equally heavily ornamented. Unlike European jewelry, though stones were sometimes etched or embossed into decorative shapes and patterns, they were not cut or faceted to remove flaws or accentuate color. The size of the stone and the elaboration of its setting rather than its depth of color or brilliance were the criteria. The back of each piece, set in heavy gold *kundan* or *jarao*, was embellished with delicate enamel ornamentation in the champlevé (raised field) technique. The design, usually exquisitely entwined flowers and birds, sometimes human and animal figures, was hollowed out, each color segment separated by a fine raised

83

gold line and the enamel painted in and fired. Each color was fired separately, in a furnace sunk deep into the ground, starting with those requiring greatest heat. The enamel colors and techniques have poetic names: *ab-e-leher*, waves of water; *tote-ka-par*, parrot's wing; and *khoon-e-kabootar*, pigeon's blood (a most highly prized deep translucent red).

Each piece of jewelry is part of a specialized chain: the *nyarriya* refines the gold, the *sangsaz* polishes and cuts the stones; the *manihar* prepares the enamel; the *sonar* makes the bezels for setting the stones and fashions the jewel, using patterned molds; the *chattera* engraves the ground; the *mina-kar* enamels and fires it; the *kundansaz* sets the stone in a mixture of lacquer and

To complicate matters further, each gem is supposed to have both positive attributes and flaws. For example, the pearl protects the wearer from evil, and a house where pearls are kept "is chosen by the ever-fickle Goddess of Wealth, Lakshmi, as her permanent abode," but a pearl of the wrong shape or color can cause leprosy, loss of sons, poverty or death. Emeralds, which cleanse a man of sin, according to Sanskrit texts, can bring wealth and success in war, and protection from poisoning, but here again, the wrong color or shade or flaw can cause disease, fatal wounds in battle, or death by snakebite!

The skilled gem-cutters of Jaipur also carve enchanting little animals and birds from rock, crystal, jade, smoky topaz and

antimony and, when it has solidified, cold-sets it with hammered gold wire. The *sonar* polishes and cleans the piece and the *patwari* puts the finishing touch of twisted gold and silk cord, with its tasseled pendant and beaded knot, twisting the threads in a flashing intricate cat's-cradle between his big toe, knee and index finger.

Stones and metals have a special iconography symbolic of the gods of the Hindu pantheon as well as the nine planets of the Indian astrological system. For example, the diamond denotes both Agni and Venus, the sapphire the god Vishnu as well as Saturn, the ruby Indra and the sun, etc. Gold and silver symbolize the sacred rivers Ganga and Yamuna.

amethyst, and you can buy intaglio beads and buttons and crystal scent bottles as well. The Rajasthani male is quite a peacock. Every inch of his splendid frame is superbly ornamented—from the stiff starched furl of his saffron or shocking-pink turban (nine yards of it twirled into convoluted folds weighing more than four pounds!) to the tips of the turned-up toes of his traditional *juthis*.

The *juthis* or slippers are made of leather flayed and tanned locally in his own village. Each village has its own community of a few families who practice this trade, collecting the dead animals from the local farmers and making *juthis* for them. For centuries they were considered outside the pale of the Indian caste system, but this did not prevent them from being consummate craftsmen. The leather was tanned and dyed by vegetable and mineral formulae handed down from generation to generation, and made into shoes and sandals, water bags, fans, pouches and saddles, even musical instruments. It was embroidered, punched, gouged, studded, sequined and stitched in a variety of intricate designs, varying from region to region—sequins and tassels in one village, brass studs and machine-stitched motifs in another. Men did the tanning, cutting and stitching, women the embroidery and ornamentation. Most of the slippers and sandals are available in the big cities—Jaipur, Jodhpur, Ajmer. They are incredibly sturdy, being made to withstand water-logged fields, wind and weather, and they pinch and squeak excruciatingly the first few days. Persevere and they become the most yielding, confortable footwear you have ever worn, and certainly the longest lasting.

In Bikaner the inner hide of the camel is put to another extraordinary use. It is scraped till it is translucent and tissue-fine and then molded into perfume bottles, water jugs, vases and lamp shades, painted with delicately gilded gesso-work floral designs.

As Rajputs decorate themselves, they decorate every aspect of their home and life. The walls of their dwellings, be they palaces or peasant huts, are painted and decorated. The palaces with inlaid mirror mosaics or marble engraved in floral bas-reliefs set with precious stones; the village homes and city walls with murals of elephants and tigers, illustrations of legends of gods and goddesses, or scenes of everyday life. Every door, window, pillar and balcony is carved and fretted, inlaid with brass, ivory or mother-of-pearl, or painted. Domestic furniture is also often carved and decorated—chests, chairs, cradles and low tables, inlaid with brass sheet-work or ivory, or painted with dancing Radhas and Krishnas and hunting scenes. Shekhavati and Jodhpur are famous centers for woodcarving. Jaipur specializes in brass-wire inlay on ebony and sheshum wood. Fine brass wires are set in intricately intertwined geometric or floral patterns and made into ornamental boxes, trays and mirror-frames. The minutely carved wood-

en blocks used for textile printing are so exquisite that nowadays they are bought by tourists for their own sake, ending up as door knobs or book ends. Udaipur is noted for its mirror and mother-of-pearl inlay, Bikaner for its plaster and gold gesso murals, Jaipur for its marble carving, while the incredibly intricate stone *jalis* (lattices) of Jaisalmer are poetry in stone.

Most of the motifs found in the painted wood and wall murals derive from the miniature and *pichwai* paintings of the 16th and 17th centuries, when every small Rajput king had at least one painter in his entourage. He was commissioned to paint court portraits, scenes from the epics, incidents from history, and make records of local flora and fauna which were then incorporated by court craftsmen into their textiles, carpets and carvings. Each court had a distinctive style of painting—the attenuated, elegant figures of Kishangarh with their soaring eyebrows and sidelong smile; the elaborately detailed court and battle scenes of Mewar; the Bikaner horses and Kota hunting scenes; the harsh simplicity of Bundi.

Done on paper made from cotton, jute or bamboo fiber polished to smoothness with an agate stone, the artist first did a line sketch in *geru* terra cotta, covering it with a coat of white. He then painted on it with mineral and vegetable colors ground and extracted from indigo, lapiz, cochineal, cinnebar, mercuric sulfite and orpiment, as well as pure gold dust, using squirrel-hair brushes often as fine as one's hair. The paintings had no perspective, but intricate details of clothes, jewelry and head-dresses were meticulously rendered, and the beauties of nature vividly portrayed, uninhibited by considerations of seasons or climatic conditions. The lion and the lamb literally lay together, just as flower and fruit grew together side by side on every tree. Both in the paintings made for the royal courts, and the *pichwai* cloth hangings used in the temples, the Radha-Krishna legend was a favorite theme, depicted in a Ragamala series, each painting linked to a musical mode in turn associated with seasons, months, days and hours and personifications of different phases of love and emotion, both temporal and spiritual.

Phad paintings, with their brilliant flaming orange, red and black stylized, cartoon-strip-type, illustrated scrolls, are a more populist art form. They are used by the Bhopas, itinerant minstrels who play at fairs and festivals to the accompaniment of the *jantar*, a two-gourd instrument joined

Young carpet weavers at work, left.

by a bamboo rod. Their songs, and the *phads*, recount the legend of Papuji Ramdeo of the Rabari tribe and his famous black mare, whose neigh warned him of danger; or of Dev Narainji, another Robin Hood-type hero.

Miniatures, *pichwais* and *phads* are all still being painted today, but are fast degenerating into slick, assembly-line copies. Simultaneously, copies of Audubon birds, Redoute roses, Japanese geisha prints and Persian manuscripts are all being turned out to meet the demand of the market. The skills are still there, the motivation and inspiration somewhat suspect.

Miniature paintings are also done on ivory in Udaipur and Nathdwara. The

Muslim artisans specialize in metal-work of all kinds, especially brass enamel. There are two types, *saadha* and *siya kalam*. In *saadha*, the brass is coated with a thin layer of tin which is then cut and engraved to reveal the pattern in the underlying brass, gleaming in contrast to the tin. In *siya kalam*, the design is left in relief, and the rest of the surface cut away. The depressions are filled with black lac or colored enamel—red, white, pink or green. When finished, the relief pattern in plain brass enamel stands out against the colored enamel. There are three different styles—*chikan*, *marori* and *bidri*, each with its repertoire of traditional motifs and designs.

Another metal inlay technique is damascening, done by the swordsmiths and

smooth, matte surface is a perfect foil for the delicate, stylized pictures highlighted with gold.

Ivory is a popular medium in Rajasthan, from the heavy bracelets worn by the tribal Bhil women, to delicate carvings and inlay work. The ivory dust is used medicinally in both the *unani* and *ayurvedic* schools of Indian medicine for abdominal disorders. Only the male Indian elephant produces ivory and with the recent restrictions on import and export, bone is being used more and more in the cheaper jewelry. Ivory can easily be distinguished by its grain and weight. It is often dyed in tea to give it an antique look or in cochineal or cinnebar for a red or green shading.

armorers of Udaipur and Alwar, whose wonderful shields, swords and armor were chased with floral arabesques, hunting scenes or calligraphic Koranic verses, depending on the tastes of Rajput or Mughal patrons. They now make cutlery, areca-nut crackers, buttons and paper knives to suit the needs of a less belligerent age. Pratapgarh gold filigree and enamel is another beautiful, unusual, but dying craft. Court, religious or hunting scenes are cut out of a fine gold sheet and the resulting silhouette relief mounted onto a backing of deep red or blue enamel and set in box tops or as decorative plaques.

Distinctive to Jaipur today, though originally Persian-Turkish in origin, is the famous Blue Pottery. It is unique in that no clay is used at all. It is a mixture of fuller's earth, quartz and sodium sulfite that needs firing only once. It is made in molds with only the neck and lip turned on the wheel. Its characteristic turquoise blue is made from copper sulfate extracted from old scrap and the deep blue is cobalt oxide. Most of the pottery made today is very poor in quality, but a visit to the studio of Kripal Singh Shekhavat, a local painter who has made an art form of the craft, is a must. Borrowing inspiration from Persian miniatures and Ajanta frescoes, and reintroducing long-forgotten pinks, greens and yellows into the color palette, he has taken classic shapes and forms and revitalized them.

All over Rajasthan, village potters turn potter turns his art to creating tiny toys and images—elephants and chariots, many-armed Devi, mounted warriors, caparisoned camels, and tiny lamps which, lit by oil wicks, will light up many homes, just as the craftsmen's art has irradiated the lives of Rajput men and women through the centuries.

The pressures on Rajasthani craftsmanship, as on all Indian traditional skills, are great. More and more of its products are deteriorating into mass-produced knick-knacks for the unwary tourist. Exploitive middlemen urge craftsmen to produce in the quickest possible time at the lowest possible price. What emerges is a rather unworthy object with just a faint flicker of its former glorious self. But the strength of

less elaborate but equally beautiful jars, water-pots, urns, and utensils for the local market. Made of unglazed red terra cotta, their simple, perfectly proportioned shapes are that miraculous blend of utility and elegance that is every industrial designer's ideal. Even more miraculous when one considers the simplicity of their creation. A lump of mud on a roughly shaped wheel, a spin and a flick of dextrous thumb and forefinger, and lo and behold, a sculptured form is ready. Come festival time, the

Left, a potter using a simple wheel creates vases for the Jaipur blue glazes. Above, a master-craftsman repairs a stone statue, Osiyan.

Rajasthani crafts is that they have always been embedded deeply in the everyday lives of the people and were not merely produced for the court or urban market. They are part of the social structure and an abiding Rajput cultural tradition. It is this that has enabled them to withstand the stresses of 20th century technology, the tourist trade and changing life-styles. They have suffered, diminished, but still persist, recognizably.

As long as Rajasthani women wear tie-dyed laheria saris and all Rajput males own at least one pair of embroidered leather juthis, and as long as Bhopa minstrels sing of Papuji, and camels still stalk the desert, Rajasthani crafts will survive.

THE ALLEGORY OF LOVE: RAJPUT PAINTING

In the 16th and 17th centuries, an extraordinary phenomenon flowered into expression in the courts of Rajasthan. An intense revival of Hindu devotionalism resulted in reaction to the severe authority of Muslim rule in north India. It brought about a vital link between poetry and drama and painting, creating vivid pictorial narratives which were inspired by contemporary literature and the dramatic pageantry of the age.

Rajasthan, or "Rajputana," included 20 feudal states in the heart of northern India. In a small tract that was 500 miles (800 km) long and 450 miles (700 km) wide, seven states contributed significantly to the impassioned fervor of medieval painting: Mewar, Bundi, Kota, Marwar, Bikaner, Jaipur and Kishangarh. Each of these courts produced a distinctive idiom, influenced of course by the royal patrons who commissioned these paintings, but also by the environment: by the undulating countryside, by the hills and shrubs, the deserts and forts and gardens in which this art form was nurtured like an exotic and perfumed flower.

Paper was introduced into India only in the 14th century. Being rare, it was used initially only in business transactions and trade. Prior to this, the manuscripts of the 12th and 13th centuries, preserved to the present day in Jain *bhandars* (libraries) of Gujarat and Rajasthan, were on palm leaf. They were inscribed with a stylus pen and adorned with tiny miniatures in a horizontal format. The value of these early manuscripts is that they often carry colophons giving dates and the provenance; but the hieratic style remains unchanged through centuries, in the *Kalpa Sutra* and the *Balagopala Stuti* texts. Even when paper had replaced palm leaf, the horizontal format continued to be used in Rajput paintings of the *Bhagavata Purana* and the *Gita Govinda*, in the 16th century.

The illustration of Hindu religious narrative received fresh impetus with the revival of Vaishnava literature. The *Ramayana* was translated into the vernacular, to become a popular source for oral recita-

tions and stage performances. In the Malwa set of paintings which can be assigned to the 17th century, the geographical location for the invasion of Lanka is mapped out with reference to the stage. The heroes Rama and Lakshmana are profiled on one side of the Indian Ocean, with the army of monkeys leaping across the great blue chasm. On the other side, Ravana, the ten-headed king of Lanka and the abducted Sita are depicted in two separate pavilions. The use of gestures and animated movement, and vivid colors to distinguish the *dramatis personae*, are essential to the dramatic narrative.

Dance dramas (*natakas*) provided a vital source of entertainment in medieval India. It was Krishna who captivated the minds and hearts of the people. Krishna, the butter thief and the miracle child, the darling of the milkmaids and the irresistible lover, became the vindication of romantic love—in an age which witnessed the seclusion of women. Earlier texts such as the *Hari Vamsa* and the *Vishnu Purana* had explored his childhood adventures. Later texts, such as the *Bhagavata Purana* and the *Gita Govinda*, dramatize his romance with the *gopis* and with Radha. These texts are still revered today, to be read out aloud in gatherings and enacted in annual pageantries, such as on the extremely popular festivals of Krishna Lila and Janmashtami.

The vibrant set of paintings of the *Bhagavata Purana*, for instance, are each "staged" in domed pavilions, with the starched contours of costumes, the use of intense dark eyes and rehearsed gestures for communication. Whether seated or standing, each figure is isolated against a red, blue or, sometimes, yellow background that acts as a brilliant back-drop or stage "curtain." The movement of figures is invariably in single file, laterally in one direction, as though on stage moving both through space and time.

Such paintings provide conclusive evidence for a miniature style that flourished in the first half of the 16th century, long before the formation of the Mughal studio of painters. It is now believed that the Mughal emperor Akbar recruited much of the talent for his new and dynamic school of painting from other court centers that existed in central India: in Gwalior, Jaun-

91

pur, Mandu, Gujarat, and in Chittorgarh in Rajasthan. This fact is confirmed not only by the overwhelming majority of Hindu artists at the Mughal court, often giving their place of origin, but also by the eclectic vigor and different idioms in early Mughal paintings of the *Tuti Nama* and *Hamza Nama*.

Yet, by what seems a curious paradox, some of the earliest surviving manuscripts of Rajasthan have been worked upon by Muslim artists. The first definitive proof of painting in Mewar, the premier state of Rajasthan, is in a *Ragamala* set of paintings that are dated to the year 1605, by a painter called Nasir-ud-din. Again, the spectacular and recent discovery of another *Ragamala* set in the Bundi style, but painted at

communication, set against flat expanses of color with a schematic treatment of trees and flowers. During the interim 30 years of warfare and stubborn defiance of Mughal authority, it is interesting to note that the Mewar Rajputs employed Muslim painters in their service, who in all probability came from the Mughal court. This subtle interaction brings a new pitch, a new sophistication to these miniatures.

Yet, from the start, Rajput painting is unmistakably different from the refined court art and book illustrations of the Mughals. It developed its own set of priorities, its own sensibility. In the early paintings from Mewar and Bundi, the colors are inflamed with pure passion, undiluted. In *Ragini Bhairavi*, a brutal, brilliant red

Chunar in Uttar Pradesh, states clearly that it was painted by three artists who had learnt their trade with the Persian masters of the Mughal atelier. Yet this set, which is dated to 1591, belongs to the formative style of Bundi, and is already imbued with the vibrant colors and lyricism of Rajput painting.

In the 17th century, all of north India lay under the rule of the Mughal emperors. It was natural that the exuberant burst of Mughal art would affect and influence the art of the Rajput courts. It seems that a seminal school of painting had already developed at Chittor in the 16th century. A set of the *Gita Govinda* may belong here, depicting the idealized lovers in intense

serves as the background to a captivating woman seated before the Shiva *linga*, performing a *puja*. White flower garlands draped on the *linga*, a triangular corner of the blue sky, the peacock on the roof, and the intensely black eyes and hair of the lady are the only accents here, in a Bundi miniature of the 16th century. The use of bold, primitive colors brings a savage intensity to these early paintings. A remarkable affinity is shared between the lady profiled and the dark peacock above, as though they indulge in the same ecstatic response to life.

These early paintings are permeated with an emotive response which shocks almost as much as it elevates the viewer to a sense of religiosity. The atmosphere is one that is "not so much mystic as almost violently vital." The critic Herman Goetz, writing about pictures of the Bundels school, expresses the idea that "as in the poems, eroticism is not a medium of mysticism, but mysticism is the pretext and disguise of eroticism. It is the loftiness not of the ascetic but of the Kshatriya."

Ragamala paintings seem, indeed, to have been the preserve and privilege of the Rajputs in north India. In the second half of the 16th century, the songs of Mirabai were sung at the Rajput courts in a surge of religious awakening. At Orcha, the *Rasikapriya* of Keshava Das had just been composed in 1594, and soon after was set to pictorial illustrations in Mewar. In the early

17th century, the hundred verses of the poet Amaru, the *Amaru Sataka*, was also set to pictures and poems of the Malwa school, in a heightened exaltation of the heroine. The depiction of the *nayika* (lover), in her different moods and situations, becomes the obsession in both poems and visual imagery. As a concept, *raga* lends credibility to the translation of sound into image. Derived from the Sanskrit root *ranja*, to color, the *raga* literally means "coloring." With reference to music, it

Left, detail from the Gita Govinda. Right, Bhairavi from the Bundi school C. 1600. Above, Nata Raja C.1650.

implies some means being used to "color" or influence the mind with a definitive emotive response, to inflame it with a certain passion. Since music then is colored and tinged with specific overtones, how appropriate to introduce color and form and visual aids to enhance the expression of a mood, or a time of day, or a season.

Every detail, from the mention of sandal paste or musk or camphor, or ashes smeared on the body, to the leaves quivering with excitement and dewdrops glistening on the lotus, to the sound of parrots in the forest, is used to arouse our sensations. It is the *physical* summoning that is vital here, which awakens us to the sound and smell and color, which contributes to the essential vitality of these paintings. Some of them, at least those that are exquisitely finished, remain as images in the mind when the music has died away.

A young lissom woman, with a waist as slender as an hourglass, her body smeared with a paste of saffron and camphor, is shown wandering through the forest with her *vina*, followed by deer who seem infatuated with her, as might be described in a verse placed above the picture. This is *Ragini Todi*, which embodies the anguish of *vipralabdha*, of being separated from her lover.

Quite a remarkable number of *raginis* portray the *nayika* as practicing *tapas*, leading a remote and austere life. Among them is *Ragini Bangali*, who has retreated from the world to assuage her ardor by focusing her mind and heart on Lord Shiva. An unusual origin is found for *Asavari Ragini*, also known as *Ragini Ahiri*, which suggests her connection with the Ahirs, the cowherd nomads living in the hills. Invariably she is seated upon a rock, in a skirt of leaves, her skin gleaming in dark blue to suggest her tribal origins. Summoned by the music of the shehnai, the inscription says, snakes desert their sandal trees and swarm up to the rocks to coil at her feet; white cranes by the water listen, enchanted; and the forest is vibrant with the sound and color of birds. In some depictions, she herself plays upon a wind instrument, the *nagasara*.

In literature and painting, there is a sensuous delight in the charms of nature: in the colors of the sky, of the rivers in space, of animals responding to the change of seasons. An entire body of literature developed on the seasons, beginning with the classic poem by Kalidasa of the *Ritusamhara*. The depiction of each month in poems and paintings is known as the

Baramasa. In the month of *Magha* (January–February), poet Keshava says, forests and gardens echo with the cries of the peacock, pigeon and koel. Bees hum around. The air is scented with musk, camphor and sandal. The sounds of the *mridanga* and other musical instruments are heard. All are celebrating the advent of spring. "If you love me," the beloved entreats her lover, "do not leave me in this month of Magha."

The theme of romantic love is celebrated in a 12th-century poem by the poet Jayadeva, who singles out Radha for the first time as the heroine. In his *Gita Govinda,* the *dramatis personae* are Krishna, Radha and the *dutika* or messenger, who serves as their confidante. The meetings of these eternal lovers in a secret grove, the anguish of their estrangements and reunion, the different phases of Radha pining for Krishna are described in successive cantos. In these verses Krishna grows to become more than a lover or a mere hero; he becomes the personification of love itself.

In the devotional literature that followed, romantic love was conceived as an exalted experience. Jayadeva's poem received instant recognition, and inspired a wide spectrum of love poems. In the west, Bilvamangala composed a genealogy on the child Krishna, known as the *Balagopala Stuti.* In Bengal in the 15th century the poets Vidyapati and Chandidasa wrote poems in which the poet identified himself wholly with the disorders of the mind, the sensations and the passions experienced by the lovers. In Mewar state the princess Mirabai composed ecstatic songs for her patron deity, Krishna, in the form of *Giri Govardhana.* The Bhakti movement, initiated in Rajasthan by Shri Vallabhacharya, established a cult center, and inspired his disciples such as Sur Das, Krishna Das and other poets.

Krishna, the cowherd boy or Gokula, dark as the clouds and beautiful, emerges from the forests of Vrindavan to lead home the cows at the bewitching hour of golden dusk. The haunting melodies of his flute fill the village girls with longing, for they recognize it to be the call to love. In the autumn nights they steal into the forest where Krishna stands before them, wearing a crown of peacock feathers and a yellow *dhoti,* his blue-black skin shimmering in the moonlight. Using his powers of delusion, he provides each girl with a semblance of himself, and they dance as the moon rises, saturating the forest.

The love play of Krishna and the *gopis,* known as the *Krishna Lila,* becomes one of the enduring elements of village life. In Vaishnava experience, the flute is the call of God, causing the souls of men and women to give up their worldly attachments and to gather to adore him. In one such incident, he steals up and carries away the clothes of the *gopis* as they bathe in the river Yamuna, and then he sits on the Kadamba tree, enticing them to come out of the water in their nakedness. The next intimate moments of passion, reflected in the relationship between the lover and his beloved, can be interpreted in terms of ecstasy, as it has been explored by Christian and Sufi mystics.

In pictures illustrating texts such as the

Gita Govinda, the artist employed poetic symbols—lotuses swaying in a stream, creepers embracing a tree trunk, trees bursting into bloom—to suggest the intimate passion of the lovers. The movement of clouds, of rain, of lightning, of rivers, were each charged with implicit meaning. In literature, they sometimes served as a catalyst, bringing lovers together.

There seems to have been a continuous exodus of artists from the Mughal court, and also from the Deccan, to feed the demands of north India. When Emperor Aurangzeb determined upon a return to Islamic orthodoxy in the 1660s, the artists of the Mughal court were set free to join and influence other centers of court painting. The impact of Mughal sophistication is keenly felt in Bikaner painting, which seems to assemble the best of both idioms. Delicate pages of a *Devi Mahatmya* are suffused with subtle tones of muted greens and grays rarely found in other Rajput painting, with a pink demon who defies the usual iconography and brandishes instead a double-barrelled musket! Once more, in the royal portrait of Shri Karan Singh of Bikaner, the drawing is tinted with pink and green wash, and illumined with pearl strands—to achieve the formal elegance typical of portraits from the reign of Shah Jahan.

A new genre of painting developed in the 18th century, to depict the pastimes, the amusements and the romantic ideals of Rajput court life. This includes a large

number of portraits in durbar, equestrian studies of rulers, and hunting scenes, especially from the smaller states and *thikanas*. Consider, for instance, a magnificent page depicting Raja Umed Singh of Udaipur enjoying a dance performance. This scene is inscribed with the names of two courtiers and of the dancer, set against vibrating patterns of red and green, in a dynamic rhythm that is quite different from the frozen assemblies in depictions of later durbars.

Left, Nayalha-Nayika theme C.1650. Right, Kishangath school C. 1750.

The Rajput rulers are now depicted in different ceremonies of state, and religious festivals. Ladies out on a hunting expedition shoot at tigers, while the sky is stained the hot orange of monsoon sunsets, and birds raise their customary clamor at sundown. Even when the ladies are shown idling away their time on a terrace, beside a game of *chaupad*, the subtle curve of the horizon and the silver moon cupped into the sky betray their secret yearnings.

The most eloquent expression of Rajput chivalry is to be found in paintings from the state of Kishangarh. In this small state that was founded only in 1609, the subjects include hunting scenes and portraits, but they also explore most explicitly the scope of courtly love. The delicate refinements and technique derive from an appreciation of the Mughal style at Delhi and at Oudh; yet the heightened sense of lyricism owes much to the sensibilities and influence of the ruler, Savant Singh. He was not only an accomplished poet, but also a religious devotee, writing poems under the name of Nagari Das, to revive once again the romance of Krishna, with a personal identification. His own romance with the bewitching singer and poet, Bani Thani, served to endorse this viewpoint, and to generate a new genre of courtly love. From 1740 to 1756 he withdrew to live in Vrindavan, in adoration of Krishna; after which he abdicated the throne in favor of his son, Sardar Singh.

During the 14 years that followed, a small group of paintings were conceived that were large in size, but exquisite in their detailing and finish. With just a few exceptions, they celebrate the romantic encounter between Radha and Krishna. The setting here may be deep in the woods, but the lovers possess the elegance of prince and princess. Figures are reduced to miniature scale, set against the vast expanse of a lake or against a carpet of towering trees— to suggest perhaps the sense of eternity that encompasses them.

The final gesture of courtly love is conveyed in a painting where, amidst their many attendants, Radha and Krishna are enthroned, against the far distant mirage of marble palaces. Male followers play upon the flute, while a female attendant offers *paan*. In Rajput etiquette, the offering of the betel leaf is a matter of social form; but the offering of *paan* by Radha to Krishna becomes a token of her deep adoration. So Krishna becomes immortalized in poetry and in painting, as the prince and the ideal lover.

A SCORE OF TRADITIONS: A SCORE OF STYLES

Rajasthan, or Rajputana as the area used to be called when it consisted of 20-odd "native states" under British paramountcy, is, literally translated, the land of the Rajputs, who were, for well-nigh a thousand years, the traditional ruling and landed aristocracy of most of the states in the area. Though a minority in term of population, their political and military dominance have left their mark, giving the whole of Rajputana an overall unity of outlook and attitudes. This persists in Rajasthan today. Historically, however, despite Rajput dominance, Rajputana seldom presented a united face to external aggression, whether of the Muslim invaders down to the Mughals or, ultimately, of the British.

So, in a sense, in Rajasthan we have 20-odd sub-histories to contend with, with all their implications in cultural and material terms. Therefore, while the contributions that follow essentially cover places, the presentation of specific historical backgrounds, to supplement the overall historical essay in Part I of this volume, cannot be avoided.

The emphasis is on leading visitors from the familiar to the less familiar, but equally exciting, byways of the destinations covered, always keeping in mind the practical aspects. The pattern adopted is coverage from a series of central, nodal points, radiating outwards, often across the old princely state boundaries and even those of Rajasthan's modern districts. This should help visitors to plan their trip on a modular basis, adding or subtracting modules according to individual interests and the time available.

RAJASTHAN

JAIPUR

Soon after he came to the Amber throne in 1699, the 11-year-old Jai Singh II went to pay his respects to Emperor Aurangzeb in Delhi. The aged Mughal, the story goes, grasped the young man's hands, and asked just how he expected to be powerful if his hands were tied. Pat came Jai Singh's reply. When a bridegroom takes his bride's hand, he is vowing to protect her for life. Thus, after the royal gesture, he would need no arms because the mighty Mughal would protect him.

Such bare-faced cheek impressed Aurangzeb. And to show how Jai Singh outshone both his ancestors and his fellow Rajputs, he later rewarded his crafty impertinence with the hereditary title *Sawai*, meaning one-and-a-quarter. Jai Singh lived up to the compliment. First he excelled at the Rajput soldiering game. Later, confident of peace and stability, he encouraged his Kachchwaha clan to change from war-loving Rajputs to peace-loving citizens. On a dried-up lake beneath his crammed hill-fort, he built a new capital, naming it Jaipur after himself—although *jai* conveniently means victory, too. It was a perfect piece of humanist town-planning. Merchants and craftsmen flocked to it. Affluence—and the famous pink color of its buildings—followed. And it continues to thrive today.

Jai Singh envisaged this first planned Rajput city as the capital of a united Rajputana, a center of government, trade and worship. Some 250 years later, his foresight brought ambition to reality. In 1948, after independence, Maharaja Man Singh II became Rajpramukh, head of the newly-formed Rajasthan Union, consolidated as Rajasthan State the following year. Jaipur became the administrative and commercial capital of a democratized collection of former princely states.

It is a busy, bustling city with busy, bustling people—over 600,000 of them. Natter and debate in the corridors of its Assembly affect the lives of more than 26 million people sprawled over 132,000 square miles (343,000 square km)—Jai Singh's state was only the fourth-largest Rajput state, a mere 15,500 square miles.

Commercially, old and new constantly clash. Traditional Jaipur crafts of jewelry, enameling, metalwork, printed cloths, handloom weaving and carving thrive side by side with engineering, distilling, shoe-making, drugs, glass and sports equipment industries. Successful *durri* makers, carpet weavers and jewelers have their world headquarters here.

In the wide avenues, quantities of bouncy Ambassador and nippy Maruti cars dart between the seemingly oblivious, haughty and splay-legged camels. A shoe trader in Johari Bazaar does brisk business with a gaggle of girls out on a pre-wedding spree, drenched in silver-edged, paint-box bright saris. Above the cabin-like shops, agile monkeys frolic about the pink-painted facades. Deep in a jeweler's cavern, the latest European designs twinkle next to traditional Jaipur baubles. And down a narrower bazaar, a top Western designer seeks out ideas, jostling with the jewel-bedecked local ladies swathed in yards of dazzling mango-orange, tomato-red, lipstick-pink and lagoon-blue cotton.

The Founder: Jaipur is a living testament to one of the most remarkable men of his age. Jai Singh II was supremely talented—politically, intellectually and on the battlefield. Indeed, the more practical historians claim he won his title of *Sawai* aged 14 at the siege of Khalna in 1702, skillfully defending Mughal interests against the Marathas.

This triumph set the tone. And by 1723, aged just 35, Jai Singh had performed a feat of political juggling. Having backed both contenders for the imperial throne after Aurangzeb's death in 1707, he was understandably thrown off his own throne by the suspicious winner, Bahadur Shah. Undaunted, he reunited the big Rajput states against the Mughal. As usual, marriage cemented the alliance. First, the Rajputs threw the Mughals out of Jodhpur. Next, they threw Bijai, Jai Singh's brother and the Mughal puppet, out of Amber and Jai Singh reclaimed his throne.

Warring over, Jai Singh left the battlefield to indulge himself and his intellectual passions: science and the arts. The result was Jaipur. And, despite its importance and activity today, Jai Singh's city not only stands as originally planned, but there is a pride in its maintenance that is all too rare in India. So it is best to explore on foot, leaving transport for the more spread out buildings outside the walls.

A good place to start is at the statue of the founder, Maharaja Sawai Jai Singh II (ruled 1699–1743). It stands just outside the southern wall. Behind him lies the city he designed with a young Bengali, an engineer and scholar named Vidyadhar Bhattacharaya.

The foundation stone was laid on November 25, 1727. Their plan was a simple grid system: seven blocks of buildings divided by very wide, tree-lined avenues. At its heart lies the palace, covering the space of another two blocks. The whole is surrounded by a crenellated wall with seven gates. Orientation is to the northeast, on two temples standing on the surrounding hills. Essentially, it follows the principles of the ancient Hindu architectural treatise, the *Shilpa Shastra*.

Pink Welcome: To these Jai Singh added revolutionary ideas: hygiene,

beauty and commerce. But Jaipur's all-over pinkness is probably not his. A few of the grander public buildings were indeed built of expensive pink sandstone. But it seems to have been Maharaja Man Singh who dressed up the rest of the city in the symbolically welcoming color when the Prince of Wales, later Edward VII, visited Jaipur in 1876. During this vast spring clean, he repaired the walls and gates and gave sloping roof verandas to the old shops. Today, every home-owner within the city is obliged by law to maintain his facade—and if he fails, the city does it and charges him.

Moving along MI Road, **Singpol** (Lion Gate) is the gate farthest west on the south wall. Like all the gateways, it has two kiosks above and machicolations over the entrance. And like all the gateways, it was until this century locked at night, leaving passengers arriving on night trains stranded until daybreak. The wall it pierces averages 20 feet (seven meters) high and a stout nine feet (three meters) thick, with plenty of bastions and towers, a parapet loopholed for musketry and holes for cannon to fire through. This was

Early postcard of Hawa Mahal

THE CHOWK AND HOWA MAHAL

not all of the city's defenses. The vulnerability of the plains was further protected by forts crowning all the important summits of the surrounding rugged hills.

Inside the gate is **Khajana Walon ka Rasta**, the market where the marble carvers work. This is the first of many *mohallas*, rectangular blocks which were each designed for a particular trade or craft. Each was planned with a precise number of shops and houses built in a distinctive style. At the top of the street, a right turn into another market, **Chandpol Bazaar**, leads to the first of three big crossroads where the widest avenues meet. **Chhoti Chaupar** is the first, where local villagers come to sell their produce.

Already, the spaciousness and formal elegance of the city is stunning. Chandpol and the other main streets are an impressive 111 feet (36 meters) broad. Secondary streets maintain their airiness at 55 feet (18 meters) and alleys are half as wide again.

Such detailed planning did not hamper speed. Lakes to supply water, the sturdy walls and the principal buildings were up in six or seven years.

Immediately, Jaipur took on a magnetic quality. Jai Singh's religious tolerance encouraged the Digamber Jains to come, who have since produced a regular flow of scholars and administrators. And his particular interest, Vaishnavism, resulted in all the major sects building temples here.

To entice more wealth, Jai Singh invited merchants to come and build houses to their own designs, so long as they conformed to the architect Vidhyadhar's general plan and high standards. They flocked here, together with bankers to serve them, so that in 1870 the British Resident wrote that "Jeypore is as it were a sort of Lombard Street of Rajpootana."

Thakurs (landowners) built smart townhouses, although they later moved outside the walls for more space. They were the maharaja's courtiers, whose lands were hereditary royal gifts or rent-free presents to a royal favorite. All courtiers danced attendance on their ruler on important festivals, birthdays and whenever they might be summoned.

In the palace corridors, they peppered the ceaseless hum with gossip

and intrigue. In the ceremonial processions, they provided color, sparkle and fine clothes. Even this century, the Thakur of Isarda would appear decked out in jewelry worth 25,000 rupees and proudly wearing his gold anklet, a privilege of the Tazimi Sardars. And at each ceremony, he and his fellow nobles knelt to offer their maharaja a gold coin in the *nazar* ritual, symbolizing a reaffirmation of loyalty.

Crossing Chhoti Chaupar, the avenue continues as **Tripolia Bazaar**, where cooking utensils and costume jewelry are sold. But down **Maniharon ke Rasta**, a lane on the right, craftsmen make multicolored, striped lacquer bangles. With astonishing speed and deftness they heat, roll, stretch and mold the tiny bands.

Back on Tripolia Bazaar, the tall tower on the left is **Iswari Minar Swarga Sal**, (Minaret Piercing Heaven). It is a proud monument built by a weak ruler Iswari Singh (ruled 1743-51). Only five of Jai Singh's multitude of children lived to maturity. And Iswari, who succeeded him, did not take after his father. Unable to face the advancing Maratha army, he committed suicide by taking poison and making a cobra bite him. But the moment was given a degree of Rajput honor by his women: three *ranis* and a concubine also took poison and 21 wives joined Iswari's funeral pyre as *satis*.

Jaipur's days of glory clouded. As the Marathas, helped by the remarkable French military expert, General Benoit de Boigne, pushed up through northern India, they kept close control over their puppet Jaipur rulers. Suddenly, the tables were turned. The Marathas quarreled amongst themselves and the British swapped sides to defend the Rajputs.

The British pincer-hold on the princes had begun to close. An alliance with Jaipur in 1803 helped counter further Maratha onslaughts but Jaipur had sacrificed independence for British paramountcy and protection.

However, life for the rulers was not bad. Massive wealth poured in. And, after 1835, Jaipur had no wars to pay for. So rulers indulged themselves and their fancies in their luxurious City Palace.

City Palace Complex: Tripolia (triple-arched) Gate, just beyond the min-

Jantar Mantar, the observatory of Maharaja Jai Singh II.

110

aret, is the grand entrance to the City Palace complex, cutting through the center of the southern wall. Maharajas, dazzling in a sun-burst of gold and jewels, would emerge here, seated atop their painted and silk-bedecked elephants. Lesser mortals now enter through **Atish Pol** (Stable Gate) to the left. After another tunnel gate and a right turn, this city in miniature begins with its **Chandni Chowk** (Moonlight Square), the courtyards of the palace stables.

Further on, huge geometric shapes dot the area on the right like forgotten surrealist stage props. This is the **Jantar Mantar** [*j(y)antra* = instrument, device; *mantra* = (magic) formula], Jai Singh's open-air observatory of outsize astronomical instruments. In mathematics and astronomy, as in war and town-planning, Jai Singh did nothing by halves—his scientific inventiveness was supposed to have emerged when, aged 13, he devised an irrigation system to water the hanging gardens of Amber Fort.

Jai Singh first built a Jantar Mantar in Delhi in 1724-27, the first observatory in India, believing size would

improve accuracy.

Later, while governor of Agra, he built three more, at Ujjain, Varanasi and Mathura, ancient centers of religion and learning. But for daily observations and constant consultations with his guru, Pandit Jaganath, he needed an observatory at home. The Jaipur set, built 1728-34, is the largest and best preserved. Not only was it built of stone, but in the 19th century Lieutenant A. Garret and Pandit Chandradhar Guleri carefully restored it. It was in use until the 1940s. For, in company with many other states, Jaipur kept its own solar time. It was read off the quadrants on either side of the vast gnomon (right angle) that acts as a huge sundial called the *Samrat Yantra* (Supreme Instrument). Size made the readings accurate down to three seconds. It was then announced to the people: less important times by a drummer at the top of the steps; more important times by a gun fired from Nahargarh fort above the city. The purposes of the other instruments are less obviously practical. The large, circular *Ram Yantras* are for reading altitudes and azimuths—distances in

ai Singh II
lso built
bservatories
n Delhi,
Mathura,
jjain and
aranasi.

the sky. The dozen *Rashivilayas* are for calculating celestial latitudes and longitudes.

Gainda ki Deorhi (Rhinoceros Gate), round the corner, leads to the main buildings of the City Palace. They are a showpiece of palace architecture, happily mingling Hindu and Mughal styles. Following the Rajput fortress pattern, a series of increasingly private rooms leads to the center of the palace. Following the Mughal tradition of Delhi and Agra, the buildings for various uses stand separate from one another. They are well ventilated to catch the breeze and are often quite small. Thus, the stables and administrative offices lead ultimately to the royal residence, the **Chandra Mahal**.

Royal Wardrobe: First comes the dazzling white **Mubarak Mahal** (Palace of Welcome), built in 1900 by Maharaja Madho Singh II (ruled 1880-1922) as a guest house. Later it served as the *Mahakma Khas* (Royal Secretariat). Now it houses part of the **City Palace Museum** and is called the *Tosha Khana* (Royal Wardrobe).

The suite of rooms on the first floor, encircled by an elaborately carved balcony, houses such treats as the special black and gold Diwali festival dress, whose *odhni* (shawl) alone has some 18 pounds (eight kg) of gold woven into it. Then there are Maharaja Ram Singh's riding clothes, Pratap Singh's wedding outfit, fine muslins, exotic striped silk pajamas and locally printed cottons.

The wardrobe also houses the royal accouterments of hookah bases, Jaipur pottery, Mughal glass, marble toys for junior royals and an exceptional collection of musical instruments. But the most extraordinary piece is the *atamsukh* of Madho Singh I (ruled 1750-68). This raspberry-pink garment of Banaras silk, glowing with gold *butti* (dotted) designs, is vast. Legend tells that its owner was 7 feet (2 meters) tall and weighed 500 pounds (225 kg).

Madho Singh II has left his mark throughout the palace, although as a ruler he was not a great innovator and merely continued to support the revolutionary improvements of Ram Singh who, heirless, had adopted him on his deathbed. In fact, the problem of heirs haunted the Kachchwaha house. When, in 1931, the first male heir for

The present Maharaja of Jaipur with courtiers.

two generations was born to a ruling maharaja, such quantities of champagne celebrated the event that the baby's English nanny nicknamed him Bubbles. And on the right wall of the courtyard, beside **Singh Pol** (Lion Gate), stand two white marble elephants to mark the great event.

But first, the **Sileh Khana** (Armory), lies behind the Mubarak Mahal. Here, one of the finest collections of Indian weaponry testifies to Kachchwaha valor. Among every kind of bejeweled dagger, sword, shield and gun, Jai Singh I of Amber's turban-shaped helmet and shield are especially opulent. Far less gentle is a steel mace in the shape of a lotus bud. Lodged firmly in the victim's stomach, it would spring open into a fan of sharp spikes.

The photographs on display are by Ram Singh, who ruled in quieter times. Aided by an Englishman, T. Murray, he put studios and dark-rooms in the palace, snapped away, and later even founded a photography school. His observant eye roams from Parsis playing Shakespeare to records of his philanthropic building projects.

Back to Singh Pol, a typically Hindu square gatehouse with delicate balconies supported by ornate brackets. Its large, bronze double doors lead into a pretty courtyard whose frilly white arches on the salmon-pink walls are 18th-century Rajput decoration. But the **Diwan-i-Khas** (Private Audience Hall) in the center is firmly Mughal, a descendant of Fatehpur Sikri. Within its scalloped arches stand two huge water flasks. Currently the largest single pieces of silver known in the world, they measure 5 feet 3 inches (160 cm) high, with a capacity of 1,800 gallons (8,182 liters). The craftsman, Govind Narain, made them for Madho Singh, using 10,408 troy oz (242.7 kg) of silver. Loyalty to the British crown had persuaded Madho to cross the dangerous seas to witness the coronation of Edward VII. So he chartered a liner, built a temple on board, flung bags of gold, silver and silk into Bombay harbor to invoke the oceans to give him safe passage, and stowed away his urns filled with Ganga water to avoid touching a drop of dirty British stuff.

To the right is the **Diwan-i-Am** (Public Audience Hall), an enclosed room built for the splendor and pageantry of sumptuous court durbars and ceremonies, watched by the ladies from behind the carved screens of the gallery. Now it forms the focus of the **Sawai Man Singh II Museum**. Founded in 1959 by the former ruling family, the museum is run by the distinguished art historian, Dr Asok Das. After the royal wardrobe and armoury, here carpets from Lahore, Herat and Agra cover the walls and one of India's largest chandeliers hangs from the ceiling. Royal palanquins and a chosen few of the magnificent collection of miniature paintings and manuscripts fill the room.

As expected, Jai Singh established the Jaipur library and gave the painting school its distinctive character. Akbar's magnificent illustrated *Ramayana* and *Razmnama* are here but rarely on view. However, you may well see a painting from the *Saras-rasa-grantha* series, such as Krishna playing *holi* with the *gopis*, painted in 1737 for Jai Singh and marking the ultimate refinement of the Jaipur style.

Back across the pink courtyard, under the delicate *jali* (lattice) work of the ladies' corridor to the Hawa Mahal,

amily
tainers at
e City
alace.

Ridhi Sidhi Pol leads to **Pritam Niwas Chowk**, known from its decoration as the Peacock Courtyard. It is a magical, enclosed courtyard with ocher walls, whose four gateways were elaborately decorated by Pratap Singh (ruled 1778-1803) to represent the four seasons. Above the parrot gate, girls would sing from the balcony.

Next, through a Wedgewood-blue hall, **Pritam Niwas** houses more Mughal glass and leads to **Chandra Mahal** (Moon Palace), the seven-tiered, pyramid-like inner sanctum of the palace. These were the royal apartments, complete with an internal garden. Crowning them, the **Mukut Mandir** has superb views.

The **Chandra Mandir**, the ground floor, has air-cooling water channels and delicate floral designs on the ceiling. From its terrace the ruler could look across the Jai Niwas garden to the **Sri Govinda Temple** where the deity was placed so he could see it. Here at the center of his creation, Jai Singh II spent his last years, seemingly alternating between pious studies of Vaishnavism and more carnal play.

Later Madho Singh II followed his illustrious predecessor in his two passions: orthodox Hinduism and sex. To satisfy his sexual appetite, Madho's three secondary *ranis* and 18 concubines were supplemented with city women. Perhaps he entertained them in his newly decorated **Sheesh Mahal** at the top of Chandra Mahal. When the floral inlaid doors are closed and the lights lit, the whole room is like an inverted medieval reliquary. Walls, ceiling, and scalloped arches are inlaid with red and green glass and mirrors, the floral designs, diamond-shapes and cartouches outlined with thick bands of gold.

Leaving the palace museum complex, the road straight ahead leads to **Jalebi Chowk** (Sweetmeat Square), where drums and the *shehnai* (a reed instrument) used to help announce Jaipur time from the **Nakkar Khana** (Drum House).

Patron Deity: In this square is Sri Govinda Deva Temple. The Jaipur rulers were devotees of Krishna. And Govinda is Krishna's name when he is a cowherd, enjoying fiery romances with Radha and other *gopis* (female cowherds). This flirtatious living was at Vrindavan, near Mathura. From there Jai Singh brought the image of Govinda and put it in his brand-new temple in 1735, establishing it as the guardian deity of Jaipur rulers. From this time, the maharaja would begin addressing his people with the words "subjects of Govinda Devji," implying they ruled merely as an instrument of the all-puissant deity.

Crowds of devout locals come daily to the temple to perform *puja* (worship), offering jolly songs, music, flowers, sweetmeats, colored powders and spices. Each of the seven pujas lasts about half an hour and marks a part of the daily ritual of the deity. Thus, Krishna's awakening is around 5 a.m., his dressing around 10.30 a.m. and his evening prayers around 8 p.m. Behind the temple there is a pleasant garden and an old tank where crocodiles were once bred.

Back through Jalebi Chowk and **Siri Deorhi Gate**, up **Hawa Mahal Bazaar** to the right, the **Hawa Mahal** (Palace of the Winds) adjoins the outside of the palace wall. It was built by Maharaja Pratap Singh (ruled 1778-1803) in 1799. A poet and devotee of Krishna, one of his couplets suggests it was

Left, Jal Mahal or Water Palace. Right, Hawa Mahal or Palace of Winds.

115

dedicated to Krishna and Radha. Its five-story, gently tapering facade of pink sandstone is encrusted with lace-fine screens and carved balconies coating its 953 niches and windows. The top three stories are just a single room thick. It served as a giant, well-ventilated grandstand from which royal ladies confined to *purdah* could see some of the Jaipur fun. Now it is another museum of Jaipur arts, with good views from the top.

Lively Bazaars: South of the Hawa Mahal, **Johari Bazaar** is the other side of the **Badi Chaupar** crossroads. Attracted by the city and court patronage, many jewelers, goldsmiths and silversmiths settled in this area and made Jaipur a major center for gem stone-cutting. And it still is, with about 40,000 stone-cutters working here. In the narrow lanes of **Gopalji ka Rasta** and **Haldiyon ka Rasta**, craftsmen sit crosslegged in dark rooms. One polishes an emerald, another cuts a ruby, while another sets pearls, diamonds and sapphires in gold.

The most fascinating work to watch is *meenakari*, or enameling. Like *champlevé* work, the delicate patterns of birds and flowers are fired in glowing red, deep green, peacock blue and white; the gold jewel is then given further sparkle with emeralds, rubies, white sapphires and dangling pearls. This painstaking, high-precision art was probably introduced into India by the Mughals and into the Amber court by Man Singh I. Today, descendants of those court craftsmen work quietly in the Jaipur lanes, taking up to a fortnight to enamel both sides of a pendant.

There are plenty of cotton shops in Johari Bazaar, too, their white-clad owners shaking out for potential buyers yard upon yard of vivid turquoise, ocher and crimson, each priced according to weight. Quite far down, past the famous LMB shop with its delicious *dahi-vada* and ice-creams, a delightful vegetable market nestles behind grand merchants' houses on the left.

Above some of the delicate facades men work on the flat roofs block-printing cotton or hanging out tie-dye fabric to dry. **Rangwalon-ki-Gali** and **Kishanpol Bazaar** are the real areas to see the two main tie-dye methods being practiced: *bandhani* work is

One of the several use of *Elephas maximus*.

dyed, knotted and bleached to make dark dots on a pale background; *laharia* work is sold as a twisted rope which, unfolded, reveals a blaze of diagonal, rippled stripes.

For the best choice of prints, turn right at the bottom of Johari Bazaar into **Bapu Bazaar** which leads into **Nehru Bazaar**. Here shop after shop is stacked high with the traditional floral prints in soft blood-reds or blues as well as current European designs of bold candy stripes. Between the fabrics, other shops stock heady Indian perfumes, banks of bangles and fun costume jewelry versions of the fine meenakari work.

Through **New Gate**, between Bapu and Nehru Bazaars, the road leads out of Jai Singh's city into its sprawling 19th and 20th century overspill. **Ram Niwas Public Gardens**, straight ahead down Jawaharlal Nehru Marg, was laid out by Maharaja Ram Singh (ruled 1835-80), its original 76 acres (31 hectares)/(now 36 acres/14.5 hectares) landscaped by a certain Dr. de Fabeck.

After 16 years of impotent rule as a minor, Ram Singh reached majority in 1851. Under him the Public Works

Department was set up in 1860, headed by a British officer who siphoned off 12 percent of the state revenue. Results were speedy. The state postal system began in 1861, carried by camels and runners but consistently run at a loss, perhaps because letters and parcels on state business went free. Seven years later, the municipality was established. In 1874, the city's piped water was turned on, pumped along iron pipes from Aman-i-Shah river west of Chandpol Gate. Street lighting came later.

The Ram Niwas Gardens are a microcosm of Ram Singh's achievements. On the left, a former theater now houses the **Ravindra Rangmanch**, the gallery of modern art. On the right, past the zoo and a crocodile breeding farm, is the **Maharaja College**. When founded in 1845, it taught Urdu, Persian and basic English. Later, Ram Singh established Oriental and Sanskrit Colleges and, in 1868, a School of Art which, with notable foresight, laid particular emphasis on the local Jaipur crafts. However, literacy in the state had only reached 2.52 percent by the 1901 census, reinforcing the horse-

City policeman attempts to control Jaipur traffic.

proud Rajput idiom that "A Rajput who reads will never ride a horse."

The focus of the gardens is **Albert Hall**, housing the **Central Museum**. As its name suggests, it was modeled on the educational Victoria and Albert Museum in London. Prince Albert's son, the then Prince of Wales and the future Edward VII, laid the foundation stone in 1876, although the collection had been forming since 1833. The building was designed by Colonel Sir Samuel Swinton Jacob (1841–1917), a British engineer who from 1867 spent most of his career here. While building the museum, the water-works and other civic buildings—with more in Lucknow, Jodhpur, Bikaner, Simla, Madras and Delhi—he published a portfolio of Indian architectural details which became the colonial architect's handy source-book for fashionable hybrid styles. A virtuoso of Indo-Saracenic style, he was later consulted for the Viceroy's Palace at New Delhi.

Inside the sandstone and white marble treasure-house there are delightful models of Rajasthan festivals, occupations and trades, and collections of puppets, costumes, ivory, pottery and jewelry. There are also sections on geology, armor and a corner for the rest of the world. The brasswork is well worth a look, the plaques, salvers, toys and vases embossed with repoussé work or engraved and lacquered. The brass shields illustrating scenes from the *Ramayana* and the *Mahabharata* with eye-straining precision are especially elaborate.

It is also well worth asking to see the magnificent Persian Garden Carpet kept under lock and key in the detached **Durbar Hall** in front of the museum building. Made in 1632 in Kerman, Persia, its fresh silks show a ravishing garden divided by fish-filled water channels and full of blossoming trees, chirping birds and frolicking animals. It is one of the earliest and best of its kind.

Further down Jawaharlal Nehru Road is a later temple to education, the **Museum of Indology**. In Narain Singh Marg, off to the right, stands the grand town house, **Narain Niwas**, which Madho Singh's emissary, Narain Singh, built in 1881. Rich in *fin de siécle* finery—Afghan carpets, chandeliers, four-poster beds and East India Com-

Central Museum, Albert Hall.

pany furniture—it typifies the taj taste that Madho Singh and his courtiers lapped up. With grandeur gone, it is run as a hotel and therefore possible to visit. In fact, several enterprising ex-nobles have followed their ex-ruler's example at Rambagh Palace and gone into the hotel trade, including the Achrols down on Civil Lines Road and the Bissaus and Khetris up at Chandpol Gate.

Palace, Prison, Treasure Trove: Back on Jawaharlal Nehru Road, at the far end on the left lies an incongruous flight of fancy, the **Moti Doongri**. It is a fort shaped like a Scottish Castle. One of its inmates in the 1930s was Lallji Moti Singh, an illegitimate son of Madho Singh. His crime was to attack a boy and chop off his testicles. Although at court *Tazimi Sardars* (senior landowners) were above the law, the British police chief locked him up. However, his food was delivered daily from the royal kitchens.

Later, during the 1970s, Gayatri Devi, third wife of Man Singh II, lived in the Moti Doongri. Although reportedly plagued by night-time mosquitoes and day-time monkeys, the views over the city from the refurbished interior compensated for any discomfort. The personal royal treasure was stored here, too. And when in 1975 the taxmen swooped, they found gold worth four to six million US dollars in one room, and piles of sparkling jewelry in another. All this was documented and legitimate. But the £19 sterling found in her dressing table was not!

But the place Maharaja Man Singh II and his glamorous wife had made famous were their home along Bhawani Singh Marg, the relatively modest **Rambagh Palace**. Here Jaipur, India and the world watched the fairytale lives of a fairytale couple known to friends as Jai and Ayesha.

The Rambagh began life as a few pleasure pavilions outside the walled city. Ram Singh later organized them into a hunting lodge, *Ram Bagh* (Garden of Ram). It was Madho Singh II who transformed it into a princely playground. On his return from England, he built deep, English herbaceous borders in the garden, still beautifully maintained. In the palace he followed the growing royal Rajput passion for

119

the latest international pleasure kits. Helped by Sir Swinton Jacob, he added a squash court, tennis courts and an indoor swimming pool, complete with trapeze swing suspended across the water. And, since Madho was a polo fanatic, he built a private polo field adjoining the gardens. Later, when a broken arm forced him to relinquish the saddle, in true maharaja style he turned to flying and, like his fellow Jodhpur ruler, built himself an aerodrome.

This fun playground was just one of many palaces Ram Singh's adopted son and successor Man Singh II inherited when he came to the throne in 1922, aged just 11 years. Later, he chose it as his principal home, enlarging and modernizing it in 1931 to be his official residence. And when in 1940 he finally married Princess Gayatri Devi, the emancipated and well-traveled beauty from Cooch Behar in northeast India, Man Singh yet again revamped the royal suites and enlarged the public rooms. Much of his palace survives today: the exotic black marble bathrooms, the boldly geometric furnishings, the Lalique fountain and the London-designed dining rooms.

From the cocoon of this luxurious lifestyle, Maharaja Man Singh II ruled Jaipur State until India's independence in 1947. He was then made Rajpramukh of the new Rajasthan Union and later served for seven years as India's first ambassador to Spain. But to his former subjects he was always their maharaja, immensely popular right up to his tragic death in 1970 which resulted from a fall while playing polo at Cirencester in England.

Like Ram Singh before him, Man Singh mixed tradition with modernity. But the extremes were fiercer. The seesaw life of feudal kingly responsibility at home and modern fun abroad set the pattern for his life. For Jaipur in the 1920s and 1930s still had an unsophisticated, medieval flavor, given piquancy by the outdated Rajput reverence for valor and honor.

The maharaja's water came from a special well outside the city walls, carried in daily by four men and guarded by a troop of soldiers. Passersby put down their umbrellas to prevent any shadow falling on the royal fluid.

Chilums **(smoking pipes) and** *surais* **(water pots) are the fastest selling items in a potter's shop.**

All traffic stopped. When Man Singh went driving, his route was closed an hour beforehand so the air would be clear of dust. Literacy, even among the *thakurs*, was around 12 per cent in the city. And court life was a continual mire of intrigue, bickering, jealousies over betrothals, wrangles over adoptions and jockeying for royal favor and position. For the king's word and wish were law. Outside the capital, in Jaipur state baby girls were frequently killed. Rajputs practiced their war-training by wrestling with panthers.

On March 14, 1931, the Viceroy, Lord Irwin, invested Man Singh with his full powers as His Highness Sarada-i-Rajaha-i-Hindustan Raj Rajendra Maharaja Dhiraj, Lieutenant-General Sir Sawai Man Singhji Bahadur the Second, Maharaja of Jaipur, the 39th and last ruler of the Kachchwaha Clan.

Man Singh now indulged his two loves: the army and polo. He created a new regiment, the Sawai Man Guards, named after that superior title and modeled on the British Foot Guards. As for polo, his playing brought him and his team worldwide fame. Today, the 61st Cavalry, one of India's few

mounted regiments, is headquartered in Jaipur and renowned for its polo skills, best seen at the **Polo Grounds** during the annual March season. "Jai" and his Rajput royals formed the legendary Indian team that arrived in London in May 1933, with 39 horses, 51 *syces* and a polo-stick maker. They turned hearts and heads with their dashing clothes and turbans and then swept up all the big trophies. It was a feat never to be repeated.

By 1958, Man Singh and Ayesha's lives were considerably less grand. Rambagh became the first palace hotel of Rajasthan, providing Jaipur with a good hotel, the palace with maintenance and Man Singh with income. The couple moved down the road to **Raj Mahal Palace**, the former British Residency—yet again easy to visit as it is now a hotel stuffed with royal knicknacks, trophies and photographs.

Here Jaipur hospitality continued. When Prince Philip, the Duke of Edinburgh, came to stay in 1965 it was *Holi*, the Hindu festival marking the arrival of spring. Prince and ex-prince were treated with traditional disre-

A typical Jaipur street.

spect. Family albums show the British prince drenched in pink, green and yellow water, but smiling broadly. His letter of thanks reveals all: "Without the slightest shadow of doubt, I have never experienced anything like last week in my whole life. Every moment was sheer joy and it's only the bruises from polo and the pink stain on my fingers which remain to convince me that the whole thing wasn't some marvellous dream (Crewe, *The Last Maharaja*)." Jaipur still gives its visitors a good time.

Trips out of Town: To see Jaipur is to see only the second part of the story. For Jai Singh II conceived it from his fortress-palace at **Amber**, where the Kachchwahas had risen to power and wealth. Amber is just north of Jaipur, with the royal *chhatris* (cenotaphs) and some of Jaipur's protective forts in the same direction, and **Samod** and **Bairat** beyond it. To the east lie the **gardens of Sisodia**, the **gorge of Galta** and beyond them **Dausa** and **Lalsot**. To the south lie first **Sanganer** with its crafts, then **Chatsu** and **Tonk**. And both eastern and southern routes lead to **Ranthambore fort** in Sawai Madhopur.

Out of Jaipur through **Zorawar Singh Gate** in the north wall, a road off to the left leads to **Gaitor** (four miles-/six km), the Kachchwaha royal cremation ground. Here, amid trees where monkeys practice their acrobatics, the white marble *chhatris* of Jaipur's rulers stand majestically silhouetted against Nahargarh hill and fort. Naturally, Jai Singh II's is the finest, the white marble dome supported by 20 pillars richly carved with Hindu mythological scenes.

Back on the Amber road, *chhatris* of the maharanis, the queens, stand on raised ground on the right. Just beyond them is **Man Sagar**, a lake with what looks like a pleasure palace but is in fact **Jalmahal**, a giant blind for aristocratic duck-shooting parties.

The road opposite twists up steeply, then follows the ridge (with spectacular views) to reach **Nahargarh** (Tiger) **Fort**. Alternatively, it is a healthy mile (1.5 km) hike up a paved pathway northwest of the City Palace. The effort is worth it: the sunset views over the city are stunning. Mostly built in 1734 to defend his new city, this was also a retreat for Jai Singh's maharanis, later

Pilgrims rest in the shade near the Govindji temple.

enlarged with an elaborate upper story by Ram Singh in 1868. Jaipur time was boomed out across the city from here. And this is where the maharaja's personal treasure was kept until Man Singh II moved it to Moti Doongri.

Amber: Back on the main road, Amber is reached through high cliffs of two ranges of Aravalli hills. It is an arresting first sight, the honey-colored palace and its snaking walls sprawled over the hill, softly reflected in **Maota Lake**, the whole protected by hills on every side with **Jaigarh fort** overseeing it all.

The Kachchwahas had eyed this superb site from nearby Daosa. They belonged to the Kshatriya, or warrior caste of Hindus. But, as usual in Rajput history, their story blends fact with fiction. Origins are celestial, traced to the sun via Kusa who was the twin son of the god Rama, king of Ayodhya and hero of the Hindu epic, the *Ramayana*. The clan migrated in the 3rd century from Rohtas on the Son river to Gwalior and Narwar in what is now Madhya Pradesh. Here they ruled, with some ups and downs, for 800 years. The mists of legend begin to lift. Taj Karan, known as Dulha Rai (The Bridegroom Prince), left Gwalior in 1128—possibly thrown out by his uncle—and married the beautiful Maroni, daughter of the Bargujar Rajput chief of Daosa. Soon afterwards, Dulha Rai's generous father-in-law is said to have given him Daosa. The Kachchwaha dynasty was established. And around 1150 Dulha Rai's descendant wrested Amber from the Susawat Minas. Stories vary. One says he got them drunk and then butchered them; another that the Minas gave refuge to a Kachchwaha who took the hospitality, then usurped the throne. Anyway, Amber remained the Kachchwaha capital for six centuries and the Minas became hereditary guards of their treasure.

The town's original name was possibly Ambikishwara—a name for the god Shiva, a member of the all-powerful Hindu Trinity—later contracted to Ambiner, then Amber. Other theories take it back to Ambarisha, a king of Ayodhya, or to Amba Mata, goddess of earth and fertility.

Relations with Delhi began early. Before the end of the 12th century, the

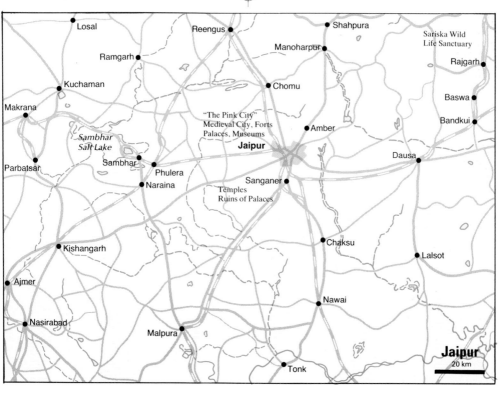

chief Pajuh is said to have married the sister of Prithviraj Chauhan, the last Hindu king of Delhi who was killed by Muhammad Ghori in 1192. But it was the special relationship between the Kachchwahas and the Mughals that brought them real power, influence and wealth.

The moment Muslim power looked like a force to be taken seriously, Bihar Mal (ruled about 1548–74) ensured he was first to pay homage to Humayun. They set the example of typical Mughal-Rajput present exchanging: Humayun gave Bihar Mal command of a 5,000–strong army, and Bihar Mal gave his daughter to Humayun's son, Akbar, and placed his adopted grandson, Man Singh, in Mughal service.

The next chief, Bhagwan Das, intensified relations. He became a good friend of Akbar, apparently saving his life at the battle of Sarnal, and in 1585/6 gave his daughter to Akbar's son, Prince Salim, who later became Emperor Jahangir. Akbar's gift was the command of 5,000 horse soldiers and governorship of Punjab. For it was under Akbar (ruled 1556-1605) that the Mughal empire expanded and

Kachchwaha power grew. The initial reason was that the pilgrimage route to the Muslim shrine at Ajmer crossed Kachchwaha territory and needed to be kept free from bandits. The Kachchwaha-Mughal alliance began.

It was two 16th-century rulers, Man Singh I and Jai Singh I, who benefited most. And with booty from the battlefield, they built and embellished their magnificent **fort-palace**, filling it with elegant court life, gardens and the song and laughter of ladies. In the hierarchy of forts, it has been ranked second only to that of Gwalior in Madhya Pradesh. It may lack Gwalior's raw stamp of Hindu originality but the setting is sublimely picturesque, the stern, rambling exterior belying the well-organized, bejeweled interior whose richness increases as the rooms go higher, opening on to striking views of the gorge.

Visitors can mount the long, steep ramparts by elephant, serenaded by a local playing his *ravanhatha*, a sort of lute. As the elephant plods up, the natural advantages of the site become clearer. With these, Man Singh I (ruled 1589-1614) had confidently begun

Amber town and Palace with Jaigarh Fort above.

building his fort around 1592.

Through **Jai Pol** (Victory Gate), there are shorter elephant rides around the large courtyard. But be careful not to fall victim to the fate of Man Singh's great-grandson, who died after a fall climbing up a ladder to mount his elephant.

Jai Singh I (ruled 1621-67) became the finest of all Kachchwaha generals. He came to the throne aged 11. By 13, he was commanding 3,000 in the Deccan. With a clear idea of where his interests lay, he first fought all over India for Jahangir's successor, Shah Jahan. Then he did some shrewd side-swapping. While Shah Jahan's sons squabbled for power, he shifted his support from Dara to his brother, Aurangzeb, promptly captured Dara who was then murdered by Aurangzeb.

For this and other loyal deeds Aurangzeb heaped prizes on Jai Singh, and the title Mirza Raja with command of 7,000 troops, the maximum permitted to non-members of the royal emperor's family. With this, Jai Singh's finest hour was the defeat and capture of the almost god-like Maratha leader, Shivaji.

Family Shrine: To the right of the huge, arched double gateway, the **Singh Pol** (Lion Gate), steps lead up from the courtyard to the **Kali Temple**. This is the Kachchwaha family shrine built by Man Singh in 1604. It is dedicated to Shila Mata, an aspect of Kali, suitably the goddess of war. Man Singh brought the deity's image back from Jessore in Bengal, housing it amid green marble pillars carved into plantain trees. This century, Man Singh II would drive up here in his Bentley and sacrifice a goat to Shila Devi with his own hands. And in 1939 he built the solid silver entrance doors as thanks for his recovery from a plane crash. Even today, a Bengali leads the *puja* (worship) with noisy bells and drums and the temple is the Jaipur family's island in the otherwise state-owned fort.

Back down, then up again to the **Diwan-i-Am** (Public Meeting Hall), where the ruler would sit on rich silk rugs and give audience to his people. Set on a dazzling white terrace overlooking the whole gorge, this is Jai Singh's masterpiece. A double row of columns have elephant-carved capitals supporting a canopy and galleried ter-

race. Its delicacy was so much to Mughal taste that Jai Singh had to cover it with stucco before the jealous Jahangir's commissioners arrived to see if the Rajput was getting too big for his warring boots. Now, as the stucco wears, the fine decoration begins to be revealed.

Ganesh Pol (Elephant Gate), a magnificent burst of color, is Jai Singh's ceremonial gate, built around 1640. It is smothered in mosaic, fresco and sculpture, with lattice-work above so the ladies could watch processions. Over the scalloped doorway sits Ganesh, the elephant-headed god of learning and good fortune.

Through this gate lies a very Mughal formal garden court. To the right is the **Sukh Nivas** (Hall of Pleasure), with aircooling water running through. To the left is the **Jai Mandir** (Hall of Victory), Jai Singh's private apartments whose sophistication is the perfect blend of Hindu and Muslim traditions executed with the highest skills. The decoration on the walls and ceilings is perhaps the finest among all Rajasthan fortress-palaces. Murals may be of bold cypresses, tiny flowers

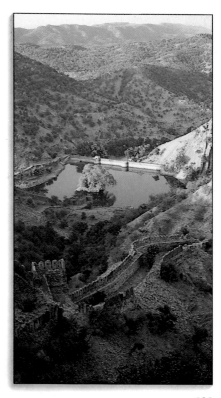

or pictures of Rajput pleasures: hunting and war. All is made silky smooth by adding powdered marble, egg shells and even pearls to the final coat. Glass and precious stones set into the plaster add royal glamor. *Taks* (niches) were filled with flowers, deities or candles, to make the jewels sparkle.

The **Diwan-i-Khas** (Private Meeting Hall) is on the ground floor, the boldly scalloped arches giving shade to a deep veranda leading to rooms decorated with delicate murals. Above, the gossamer-fine *jali*-work of the alabaster windows in **Jas Mandir** (Hall of Glory) are at ground level so reclining royals could enjoy the superb views. But the jewels is the **Sheesh Mahal** (Hall of Mirrors), whose interior is encrusted with tiny mirrors. With doors closed and candle lit, it is like being inside a vast twinkling diamond.

Behind the garden court lie Man Singh's apartments, the oldest parts of the palace. In the *zenana*, Man Singh's dozen wives each had a separate suite. Murals of Krishna and Radha still decorate some of them. Brightly striped *durries* would have been laid in their large open hall, where the evapor-

ating water in the shallow ponds cooled the stifling Rajasthan air.

Back in the courtyard, the path through an archway leads down to old **Amber village**. Of the several Hindu and Jain temples, the most interesting was built by Bihar Mal and dedicated to Sri Jagat Saromanji, with stone elephants to guard its marble gateway. The Amber rulers' *chhatris* stand nearby. On the banks of Maota Lake the beautifully restored **Dilaram Gardens** are almost encircled by water. A small **Archeological Museum** is housed among their buildings and verandas. Indo-Greek coins, fragments of Ashoka pillars and decorated pottery from Bairat are among its exhibits.

Kachchwaha Treasury: Hovering above Amber like a watchful eagle is **Jaigarh Fort,** built by Jai Singh II in 1726. Romantic legend fills its palatial rooms, courtyards and reservoirs. For Jaigarh housed the legendary Kachchwaha treasury. The loyal Mina tribe, former rulers of Amber, guarded it, using their skills as archers and mountain fighters. The massive **Jaiwaan cannon,** one of the largest in Asia, gave added protection. It was said that the

Left, gaily painted elephants take visitors to the Amber Palace. Right, the Ganesh Pol, built C. 1640, Amber Palace.

Minas would take each Kachchwaha chief, blindfolded, into the treasury just once, where he could choose one item from all that booty from Mughal warring. The legend lived on, and in 1976 the taxmen spent six months and some £75,000 digging for it. They found nothing. Some say Jai Singh II used treasure amassed by Man Singh I to build his model city. Others say it is still there.

Beyond Amber, a pretty road leads to the ancient city of **Bairat** (53 miles/85 km from Jaipur), or **Viratnagar**. It is an archeologist's delight. Two rock edicts of the ruler Ashoka (272 B.C.–232 B.C.), hoards of Greek and Indo-Greek coins, remains of a large Buddhist monastery and *chaitya* (temple)—together with the Chinese pilgrim, Hieun Tsang's travelogue—all point to Bairat being a major Buddhist center in the third century B.C. In Hindu legend, Bairat is believed to be Biratpuri, where the Pandavas, heroes of the epic *Mahabharata*, spent their 13th year of exile. So the Minas tribe celebrate these heroes with song and dance here at the annual Benganga Fair. Beyond Bairat is Sariska wildlife sanctuary.

Another delightful trip north from Jaipur is to **Samod** (25 miles/40 km)—it is even possible to go by camel. The narrow lanes lead up through massive gateways to a delightful palace built by Jai Singh II's finance minister. The grand staircase leads to rooms elaborately decorated with murals set between panels of fine mirror work. Downstairs, the magnificent durbar hall has delicate paintings and quantities of gilding. Samod is yet another palace-turned-hotel, run by the minister's descendants. It is easy to visit and makes a good stop en route to touring Shekhavati.

Heading east from Jaipur, out of Surajpol, a branch to the left reaches **Ramgarh** (15 miles/25 km), a Kachchwaha hilltop stronghold which now overlooks Jaipur's main water supply: a six-sq-mile (15 - sq - km) lake good for boating and picnics. Back on the main road, the temple-filled gorge of **Galta** (six miles/10 km) plunges down from the Aravalli hills. The **temple of the Sun God** on its summit (yet more stunning views) can also be reached from the other side by a short hike

from Jaipur. Waters from the Go-mukh, believed to have curative pro-perties, flow from the mouth of a stone cow to fill the seven tanks set amid pavilions.

For some more picturesque treats, leave Jaipur by Ghat Gate. First comes **Vidhyadharji ka Bagh** (five miles/eight km), a garden named after Vidyadhar Bhattacharaya, Jai Singh's architect. Next, **Sisodia Rani ka Bagh** (five miles/eight km) built by Jai Singh II for his Udaipur queen, the one he took to cement the revived Rajput alliance. The glorious murals of the domed palace show hunting scenes, strolling lovers, polo playing and moments from the life of Krishna. Peacocks strut in the fine terraced garden with foun-tains and statues surrounding it. At about 4 each afternoon, crowds of langurs come to the hillside temple dedicated to *Hanuman,* the monkey god, where the priest feeds them sweet-meats. The crowds are even bigger on the god's special day, Tuesday. Galta's **Sun Temple** is on the hilltop.

Beyond, en route to Agra, **Daosa** (30 miles/50 km), was the first Kachch-waha capital in the area known as Dhundhu. And to the south lies **Lalsot** (a further 25 miles/40 km), where the Jaipur and Jodhpur forces defeated the Marathas under General de Boigne in 1787 in the Battle of Tonk.

From here, the road leads to the remarkable **Ranthambore fort** (See page 259). And game reserve. And one final good trip out of Jaipur, this time southwards, leads here too.

Prints and Paper: Leaving by Ajmeri Gate, the road towards Jaipur airport leads to **Sanganer** (10 miles/16 km). (10 miles/16 km). Within the majestic **Dausa Gate,** amid the camel-filled alleys, lie an **old palace**, a **Krishna temple**, some statue-packed **Jain tem-ples**, and the homes of several thou-sand craftsmen whose ancestors made Sanganer the "metropolis of calico printing." The delicate flower, bird, tree and animal prints for the gathered Rajasthani skirts could easily be made fast because the waters of the Aman-i-Shah helped to fix them. Even if chemicals have replaced both the local waters and the vegetable dyes, the work is fascinating to watch. Each craftsman practices one particular art. The designer separates the colors, a

Jian temple, Sanganer.

second man cuts the woodblocks, and a third, a *chippa,* prints each color down the whole length of his fabric. Finally, after fixing, some fabrics are dollied up with *kari*-printing—embossed printing with gold or silver. Their turnover is about 20 times as fast, but it is also interesting to watch.

The spin-off from printing is paper-making, using the offcuts of cotton or silk to make bright pink or yellow sheets, some polished silky smooth and speckled with gold and silver. Whereas little rivulets of color are the clue to finding some fabric printing activity, sheets of paper pegged out on a washing line leads to a paper-maker. The other main craft of Sanganer is Jaipur blue pottery. Traditional designs are distinctive for their special inky cobalt-blue glaze which serves as a background for rich floral arabesques painted in white and copper oxide green.

Bagru (20 miles/35 km from Jaipur), just west of Sanganer, is also famed for its block-printing, especially large, floral, circular designs printed in deep rich colors using the traditional vegetable dyes. South from Sanganer lies

Chaksu (27 miles/43 km from Jaipur), where Vikramaditya, legendary king and founder of the Samvat era (57 B.C.), is said to have lived, surrounded by a wall of copper. The annual March fair honors Sitala Mata, goddess of fever diseases, especially smallpox—traditionally, if a Hindu died of smallpox, he was not cremated for fear of injuring the goddess who possessed him.

Tonk (60 miles/96 km from Jaipur) was once ruled by the Buner tribe of Pathans from Afghanistan. The old walled town, supposedly built in 1643 by a Brahmin called Bhola, is picturesquely perched on the slopes of a small range of hills. To the south, the grand new town is enriched with the mansions and painted mosques of the Muslim nawab descendants of the Pathans. **Sunehri Kothi** (Golden Mansion) is an especially fine one, its exterior simplicity contrasting sharply with interior splendor: polished floors, stained glass, mirrors, stucco and gilt. In addition, as a former British headquarters, there are fine colonial buildings. From here roads run down to Bundi and Kota or across to Sawai Madhopur.

ALWAR: A TREASURE OF SURPRISES

A visit to Alwar is in a sense, a re-entry into historical chapters of great antiquity, a return to a time when warfare was a way of life and peace a brief interlude to gild the state with splendor. A fort, a palace, a lake, a temple, and a garden were the five attributes of great Rajput princes: a dictum which Alwar's rulers took seriously to heart, judging by the plethora of creative activity they sponsored.

A short drive south from Delhi (100 miles/ 170 km) or from Jaipur (90 miles/148 km) brings one to Alwar, shielded from the desert by the Aravalli range. What Kipling called the "tumbled fragments" of these hills reach up here into peaks loftier than anywhere else in Rajasthan. Chiseled from crystalline rock, they are covered with tropical dry, deciduous, scrubby-looking forests which are transformed almost overnight by the monsoon rains, which seem to drench them from an unseen palette of infinite shades of green. Alwar's ambience of undulating hills and deep valleys, populated by plentiful wildlife and interspersed frequently with lush oases, perennial streams, and hot and cold springs—so unusual in Rajasthan—cradled many civilizations. From Matsya to Machari to Mewat, successive stages of its history moved until it settled finally in Alwar city.

Around 1500 B.C. most of Alwar was included in the territory of the Matsyas known as Viratnagar. Their polity known as the Matsya *maha janapada* is Rajasthan's oldest recorded kingdom. The Pandavas, heroes of the great Indian epic, the *Mahabharata*, are said to have spent the last year of their exile in disguise at the court of King Virata. It was here that their Kaurava cousins arrived to steal cattle, initiating, when all efforts at mediation failed, the epic war in which the Matsyas sided with the Pandavas. The fast-expanding Mauryan Empire, however, seems to have eclipsed the Matsya state by the third century B.C.

Hiuen Tsang, the Chinese traveler, makes brief mention of this area as being under a powerful king in the seventh century A.D. Shortly afterwards, it was incorporated, along with Dausa, into the large kingdom of Machari, south of Alwar, and ruled by the Bargujar Rajputs. Inscriptions of Machari kings are found up to the 14th century, when it was swallowed up by Amber.

History's mainstream meanwhile shifted north and the crucial interplay of events to Mewat, bordering Delhi, then including both Tijara and Alwar city. Mewat was governed by the famous Khanzadas, fiercely independent Muslim aristocrats. Hasan Khan Mewati, their most important ruler, preferred an alliance with the Rajputs to siding with his Muslim brethren at Delhi and rejected Babur's many overtures. Amongst his people were the Meos, also known as the "bandit Mewatees" whose raids so terrorized the people of Delhi that sultans and Mughal emperors had to resort to punitive raids against them. In this turbulent situation, with Delhi under constant threat, Alwar city, holding as Major Thorn wrote, the keys to the southern gates of Delhi and the plains of northern and central India beyond, assumed great strategic significance. The Mughals conquered it with great difficulty and were fiercely challenged by the Kachchwahas of Amber and the Jats of Bharatpur, with the British and the Marathas also joining the fray.

From the disorganization and incessant warfare of the 18th century emerged a leader called **Pratap Singh**. By shrewd realpolitik involving astute juggling of alliances this remarkable *Thakur* (noble) was able to establish an independent state by throwing off Jaipur's suzerainty over the south, ejecting the Jats from Alwar, repudiating the Marathas and having his gains ratified by the Mughal emperor. From a mere two-and-a-half villages of Machari he expanded his dominions to include almost all of Alwar state. He founded the Naruka dynasty, distantly related to the Jaipur family which gave Alwar esthetes and epicurians for kings for almost two centuries.

Pratap Singh's successors consolidated their rule by lending assistance to the infant British Empire at the historic Battle of Laswari (1803) fought at a 12-mile (20-km) distance from Alwar, against the Marathas, and were rewarded with the title of Maharaja and substantial territory. British

Preceding pages, village fair. Left, Kankwari Fort, Sariska.

feelings of gratitude were soon subverted, however, by increasing interference in Alwar's internal affairs in the 19th century, climaxed by the appointment of a British Resident. As the momentum of the Indian freedom struggle grew its reverberations could be discerned in Alwar's middle class and rural peasant movement of the 20th century spearheaded by the Alwar Rajya Prajamandal. After independence a short-lived experiment at limited monarchy was made in a union of the princely states of Alwar, Bharatpur, Dholpur, and Karauli. But eventually this United State of Matsya, headquartered at Alwar, merged with the new state of Rajasthan in May 1949.

Alwar is now the headquarters of one of the premier industrial districts of Rajasthan and a part of the national capital grid, seeking to divert towards itself overcrowded Delhi's prospective immigrants. It offers a treasure of surprises to the tourist—wildlife, ancient temples and sculptures, medieval forts, exquisite palaces and cenotaphs and tanks, dams and gardens galore, set in a mosaic of mystery and folklore.

Amongst its people are the **Meos**, a unique instance of Hindu-Muslim cultural synthesis. Notwithstanding their dress—notice their women in colorful pajamas and long shirts, different from the full skirts Rajasthani women normally wear—and the Muslim religion they profess, they share their Hindu neighbors' rituals, customs, festivals, gods, saints, and superstitions. Alwar also has several rare, but unfortunately declining, folk and classical traditions of music and dance, quite distinct from the more publicized folk entertainment of western Rajasthan.

Alwar City: On a steep cliff, presiding over the city of Alwar, stands **Bala Quila** (fort). As a police wireless station is located here prior permission to visit the fort must be obtained from the district authorities. The steep, bumpy drive (negotiable only by 4-wheel-drive vehicles is compensated by the spectacular view it offers of the city 1000 feet (300 meters) below. The fort, whose ramparts flank a cliff along 3 miles (5 km), was originally constructed by the city's oldest inhabitants, the Nikumbha Rajputs. Their old town known as **Ravana Devra** lies in ruins at

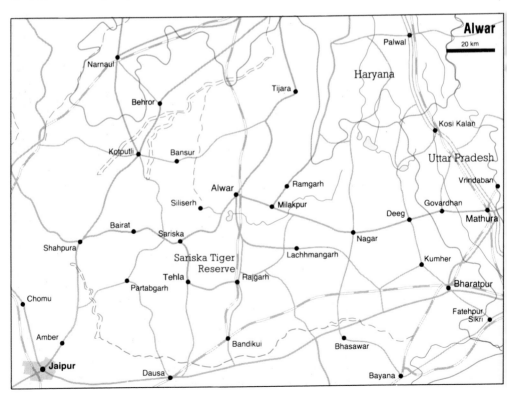

134

the foot of the hill amidst a bustling village.

Bala Quila was occupied successively by Khanzadas, Mughals, Pathans and Jats. In 1775, Pratap Singh ousted the Jats from the fort. His successor, **Bakhtawar Singh** added to the existing structure the rooms of the palace, and some fine gold leaf painting on the ceiling. Being quintessentially Hindu in style, the fort is one of the few examples, in Rajasthan, of pre-Muslim fortification. According to old manuscripts on Alwar, Babur spent a night here after crushing the unique Khanzada-Rajput alliance at the decisive battle of Fatehpur Sikri, and handed over its treasure to his son Humayun. A proposed deer park will perhaps attract more visitors to this somewhat forsaken ancient monument.

Below the fort, in the heart of the old city, is the magnificent **City Palace**. Five massive gates were once closed and caged tigers let loose at night to keep intruders at bay. Today the fabric of democratic authority has been woven into this originally feudal seat of authority. Alwar's district government inhabits the rooms of the former armory, library and treasury. In the grand courtyards where girls once danced in the light of the full moon to entertain the maharaja and his courtiers, crowds now seek succor in the offices and courts of the district administration. The palace is particularly noted for its darbar room (access to it now requires the permission of the former maharaja, resident at Delhi's Alwar House) decorated with a frieze of miniature paintings and an upper chamber of mirrors set in gilt. Previously used on state occasions, a contemporary British art critic once wrote that "a durbar at Ulwur recalls the dreams of magnificence which the European is accustomed to indulge in with regard to the East."

Wealthy and exploitative as Alwar's rulers were, they owned legendary objects like a solid silver dining table, a cup carved from a solitary emerald, a golden limousine, inside and out. Some of these objects are still in the possession of the erstwhile royal family, others are displayed at the **Museum**, located in the upper story of the palace (closed on Fridays). The Alwar court, renowned for its patron-

Alwar Palace complex.

age of the arts and scholarship, attracted famous writers, painters and artists. A copy of the *Mahabharata* minutely written on a single page, 80 yards long, an illuminated *Koran* and an exclusive copy of the Persian *Gulistan*, lovingly created over 10 years, are the gems of a choice collection of manuscripts in Sanskrit, Arabic, Persian, and Urdu. The armory section has weapons dating back to the days of Hazrat Ali, the Prophet Muhammad's son-in-law, and as renowned as the swords and armor of Muhammad Ghori, Akbar and Aurangzeb. The daggers, swords, shields and sabres on display are often richly ornamented and encrusted with jewels. Art objects in jade, ivory and sandalwood are delicately filigreed, inlaid and enameled and a silver table with a trick impression of colored fishes floating in channels of water across it are other highlights of its collection. The museum is most reputed, however, for its miniature paintings, particularly a rare folder of the Bundi school. The juxtaposition of the Mughal and Rajput schools shows their respective treatment in the *ragamala* (garland of music) series of the sensuous mood evoked by a particular musical mode or *raga*.

While at the museum, remember to look out of the windows, for another "miniature"—the spectacular view of a huge tank below, lined by a chain of temples on one side and dominated by a marvelous cenotaph, all cradled in the lap of high hills crowned by the ramparts of the fort. The impressive **Moosi Maharani Chhatri** (cenotaph) is popularly identifed and named after Bakhtawar Singh's mistress who performed *sati* here. Her footprints, it is said (although they seem rather small), are embedded in the ground and water washed from them is considered to have medicinal value for children. Resting on a pillared, red sandstone story, the upper portion in marble with columned pavilions and domed arches is embellished with floral tracery. Like the palace, it is in an Indo-Islamic style. Mythological and court themes in fading gold-leaf painting and sculpture adorn the ceiling. This memorial is regarded as one of the finest of its class. The tank or *sagar* is a concrete catchment one with a pattern of stairs and tiny kiosks in perfect symmetry along the sides.

The Environs: On a diversion six miles (10 km) away, on the road to Behror, is **Vijay Mandir Palace**, the later royal residence. Uninhabited except for old retainers and with decay fast setting in, this palace is nevertheless a window to the lifestyle of the princes. Owned by the former maharaja, entrance is subject to his permission. But even if it cannot be seen from inside, the drive to the palace and back is highly recommended, particularly if, on return, the circuitous route (previously meant for the exclusive use of the women of the royal family going to and from the *zenana*—women's quarters—of the 'City Palace), leading behind the fort is taken. It is from the vantage point of this drive that the charming character of the palace, modeled like a ship at anchor, beside a lakelet where migratory birds and waterfowl feed on fish, is evident.

Jai Singh (1892–1937), the builder of this palace, was Alwar's most controversial ruler. Talented in many ways and popular, indeed beloved of his people, responsive to their problems and patriotic, he is nevertheless the subject of many a wild tale. He gave, it is whispered, orders to pickle his dead guru, used babies as tiger bait, sprang a tiger trophy with a hidden mechanism on an unsuspecting viceroy, and was known for his extravagant and eccentric ways. With a penchant for palaces, he also built the Itarana and Sariska Palaces, constructed a club, dams, gardens and roads to the city. Near the exit to the Jaipur road still stands the interesting **Moti Doongri fortress**. Landsdowne, a palace, once graced the flat hill which the fortress still girdles. It was inexplicably dynamited out of existence by Jai Singh, some say in search of hidden treasure, others, because he wanted to build a better and bigger palace in its place. A short drive to the top of the Moti Doongri, on whose slopes a park is being landscaped, is worthwhile for a circular view of the city.

If *Alpur* or *Arbalpur*, meaning fort on the hills of the Aravalli, is the original derivative of the word Alwar, it should certainly be used in the plural since its rulers built forts at the drop of a hat. Of these, the fort of **Rajgarh** 22 miles (36 km) southwards is historically and architecturally the most significant. An hour's drive brings one to this old capital of Alwar, a town of old *havelis* (mansions), citrus fruit gardens and a lake over which presides the fort known for its secret passages (now unidentifiable), and frescoes. It was built by Alwar's almost legendary founder-king, Pratap Singh, on the site of an old fort belonging to the Gujar-Pratiharas. The latter ruled around the third century A.D. from Rajorgarh nearby which Tod describes as "a city of great antiquity."

More City Sights: Back to Alwar city once again, one can drive briefly past the **old Railway Station**, adjacent to the new one, and the **Fateh Jang Gumbad** (both having examples of local stone tracery) and into the **Vinay Vilas Palace**. This resplendent residence, in a composite style, was once characterized as the Garden Palace because of its long driveways, ornamental shrubs and profusion of flowers, vegetables and fruits including, unheard of in Rajasthan, peaches and strawberries.

This garden and Jai Singh's **Company Bagh** with a rare greenhouse known as **Simla** (named after the summer retreat of the viceroys because of the welcome relief it provided Alwar's residents from the terrible heat) were watered by the Silliserh water reservoir eight miles (13 km) away, via a long aqueduct. This solid stone masonry structure, which transformed the barren soil of the city, is still visible along the road to Silliserh. The disuse of this traditional facility has spelt death to many a garden in the city.

In and around Sariska: On the road to Jaipur is Silliserh's enchanting waterpalace. Built as a retreat by Vinay Singh, Alwar's third ruler, it is one of the most popular and picturesque spots near Alwar. A delightful evening can be spent here, sitting upstairs on the terrace of Rajasthan Tourism's hotel-cum-restaurant to watch the tranquil waters of the lake, or paddle-boating on it. From the lake, one can view the palace tucked away amidst the dark, green hills set aglow in the light of the setting sun.

The strength of myth and the unwritten word in India has to be experienced to be believed. Twenty-one centuries after King Bhartrihari wandered about in exile in these parts in penance for his suspicions against Vikramaditya (his younger brother, and the famous king

The *sagar* or tank—perfect symmetry of steps and kiosks.

of Malwa), he is still greatly revered. A little away from the Alwar-Jaipur road the **Bhartrihari temple** is dedicated to him. Both a fair and an epic musical drama lasting six hours—are massively attended in Alwar in the months of September and October.

Traveling further along the same road, a diverison of six miles (10 km), takes one to **Talbraksha** past the **fortress of Kushalgarh.** In a clearing above a dense palm grove are several ancient temples of indefinite antiquity. Amid the tinkling music of temple bells and with hordes of naughty pale-faced red-bottomed monkeys strolling about, numerous pilgrims take a dip in the hot and cold springs. A famous icon of the blue-blooded Krishna, appropriately in sapphire, was once stolen from here, and although recently recovered, has not been re-installed. The huge ancient earthenware urn which stands here was unearthed from a field and was found to be filled with gold coins. It is considered to belong to the Mauryan era.

At **Sariska** within a radius of 26 miles (42 km) from the wildlife sanctuary's gate, for the adventurer prepared for a bumpy Jeep (on hire at the Palace Hotel) ride, there are many delightful spots to fascinate the wildlife enthusiast as well as the connoisseur of art and archeology. A couple of days are required to visit them and it is advisable to make Sariska one's base.

The **Sariska Palace**, the old watchtowers of Bandipul, small dams and bridges are survivals from the times when Sariska was the private game preserve of the rulers. The palace itself was previously a hunting lodge or the *place de nature* of the princes, originally built in honor of the Duke of Connaught, Queen Victoria's son, at the end of the 19th century. Presently a hotel, it has an old-world charm with its wonderfully restored period furniture, quaint bathroom accessories and rolling lawns.

The typical Sariska "beat" takes one to **Pandupol**, only 15 miles (24 km) away, but involves a long drive punctuated as it usually is with numerous stops to watch animals in their natural habitat. A tiered stream with a delicate trickle and deep waterholes accompany the drive up the hills on either side. The Pandava brothers found the

The City Palace now houses an impressive museum.

dense forests of this area a good place to hide from their enemies in the 13th year of their exile. At Pandupol, the story goes, Bhima, the strongest of the five brothers, smote the rock face of a cliff with his mace to clear their passage. A little below Pandupol is the old temple called **Budha** (old) **Hanuman**. The newer one further down, however, is more popular and is known for its unusual reclining image. In September devotees crawl, fully stretched out on the ground, all the way from Alwar to attend a crowded fair here.

On the outskirts of the sanctuary (28 miles/45 km), nestling in a green valley towered by hills and facing the plains, are the rarely visited, but breathtaking ruins of **Bhangarh**. Madho Singh, younger brother of Amber's Man Singh (Akbar's famous general), enthralled by its natural beauty, established an extensive city here of some 10,000 identifiable dwellings in 1631. Even in ruin, the attempt at town planning structured in accordance with caste hierarchy is discernible. At the apex, along the hillside, is the former residence of the king. At its base, the mansions (now remnants) and rooms

The Sariska Palace is now a hotel.

around the verandas of the temple were probably meant for the clergy and aristocracy. Along the main road, for half a mile, are symmetrical rooms on either side indicating a remarkable market-place of a prosperous urban center. Gates flanking it at both ends suggest the limits within which the trading and commercial classes were normally restricted. Beyond this, on the periphery, most likely, were the houses of the lower orders.

Specially worth attention are Bhangarh's two **temples**. One of them beside which a perennial spring trickles into a concrete tank emerging from the backdrop of a lush screwpine forest, has a particularly beautiful setting. Both temples are ornately carved in stone and marble with floral friezes decorating walls, ceilings and pillars. Images of ancillary gods, of the main deity, Shiva, in a Rajasthani variant astride a camel or peacock, and of typical entrance guardians, river goddesses and musicians grace the shrine. In fact, the contrast between Bhangarh's religious and secular architecture is quite startling. While the latter now consists mainly of crumbling stones, the former

is still well-preserved. This and the strong similarity in both architectural and sculptural aspects to the temples excavated at Neelkanth, affirm that Bhangarh's temples are much older than the early 17th century, the period to which they are attributed.

Famine, war, pestilence, a slow decline, or perhaps a queen's curse, led its population to abandon Bhangarh suddenly and it remains hauntedly desolate even today, except for ubiquitous peacocks and rare visitors. Internecine quarrels had, however, already caused the shifting of the capital of this large kingdon to **Ajabgarh**, founded by Ajab Singh, Madho Singh's grandson. In this picturesque valley 20 miles (32 km) from Bhangarh, once regarded as the richest tract in the state, old temples are still to be seen.

Another immensely rewarding excursion, off the regular tourist track, is to **Kankwari** and **Neelkanth** 21 miles (35 km) in the interior of Sariska. Kankwari (12 miles/20 km) is an exceedingly picturesque fortress overlooking a lake, surrounded by forest-covered hills on all sides. Legend has it that Dara Shikoh, heir to the Mughal throne after Shah Jahan, was held captive here by his usurper brother, Aurangzeb.

Imprisonment so remote from civilization is credible but it is indeed a wonder how an extraordinary fortified temple town like Neelkanth thrived 10 centuries ago, surrounded as it was by a thick forest, populated by dangerous animals, access through which is difficult even today. Contemporary to Khajuraho in Madhya Pradesh (950 A.D. – 1050 A.D.), another great artistic genius here chiseled the same number of 80 temples. Unfortunately, only a fourth have been excavated and in spite of substantial theft, the sculpture lies neglected at the site. They testify to a variety of religious cults and influences, Hindu, Buddhist and Jain. A colossal statute of the 23rd Jain Tirthankara, Parshvanath, an image of the traditionally bachelor god Ganesh with a woman on his knee, and of Vishnu reclining are quite unique. The rare image of Vishnu in his Varaha (boar) incarnation is a theme repeated at Bhangarh and in a black marble statue excavated from Talbraksh which seem strongly to indicate the geographical spread of this Bargujar-Rajput state.

En route to Jaipur (40 miles/66 km) is **Viratnagar (Bairat)**, one of the most ancient sites in Rajasthan. Eight miles (13 km) away is **Dhigariya** where caves, rock shelters and stone tools of the paleolithic age have been excavated. Nearer the village, which still reverberates with legends of the Pandavas' stay here, are five huge rocks (representing the five brothers) and atop them are temples dedicated to Bhima and Hanuman—the only instance in India of the monkey god depicted in a human form—thus venerating the heroes of both the epics, the *Mahabharata* and the *Ramayana*. In the third and uppermost layer of history at Bairath are stone inscriptions of the great Mauryan emperor, Ashoka, and a **Buddhist temple** with multiple pillars dating back to the 3rd century B.C.

To the northwest of Alwar on the main Delhi to Jaipur road (NH 8), restoration work has begun on the fort and small ruined palace of **Neem Rana**. Situatuated one mile to the west of the road, it is six miles (10 km) south of the state border with Haryana. In the village below the fort is an ornate step-well, still in use.

The Silliserh Palace overlooking a 19th–century reservoir.

140

SARISKA TIGER RESERVE

On the main highway to Jaipur 21 miles (34 km) south of Alwar, lies the Sariska Tiger Reserve and National Park. Sariska is one of the few remaining pockets of forest in the Aravali range of hills and the area now covers 308 square miles (800 square km) is the core area. The reserve has been under Project Tiger since 1979 and before that, since 1955, a smaller sanctuary. But earlier still it was a hunting area for the Maharajas of Alwar and was strictly protected.

The forest is mainly hilly with two extensive plateaus, Kankwari and Kiraska, and a wide valley starting at the Baran Tal Gate and running south to Thana Gazi. At the northeastern corner, just off the road between Alwar and Sariska, is the Siliserh Lake. Although game viewing in the lake area is poor, crocodiles are often seen and, during the winter, there are many migrant water birds.

In spring, the surrounding hillsides are filled with color as the "flame of the forest" and other flowering trees bloom In the summer the park is parched and brown but with the coming of monsoon becomes lush and green. In the few more moist areas, bamboo is found and, along the banks of streams, jamun and arjan.

Among the undulating hills and wide valleys of Sariska is a rare combination of natural history and archaeology. The ruined temples of Neelkanth (20 miles/32 km from Sariska), are from the ninth and 10th centuries. The medieval fort of Kankwari was used throughout the Mughal period. At Sariska, opposite the Baran Tal Gate of the reserve, is a large palace built in 1902 by Maharaj Jai Singh of Alwar as a base for his elaborate shoots. The palace is now a hotel.

Sariska has a good network of metaled roads. From these main arteries. forest racks lead into side valleys.

With a low average rainfall of 25 inches (65 cm), water becomes a major limiting factor for the animals. The forest department has provided many artificial water holes along the main roads which attract the animals and makes wildlife observation from vehicles in the morning or evening comparatively easy. Because of the scarcity of water, viewing from hides overlooking waterholes at Salopka and Kalighati ofter numerous opportunities to watch, photograph and study many of the species, especially during the late afternoon in the summer months of April, May and June.

The dry open deciduous and thorn forests support increasing populations of ungulates including **sambar**, **nilgai**, **chinkara**, **chausingha** and **chital**. The predators include **leopard**, **hyena**, **jungle cat** and **jackal**, apart from **tiger**. Also found are **porcupine**, **wild boar** and, occasionally, **ratel**, but with the exception of the jungle cat, the carnivores are elusive and are usually only seen at night. Daytime tiger sightings are becoming more frequent. Sariska has large populations of **rhesus macaque** and **langur** monkeys.

The range of habitat also supports a rich variety of birds including **shrike**, **parakeet**, **gray partridge**, **golden backed woodpecker**, **peafowl**, **owls** and the **crested serpent eagle**. **Babblers**, **tree pies** and **bulbuls** are often seen from hides and around the forest department buildings.

A male Nilgai or Bluebull.

141

AJMER AND PUSHKAR

Ajmer is located 80 miles (130 km) west of Jaipur, in a picturesque valley surrounded by the hills of the Aravalli range. Of strategic importance in erstwhile Rajputana, it is today an important center of pilgrimage for the Muslims of the sub-continent, due to its association with the great Sufi saint Muin-ud-din Chishti.

Ajmer was established in the early seventh century by Ajaipal Chauhan. He named the place *Ajaimeru*, the invincible hill, because here he built India's first hill fort, **Taragarh**. Ajmer was a Chauhan stronghold till 1194. The only remains of their times are the fort and the beautiful **Anasagar Lake**, built in 1150 by Anaji. The legendary Prithviraj, last of the Chauhans, is the inspiration for many heroic ballads sung even today in the villages of Rajasthan. The most popular of these dwell upon his daring elopement with Princess Sanyogita, daughter of the King of Kanauj.

It was during the reign of Prithviraj, in 1191, that Muhammad of Ghori invaded India. Prithviraj died fighting the sultan's army, and with the establishment of the Sultanate in Delhi, a new era began.

Ajmer remained under the Sultanate till 1326. Thereafter, it became a bone of contention between the Sultans of Delhi, the Ranas of Mewar, the Rathors of Marwar and the Sultans of Gujarat. Peace was restored with the accession of Akbar to the Mughal throne in 1556. He made Ajmer a full-fledged province, and, in pursuance of his policy toward the Rajputs, the base for his operations in Rajputana. He fortified the city, but only parts of the 4045-yard (3735-m) long wall remain. His palace, the **Daulat Khana**, houses the **Government Museum**.

Mughal Center: Akbar's son, Jahangir, lived in Ajmer from 1613 to 1616. His palace, the Daulat Bagh, is now in ruins. The celebrated English ambassador to the Mughal court, Sir Thomas Roe, was received here by the emperor. During the course of his extended stay, Roe met the emperor several times and showered him with gifts varying from maps to a coach. But he failed to conclude a commercial treaty between England and the Mughal empire. Roe's detailed journal contains descriptions of Jahangir's palaces in Ajmer.

In 1659 a battle was fought in Ajmer between the Mughal princes, Aurangzeb and Dara Sukoh, during which Taragarh was greatly damaged. In the first half of the 18th century, Ajmer was affected by the political chaos in Delhi. At times it was the Rathors who reigned here, at others the emperors of Delhi. In 1755, the situation became more complex with the involvement of the Marathas. Finally, in 1818, the Marathas ceded Ajmer to Sir David Ochterlony and, as part of the British empire, it remained under the care of successive superintendents. With the reorganization of the princely states in 1947, Ajmer became a part of Rajasthan.

Commercially, too, the city has been of importance, especially since the 13th century. For it was on the main trade route between Delhi and the ports of Gujarat (it is still on the Delhi/Ahmedabad highway) and taxes were levied on transit goods. The area is also rich in mica, lead and garnet. The 19th century was a very prosperous period, during which several royal families and wealthy *seths* (merchants) came to Ajmer. They built *havelis* to live in with ornately carved facades and some of these may still be seen off the narrow lanes in the old city.

Ajmer was also considered by the British as an appropriate place to establish a school for Indian princes. In 1874, Mayo College was opened with one pupil—H.H. the Maharaja of Alwar. He was attended by a retinue of servants and set out for school each day on an elephant and with considerable fanfare. In 1947 the school was opened to commoners, and is today one of the leading educational institutions in the country.

Islamic Shrine: It is, however, as a religious center that the importance and vitality of the city endures. For the **Dargah Sharif**, where Khwaja Muin-ud-din Chishti lies buried, draws pilgrims from all parts of the Islamic world. The saint was born in Sanjar, Persia, in 1142. He became absorbed in matters spiritual at an early age. It is said that, while in Mecca, he had a prophetic vision directing him to go to Ajmer. He came to India around 1191.

145

probably with Ghori's army, and settled in Ajmer, where he established the Chishtiya order, to date the foremost Sufi order in India. Through his message of love and his devotion to the poor he was able to spread the word of Islam more effectively than Ghori's army. He came to be known as Khwaja Gharib Nawaz, the protector of the poor, and beggars, even today, plead for alms in his name. Along with fakirs, they seek shelter at his shrine.

Chishti died in 1236 and his devotees now extend beyond the pale of Islam. The Dargah Sharif is considered a wish-fulfilling shrine. Akbar is known to have walked on two occasions from Agra to Ajmer in thanksgiving for boons granted. There is a steady flow of pilgrims to the Dargah throughout the year, but during the *Urs* (death anniversary ceremonies) of the saint, celebrated between the 1st and 6th of Rajab, the seventh month of the lunar calendar, lakhs of pilgrims from all parts of the subcontinent converge upon the shrine.

The **Dargah** and its surroundings have a vitality and character quite apart from colonial and modern Aj-mer. The shrine is approached through **Madar Gate** and past the **Dargah Bazar**. The bazar is stocked with ritual offerings—dazzling coverlets for the grave, incense, sweetmeats, rose petals and *attar* (perfume). Ajmer is famous for its pink roses and it is here that *attar* of roses was discovered at the time of Jahangir.

The Dargah lies at the foot of the northeast spur of Taragarh hill and is separated from it by a 19th-century water reservoir. The simple brick tomb in which the saint was buried has since been embellished by the lavish gifts of wealthy and powerful devotees, and several mosques, pavilions and gateways now surround the mausoleum. To its north lies the **mehfilkhana**, built in 1888 by the Nizam of Hyderabad. It is the scene of all-night *qawwali* (devotional songs) during the *urs*. Adjacent to this is the **mosque built by Akbar**. **Shah Jahan's elegant mosque** in white marble is well preserved and lies west of the mausoleum, while to the east is the ornate **Begami Dalan**, the portico built by Princess Jahanara, the emperor's daughter.

The saint's grave is enclosed by a

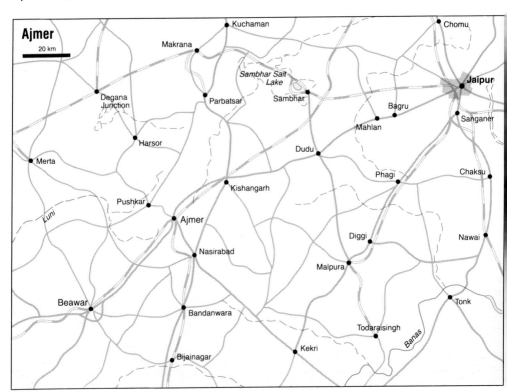

silver railing and lies in a domed chamber, partially surrounded by a marble lattice screen. *Qawwals* sing in praise of the saint, eccentrically attired fakirs plead for alms, while the *khadim* ("servants" of the saint) keep a look-out for pilgrims.

Of particular interest in the Dargah are two huge *deg* (cauldrons) originally presented by Akbar and Jahangir but replaced in the 19th century. The looting of the *deg* is a unique phenomenon which takes place when enough rice has been donated to fill them. (The large *deg* is over nine feet in diameter.) Once the rice is cooked and the names of the donors announced, professional looters empty it with lightning speed, even jumping into the boiling cauldron to scrape the dregs. The event is over in a few minutes and evokes great excitement. The rice is then sold as *tabarrukh* (sanctified food) by the looters.

West of the Dargah Sharif lies the immense **Adhai din ka Jhonpra** (the two-and-a-half-day hut). Originally a Sanskrit college built in 1155, it was restructured into a mosque by Sultan Ghori in 1198. It is one of the finest monuments of medieval India, espec-ially noted for the beauty of its surface decorations and ornate calligraphic inscriptions. The pillars retain Hindu stylistic elements but the screen and arches were added in 1266. In the 18th century, fakirs used to assemble here for the *urs* of Panjaba Sahib, which lasted two-and-a-half days, hence the name.

Hill Fort: Taragarh, the star fort, rises 800 feet (250 m) above the valley. It is accessible by road via Nallah Bazar and a bridle path from behind the Dargah. Between 1860 and 1920 it was used as a sanatorium by the British. It affords an interesting view of the Dargah and of the valley to the west. The saint's daughter, Bibi Hafiz Jamal lived in this valley which is named after her. Jahangir built a hunting palace and tanks here, the ruins of which are also visible. Taragarh is important for a mosque and the **shrine of Miran Sayyid Hussain**, governor of the fort. He died in 1202, but sanctity was attached to him only four-and-a-half centuries later, when Akbar visited his grave.

Within the walled city, off Station Road is Akbar's red sandstone palace,

the **Daulat Khana** (Abode of Wealth). It served the British as the Rajputana arsenal between 1818 and 1862. The central audience hall is now the **Government Museum**. It is especially rich in arms, both Mughal and Rajput, sculptures dating from the fourth to the 12th centuries and Hun, Bactrian and Kushan coins.

Glimpses of Ajmer's colonial past are had at the **Edward Memorial Hall** and **Golden Jubilee Clock Tower**, both on Station Road, as well as the **Ajmer Club** situated near the spacious **Kalka Bagh**.

At the junction of Station Road and Kutcheri Road is the ornate 19th-century **Nasiyan** (red) **Jain Temple**. Its interior is embellished with rich depictions of Jain mythology.

A little over a mile (two km) from the Tourist Bungalow, past **Subhash Bagh**, is the tranquil **Anasagar Lake**, situated between hillocks. It is almost eight miles (13 km) in circumference and its beauty is enhanced by Shah Jahan's white marble embankment and pavilions. This pleasure resort of the emperor was used by the British for official purposes, and Tod and Bishop

Herber stayed here. Fortunately, some of the pavilions are well preserved and it has again been restored as a place of extraordinary scenic beauty.

Ajmer forms a convenient base for visits to nearby towns of interest. Foremost among these is **Pushkar**, the road to which skirts Anasagar Lake.

Just 11 km northeast of Ajmer is Pushkar, a small town sacred to the Hindus and now a tourist attraction for its annual camel fair, the largest in the world. The sanctity of the lake for Hindus is equal to that of Mansarovar in Tibet and according to tradition, a bath in its waters is as essential as pilgrimages to Badrinath, Dwarka, Rameswaram and Puri, the traditional "at least once in a lifetime" places of pilgrimage.

The *Padma* (lotus) *Purana* (sacred legend) describes Pushkar as the place where Brahma, Lord of Creation, killed a demon with a lotus. The petals fell at three spots where lakes emerged. Pushkar is the most important of them, for Brahma performed a *yagna* (sacrifice) here on the full moon of Kartik (October/November). His consort, Savitri, could not be present on the

Muslim pilgrims at the *dargah*.

occasion, so Brahma hastily married a Gurjar girl, Gayatri. When Savitri appeared she was furious. She cursed all those present, and said that Brahma would be worshiped at Pushkar only. Brahma countered this by assigning Gayatri the status of goddess, with powers to undo the curse. However, his temple here remains one of the very few dedicated to this deity in India. Savitri retreated to a hillock north of the lake, where a temple is dedicated to her. On a hillock opposite is another dedicated to Gayatri.

Epics, religious texts, coins and inscriptions bear evidence to the sanctity of Pushkar. Over the centuries it grew into a temple town, and today there are as many as 400 temples in Pushkar. The present town was renovated in the ninth century by a Parihar king of Mandor, when he was cured of a skin ailment after a dip in the lake.

Pushkar is a maze of temples, *ashrams* (hermitages) and *dharamshalas* (rest houses) and one is never far from the sound of worship, from ascetics and devotees. The most important temples are dedicated to Brahma, Shiva, Badri Narayan, Varah, Savitri and Gayatri. The *dharamshalas* are for specific castes, tribes and sects. Pushkar is frequented most by Rajasthani peasants, by Gurjars in particular, who naturally have a special feeling for Gayatri.

The lake is bounded by 52 ghats, built over the centuries by kings and nobles. (Photography is prohibited on the ghats.) Of these, **Varah**, **Brahma** and **Gau Ghats** are the most revered. Varah Ghat is specially sacred as Lord Vishnu is believed to have appeared here in the form of a boar. A dip in the lake by a woman absolves both her and her husband. For a complete cleansing of sins, three twilights must be passed at Pushkar with baths at the three important ghats.

The Pushkar Fair: Throughout the year, life is centered on the lake and temples, and Pushkar has the atmosphere of an ancient religious town, peaceful and secluded. But for 12 days in the month of Kartik it is transformed into a spectacular fairground that spreads over the dunes west of the town. The *mela* is an event of religious and commercial importance. Thousands of men come first, with their camels and cattle, and camp on the dunes to transact business. Three days before the full moon, the women start coming, gorgeously attired. The beauty of rural Rajasthan gets concentrated within the radius of a few miles. The peasants bathe and worship, are variously entertained, and delight in the dazzling wares of hundreds of roadside stalls, while on the dunes camels are bought and sold, beautified, raced and paraded. The fair is overwhelming in its magnitude and in its visual impact.

Apart from the tranquil tourist bungalow on the shore of the lake, a miniature tent city is put up during the fair for the convenience of tourists. Pushkar also has several boarding houses because it has lately become a popular retreat for hippies.

Kishangarh, painters' haven: Kishangarh, a charming town well worth a visit, lies 19 miles (30 km) before Ajmer on the Jaipur road. It was founded in 1611 by Kishan Singh, brother of the Raja of Jodhpur. Politically unimportant as a princely state, it has won international renown for having nurtured the finest school of miniature painting in 18th-century India.

Rajput princes had adopted the

dhai Din ka hopra has ne of the nest xamples of Iamic alligraphic iscriptions.

sophisticated and luxurious lifestyle of the Mughal court, of which miniature painting had become an integral part. By the mid-17th century, artists were already working in the ateliers of Kishangarh. A few decades later, Kishangarh also provided a haven to artists fleeing the puritanical severity of Aurangzeb's court and among those who came were the renowned Bhavanidas, Surat Ram and Nihal Chand.

The greatest patron of Kishangarh art was Raja Satwant Singh. He was himself a painter and poet and wrote verses under the pseudonym of Nagaridas. He fell in love with a court singer, Bani Thani, who subsequently became his mistress. It is said that the famous Kishangarh Radha is made in her likeness, but in fact the lotus-eyed woman had long been the Rajput ideal of feminine beauty. In 1757, Satwant Singh abdicated and left with Bani Thani for Vrindavan. By then the excellence of Kishangarh painting was equalled only by those of the Kangra school of Himachal in the Himalayan foothills. The artists were obsessed with the *Krishna leela* theme, but they portrayed Krishna in a courtly instead of a pastoral setting. Hunting scenes were also popular, as were equestrian portraits. The paintings belonged to the Rajas of Kishangarh and were first seen by the outside world in the 1940s. Some of these exquisite masterpieces are now on view at the National Museum, New Delhi.

The old city of Kishangarh still has the flavor of the magic world created by the artists. Modern Kishangarh is bustling and crowded, important as a wholesale market for red chillies and a cotton-weaving center. But Kishan Singh's city is about 2.5 miles (four km) away, on the fringe of an enormous lake. A road leads to the fort and buses and *tongas* ply regularly.

The **fort** and **palaces** overlook the lake in the center of which is another palace, accessible by boat. The area is especially beautiful during the monsoon when the lotus blooms, and herons, egrets and ducks are to be seen. And though the pleasure gardens are overgrown and the palaces unkempt, there are exact locations which can be recognized in the miniatures. A walk through the cobbled streets is rewarding. The ambience is decidedly medi-

Rose petals being dried, Ajmer.

eval, and in many *havelis* painters of miniatures are still at work. The quality, however, has deteriorated and their art bears no relation to the original. There is also an interesting little bazar, where, amongst other things, goldsmiths and silversmiths can be seen at work, crafting traditional jewelry.

Marble Quarries: Due north of Kishangarh and 40 miles (63 km) away via Parvatsar are the marble quarries of **Makrana**, famous for having supplied the white marble for the 'Taj Mahal and the palaces built by Shah Jahan. More than a century ago Tod wrote: "The quarries, until of late, yielded a constant revenue but the age of palace building in these regions is no more and posterity will ask with surprise the sources of such luxury." However, marble is being increasingly used in contemporary architecture. Today, Makrana is the biggest center for marble trade in India and the entire population of the city is associated with it.

The quarries, most of which have been privately owned over several generations, vary in size and stretch over a distance of 12.5 miles (20 km). The finest marble is pure white, followed by white-grained, pink, gray, and gray with blue streaks. Quarrying techniques are mostly primitive. Blocks of marble are often raised by hand-operated pulleys. The stone is dressed for sizing at the site and transported on bullock carts to factories where it is sliced, washed and polished. There are about 500 factories in Makrana which supply marble slabs to all parts of India. Marble is also sent to Agra for inlay work, often pre-shaped on lathes in Makrana itself. There are about 40 carving centers in Makrana as well, and craftsmen can be seen working on statues, containers, vases and pedestals. It is fascinating to watch the entire process, to see a town where interest lies in marble, to the exclusion of all else.

Twenty miles (32 km) east of Makrana, is an area of inland drainage, is the **Sambhar Salt Lake**. After the monsoon, an area of 90 sq.miles (233 sq. km) becomes an area of shallow water. By the next summer, the water evaporates and salt is collected for distribution throughout western India.

Red chilies being dried, Krishangarh Fort.

SHEKHAVATI'S PAINTED WALLS

Shekhavati lies in a triangle between Jaipur, Bikaner and Delhi. With the exception of the rocky Aravalli range that divides Shekhavati diagonally, showing its jagged face here and there, the countryside is flat and almost monochromatic. Today, Shekhavati comprises the administrative districts of Sikar and Jhunjhunu, which are together one-fifth of the Jaipur Division.

Since the middle of the 19th century, the inhabitants of Shekhavati have patronized the art of fresco painting compensating, in a way, for the lack of color in the landscape of their homeland.

The Rajputs seem to have been the first patrons, ordering a frescoed room in a fort or on a *chhatri* (cenotaph) commemorating a hero. The Marwaris, the merchant community which prospered on the trade routes between Delhi and the coast and between Central Asia and China, later became

even more extravagant patrons.

The roads of Shekhavati, now like any other, were once caravan routes "where the productions of India, Cashmire, and China, were interchanged for those of Europe, Africa, Persia and Arabia."

Even though trade rivalry with the British had pushed the Marwaris from Shekhavati to the ports, they never ceased to think of Shekhavati as their own land. And this explains the enormous structures raised in nostalgia.

The merchants built for the community: wells and reservoirs, *dharamshalas* (caravanserais), schools, *gaushalas* (shelters for cows), and temples. In memory of their ancestors they constructed cenotaphs, and for their families large *havelis* (mansions).

Framework for a Way of Life: The word *haveli*, which is of Persian origin, mean "surrounded" or an "enclosed place." It has no exact equivalent in the English language. Perhaps "mansion" comes close enough, suggesting the spacious residence that *haveli* connotes, but it fails to capture the essence of a way of life that was more than just a form of architecture. In Mughal times it signified a residential block, usually three to five stories high, around an open courtyard. It normally accommodated several families who lived together as an economic, civic and social unit, sharing many common amenities. The density of occupation was balanced by the open court that would usually accommodate a common well for drinking water, space for washing and drying clothes, and a play area for children. Just as the joint family system was the smallest economic unit in the social structure of medieval India, a *haveli* was the smallest survival unit in the urban civic structure.

Havelis are generally town houses, as opposed to *kothis* or garden houses of the suburbs. The original function of a *haveli*, apart from providing a residence, was to wall-in the domestic life of a family. Secluded from the outside world, a *haveli* set its own pace of life. All through royal and feudal India the *havelis*, whether inhabited by Hindus or Muslims, represented the rigid lifestyle of a society that segregated its men from its women. The architecture of the *haveli* was conceived around this social norm. Unlike the Mughal *have-*

lis, the typical *haveli* in Shekhavati consisted of two courtyards, an outer and an inner. The grander ones sometimes had three or four courtyards.

Today, life in the *haveli* continues on much the same pattern, though there are fewer inhabitants. The outer courtyard serves as an extended threshold, since the main gate is seldom shut. The inner one is the domain of the women who are entirely occupied with household chores. In days gone by, their routine began before dawn with the worship of *tulsi* (holy basil), followed by the milking of the cows in the *nora* (pen), the churning of butter, cooking, and collecting and storing water in a special airy room called the *parinda.* When male guests entered the house, the women, who normally remained in *purdah* (literally, "behind the curtain"), retreated briskly into the *zenana,* their private apartments. And from their fretted *zenana* windows they peeped into the men's world.

The *havelis* are guarded at the entrance by large wooden doors reminiscent of medieval forts. Within these, a smaller door is normally used for daily movements. Intricate wooden carvings with fancy brass and iron fittings demonstrate the owner's wealth. The ground floor is normally recessed in such a way that balconies overhang the street. It was from the latticed windows on the balconies and over the courtyards that women were able to get a glimpse of the men's world. The facade, the gateways, the courtyard walls, the parapets and ceilings, were all covered with frescoes.

Wall Paintings: The frescoes on the earliest *havelis* date back to the early 1800s (though some on the forts, *chhatris* and temples are dated around 1750). The majority were painted between 1860 and 1900. Starting from purely religious themes, the frescoes move on to ornamental designs, and after 1900 when these became widely available, to imitations of European lithographs and etchings.

The technique of fresco painting in Shekhavati was not primitive or unique to the area but very close to the Italian fresco (fresh) technique developed around the 14th century. Whether this technique traveled to India through the Mughals, who knew of it from Persia, or whether it was the **The Char Chowk Haveli, Lachhmangar**

missionaries to the Mughal court who first introduced this at Fatehpur Sikri, is not known for certain. But the local Shekhavati mason had definitely mastered it to give us the true fresco *buono* on wet plaster.

Driving through Shekhavati: By road or by train, Shekhavati can be approached with equal ease from Jaipur, Delhi or Bikaner. Let us begin from Jaipur, on the road that armies and caravans once took—the Jaipur-Sikar road.

The first little town we pass on our left is **Chomu**. A moat and a sturdy medieval wall with machicolations remind us of the bloody times gone by. At the fort, a large iron lock still hangs from its entrance door. The Chomu fort is now a granary, its high walls and large covered spaces providing easy storage and shelter. From Chomu turn right to **Samod**. This detour into what may seem a ghost settlement is well worthwhile. The road winds through a narrow abandoned street, under several gates, up to a late 19th-century palace with stables and European lamp-posts for lanterns.

Climb a flight of stairs and you enter elaborately painted rooms, most of which are still in fairly good condition. The Darbar Hall of the Samod palace is known for its *meenakari* (inlay of glass mirrors and stones), its stucco work and its gilded strappings. Notice that the windows have adjustable louvres. Behind these, the ladies and their retinue once watched and listened, and perhaps commented among themselves, while the men held audience.

Sikar, the next stop, was the largest *thikana* (feudatory state) under the Jaipur State. It is now one of the two districts of Shekhavati, the other being Jhunjhunu. Drive through Sikar's large market to the **Clock Tower** and the older quarter where the painted **Biyani Havelis** will delight your eyes. There is one painted only in blue, reminiscent of the typical Chinese blue-and-white porcelain.

The obsession with blue is understandable, once we know that synthetic blue began to be imported from Germany around 1870. For a wealthy patron, using only blue must have been a step ahead of the others. Then, as now, possession of imported goods was a status symbol.

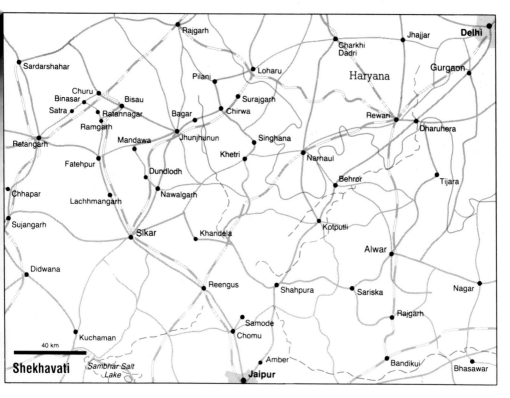

Sikar has a **Jubilee Hall**, and a palace-turned-temple where ladies gather and chant prayers all day. The **Sikar fort**, though neglected, is not without charm. Its meandering stone ramps with chevroned patterns lead you to private terraces, painted rooms and fretted windows. The later additions have wrought-iron fences that frame oval portraits of Queen Victoria, Empress of India.

From Sikar to **Nawalgarh**, a fascinating town founded by Nawal Singh in 1737. Nawalgarh has a college with a very British clock tower; and hundreds of painted *havelis*, old and new. Many of the better known Rajasthani merchant families come from here. The *Thakurs* (nobles) of Nawalgarh also had a great passion for building. Many structures of the early 20th century still stand. Among them is **Roop Niwas** (with its drive around a fountain) where tourists can stay in comfort. Also worth seeing is the **Saat Haveli** complex.

Walking through Nawalgarh's streets, there is much to discover. Try and see the Shiva Temple with a multi-headed *lingam*; the frescoed telephone exchange; the recently tiled cenotaph near the railway station; the "Company School" paintings (ie. those showing signs of the English influence of the East India Company. 1760–1880). If you can manage to secure the keys, see the painted dome in the fort on which an aerial view of Jaipur has been drawn in great detail. *Trompe l'oeil* frescoes characterize Nawalgarh. A colorful bazaar surrounds the old fort. In Jaipur, the Nawalgarh family has one of the best private art collections.

An excursion from Nawalgarh will take you to **Parasrampura** where some of the earliest frescoes (around 1750) are to be seen in the interior of a temple and inside the dome of the *chhatri* of Shardul Singh (the eighth descendant of Rao Shekhaji, founder of Shekhavati) who expanded his territories by ousting the Kayamkhani *nawabs* from Jhunjhunu (1730) and Fatehpur (1731), putting an end to three centuries of almost unbroken Muslim supremacy over large areas of Shekhavati.

From Nawalgarh, the more adventurous can tour the Aravalli region

Noblemen chase wild boar.

where they will be rewarded by extraordinary sights of towns like **Chirana**—with an elegant fort and grand *havelis* against a rocky backdrop; **Lohargal**, where the mace of Bhima—a hero of the Mahabharata—is said to have been cast, giving it its name (*lohargal* literally means "iron smelting"); **Raghunathgarh**—which seems to stand at the end of the habitable world; and **Udaipurvati**—historically one of the most important towns, as the Confederation of the Shekhavats used to meet here to decide on joint action in times of danger.

Close by is the small and charming town of **Dundlod**. Here an enlightened *thakur* had modernized his rugged fort (dated around 1765). It now houses a well-stocked library with European-style portraits and chandeliers. Here, too, the tourist can stay in large rooms with four-poster beds and imitation European furniture. Don't miss the **Goenka Haveli**. Very close to Dundlod is **Mukundgarh**, a town built around a temple square, outside the sloping fort walls. Here you can shop for local handicrafts in a charming white-colonnaded market. Besides textiles, its

renowned brass and iron scissors are Mukundgarh's highlights. The **Kanoria** and **Ganeriwala Havelis** deserve a visit.

A few miles away, **Lachhmangarh** offers one of the best forts of the area. It commands an aerial view of the town, the only one to have been planned on the model of Jaipur, with roads at right angles and roundabouts. The **Char Chowk Haveli** with four courtyards is the most imposing one in Shekhavati.

Next **Mandawa** emerges like a mirage. A medieval fort (dated around 1750) gradually rises on the horizon. A painted, arched gateway adorned with Lord Krishna and his cows leads to the bazaar. Later, three large gates lead you to the cannon-guarded interior of the fort. Here the visitor can ride a camel and stay in rooms that retain a strong medieval flavor. The terrace of **Castle Mandawa** holds a breathtaking view of the town and the semi-arid plains beyond. The stables are now rooms that face the luxury of a desert garden. In the great timelessness of the desert, a gong announces time by the hour. The Mandawa bazaar has many painted houses, parts of which have

emoiselle ranes, Tal happar, ear Churu.

now been turned into shops. Hand-painted and tie-and-dye fabrics flutter in the wind, tailors oblige you with a shirt in a day, skilled hands craft colorful bangles in lac and cobblers make shoes embroidered with gold thread. Though the *havelis* of the Chokhanis, the Goenkas and the Sarafs are extravagantly painted, one of the oldest frescoes is within the fort itself. The Mandawa family has a small collection of traditional ceremonial costumes and precious arms with handles of jade and gold. On the outskirts of the town, a temple built by a jeweler has an enormous natural crystal in the shape of a *lingam*. The Mandawa family has built a desert camp for tourists who would prefer to live in village ambience on a dune. Three groups of very ethnic cottages symbolize the villages of potters, weavers and peasants.

A short road links Mandawa with **Fatehpur**, a town once ruled by Muslim *nawabs*. The frescoes on the **Devra** and **Singhania Havelis** of Fatehpur are matched by few others. As later, more hybrid examples, the two **Bhartia Havelis** are impressive. These are adorned

with mirrorwork on their entrances and Japanese tiles patterned with Mount Fuji! Drive through Fatehpur's confusion of roads that link with each other when you least expect them to. See the English-style portraits on the crumbling fort and the intricately painted room of a **Goenka Haveli**. Here, there is no place to stay. Not far off, is **Churu** with its imposing 18th-century fort and large painted *havelis*.

From Churu you can branch off southwest to Bikaner or east to Delhi. As you drive to Delhi you will pass **Bissau** with one of the nicest painted *chhatris* near a massive fort. From here you take a detour to **Mahansar** which has the single most exquisite room painted in gold (*Soney Chandi ki Haveli*). This was once a showroom for a family of goldsmiths. At nearby **Ramgarh**, the entire *Ramayana* is illustrated on the interior dome of the Poddar cenotaph. The frescoes on the **Shani Temple**, dedicated to the Saturday god, have been painted with devotion and delicacy.

From Bissau to **Jhunjhunu** the road goes up and down the dunes till it finally straightens out. This too, was under Muslim rulers till the brave Shardul Singh recovered it for his Rajput Shekhavats. Besides the painted *havelis* (the **Tibdiwala**, the **Modi** and the **Chhe** (six)-Haveli complex), the stark pure **Khetri Mahal** is very refreshing and offers a complete view of the town. Among the sands, discover a famous mosque, or just off the road, gaze at the completely *kitsch*, **Rani Sati Temple** where the Marwaris, the mercantile community of Rajasthan, gather once a year for a fair.

En route to Delhi, stop at **Baggar** to admire the gigantic *havelis* of the **Rungtas**. Farther, at **Chirawa**, are more stunning *havelis* of the **Dalmias** and the **Kakraniyas** (where visitors are shown a bench on which, Queen Victoria is supposed to have sat—although she never came to India!).

And so back on to the Delhi—Jaipur road. Stop at **Dharuhera** for a snack and you will find yourself back in the present. For, even though Shekhavati's fort and palace hotels have most of the facilities of the modern world, its medieval charm dominates—at every turn, in every street, when the visitor faces painted walls that re-enact the past before his eyes.

Left, gateway to mosque, Jhunjhunu. Right, painted doorway depicting scenes from Indian mythology.

BIKANER: JEWEL IN THE SUN

Bikaner: This desert city was a major trade center on the old caravan route linking Central Asia and North India with the Gujarat seaports long before a Rathor prince, Bika, conquered it in 1486 A.D., and called it Bikaner. When Muhammad Ghori destroyed their Kanauj kingdom in 1193, the Rathors re-established themselves in the wilds of Marwar. Bikaji was the second son of Rao Jodhaji, the real founder of Jodhpur state, its magnificent fort and city. Bika left Jodhpur in a huff with a few kinsmen and followers because his father taunted him in open durbar about concocting expansionist schemes with his uncle, Rao Kandhal.

Fortunately for his descendants, no enemy could withstand the harsh desert that surrounds this rich city and disrupt its leisurely lifestyle, which still prevails. Here, medieval settings, customs, and attitudes are natural, and modern ways rather alien. Bikaner has a special quality, an authentic medieval flavor that immediately draws the outsider's attention.

The bazaars round **Kote Gate** bustle with activity. Jeeps jostle camel carts and one-horse tongas for space. Cars inch past cyclists and pedestrians choking narrow roads. Rustic women in colorful *lehenga-cholis* (flared ankle-length skirts and midriff-baring blouses) and hand printed *odhnis* (veils), wearing massive silver anklets and ivory bangles up to their elbows, seek bargains at the pavement stalls. Turbaned men wearing gold earrings stride purposefully into cool stores where *baniyas* (merchants) sit cross-legged on white sheets, leaning against bolsters, checking accounts or showing bolts of cloth to customers. TV sets, VCRs, tape recorders, toys, and knick-knacks crowd show-windows. Sari shops, readymade garment stores, *zari* (gold and silver embroidery) shops, tailors, jewelers, photographers, furniture maaers, booksellers, *pan* (betel leaf) *wallahs*, barbers, boys selling *kulfi* (ice cream) out of vacuum flasks, boys flying kites, students pausing for soft drinks, people buying vegetables and fruit, donkeys loaded with clay pots, stray cows, dogs, and hawkers calling out their wares fill the space between the **Vishwa Jyoti** and **Prakash Theatre** cinema halls.

Several local handicrafts and souvenirs are available in the bazaar. Lacquer-work wall panels on camel skin are a Bikaner speciality. In fact, camel skin is used for making all sorts of useful or ornamental things like embossed water-bottles, slippers, handbags, purses, bookmarks, cushions, and lacquered lampshades. Charming gold-lacquered pottery, trays, handblocked ethnic prints, and tie-and-dye fabrics, bedspreads and table linen, exotic silver and gold jewelry and key chains, are also good buys. Handwoven cotton *durries* (rugs), camel-hair blankets, and silk carpets are local specialities, which have long been export items.

Bikaner can be very uncomfortable in summer, which lasts from April to September. There are three distinct seasons in Rajasthan—the long hot summer, a short rainy spell when everything turns miraculously green and the lakes fill up, and the cold bracing winter. People who want to enjoy their visit to Bikaner should plan their trips between October and March. The festival of Holi generally falls in March, and for nearly three weeks before that, people start singing Holi songs to the beating of huge tambourines called *duffs*. This is the mesmerizing music of the desert stretching from the Horn of Africa, across Arabia, to Sind in Pakistan and to Rajasthan. Suddenly one night, on a date declared auspicious by astrologers and priests according to the lunar calendar, you hear the first bold *duff* begin, then others picking up the rhythm, and male voices from different parts of the city and the surrounding villages joining in. As the singers collect round campfires in various courtyards, you know that winter is ending, and the wheat crop is ready for ritual harvesting on the day of Holi.

Bikaner's villages are very thinly populated, and most of the people live in urban centers. Several charming *havelis* (mansions) belonging to distinguished merchant families stand in the old quarters of the walled city. Bikaner was a safe haven for rich traders and bankers in strife-torn medieval,

Mughal, and British India, where they could leave their families while carrying on their commercial ventures in distant places. Two *havelis* in particular, belonging to the super-rich Khajanchis and Kotharis, are worth visiting—after prior appointment, because they are lived-in examples of centuries-old Marwari domestic architecture. Both also contain excellent art collections. Remarkable carved sandalwood doors and windows, airy sandstone balconies, balustrades, and lacy *jharokhas* (latticed stone windows) enclose an old-fashioned world where the generations overlap, and Ivy League or Oxbridge-educated tycoons and their unassuming cotton-clad wives with diamond solitaire ear and nose rings offer guests hospitality and stimulating conversation. This ready welcome awaits you everywhere, in dignified Rajput *deras* (mini-forts), modest village homes, or Jat farmhouses. Desert hospitality has always been a great tradition.

Jain Temples: The oldest existing structures in Bikaner are the 14th-century Jain temples built by two merchant brothers, Sandeshwar and Bhandeshwar. Neither had a son to carry on the family name, so each built a temple. The **Bhandeshwar Temple** stands on a high-walled plinth and has a shallow sultanate type of dome over the main entrance. Carved wooden columns with dancing figures surround a dark sanctuary with checkered gold designs, and there is a mass of reflecting mirror-work behind the marble Mahavir. The circular *mandap* (pavilion) features astonishingly well-preserved frescoes of battles, local historical events, and parades of elephants and camels.

The nearby **Neminath Sandeshwar Temple** is entirely different. Its chief features are stylized enamel and gold-leaf wall paintings, and an interesting vaulted and arched ornamented ceiling. Rows of white marble statues of Jain saints line two marble altars beneath the raised lotus pedestal on which Neminath sits meditating.

Camels are to be seen everywhere in Bikaner, carrying people, transporting goods, pulling carts, plowing fields, plodding patiently through trackless sands, or sitting still in camps after a hard day under the blistering sun.

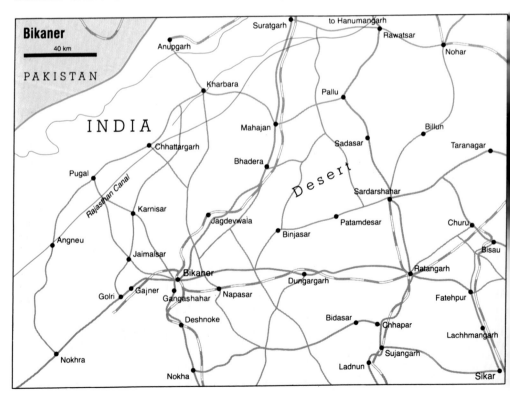

Camels are still very important in Rajasthan's daily life. At festivals, fairs, and weddings, people show their appreciation by decking their camels in colorful *gorbunds* (ornamental harness and camel accouterments) dripping cowrie shells, coral beads, silver chains, and silk tassels. It's worth spending a little time watching the huge camel herds being watered, fed, and exercised at the **State Camel Breeding Farm** near **Shiv Bari**. A camel ride over the sand dunes is an exhilirating experience, but not for faint hearts.

Junagadh Fort: Akbar's contemporary, Raja Rai Singh, began building Bikaner's Junagadh Fort in 1587. It is one of the finest of Rajput monuments, even though it lacks the commanding hilltop site of the forts at Jodhpur, Jaisalmer, Amber, and Chittor.

Rai Singh's brother, Prithviraj, a poet, scholar, and wit, was one of the distinguished Nine Gems of the Mughal Emperor Akbar's court. And Raja Rai Singh's eccentric youngest son, Kishen Singh, ventured forth from Junagadh to establish a branch of the Bika dynasty at copper-rich Sankhu.

Junagadh is one of the few forts in India which has never been conquered, though it was often attacked. Sati queens down the centuries left their handprints on the wall facing the huge spiked gate leading to an eerie enclosure which opens on the main courtyard. Thirty-seven palaces, pavilions and temples built by different kings stand protected by massive ramparts and round towers. They are all connected by paved courtyards, painted galleries, narrow staircases which could be defended by a single warrior, and terraces. Two marble fretwork windows set in a soaring sandstone wall leave a strong impact on anyone going into Junagadh. Bikaner's crimson and saffron standard still flies over this Rathor stronghold, cared for by a family trust. But the kettle-drums which signaled the ruler's arrivals and departures are now silent.

Behind the multi-storied Anup Mahal facade lie incredibly well-preserved chambers where able rulers who created so much splendor in the sand lived, surrounded by relations and retainers. From the latticed windows women watched the outside world without

painter
uts the
nishing
ouches
o his
aasterpiece.

breaking *purdah*. For four centuries Junagadh was the heart of an important autonomous kingdom where the public came daily, as a matter of right, to lay their problems and petitions before their *maharaja*, or to eat at the communal kitchen from which no one could be turned away hungry. But now the silence is broken only when visitors come to see and photograph the historic treasures on public display. The rarest of these is the ancient *Pugal* or sandalwood throne of the Kanauj kings, probably the oldest piece of furniture existing in India. This was one of the Rathor heirlooms brought from Jodhpur by Bikaji after the deaths of his father and elder brother. Another is Bikaji's small silver-legged bed. Remembering how his grandfather, Rao Riddmall, was tied to his own bed and treacherously killed at Chittor by enemies who had hidden under the bed, Bika always slept on a low, narrow bed under which no one could hide. Sitting or sleeping on this bed is strictly taboo even for members of Bika's dynasty.

The huge **Ganga Niwas Durbar Hall** with its carved walls and ceiling, was a splendid setting for ceremonies in the old days. Royal marriages, births, and the yearly Gangaur festival are still celebrated in the **Har Mandir** facing the Anup Mahal courtyard, where the ancient Hiranyagarbh idol of Lakshmi-Narayan, the Nav Durgas seated on a nine-petaled gold lotus, the holy Dakshina-Vrat Shankh (conch shell), and the sacred Karand casket are housed. Daily worship is performed here by hereditary priests who still serve Bikaji's descendants.

From the fort's roofs and ramparts there is a magnificent view of the crowded city, with the great **Ratan Bihari Temple** in the foreground. In the *zenana*, shady balconies and kiosks surround colorful mosaic courtyards, each different—some studded with pools and fountains to refresh the queens and princesses in the summer months. Each exuberant *chaubara* (four-sided open pavilion), *panchbara* (penthouse), and *sal* (gallery) is ornamented with lacquer-work, mirrored niches, floral panels, portraits and mythological scenes. The vaulted, arched, or paneled ceilings and decorated doors, each different, have to be

Junagarh Fort.

seen to be believed. The **Gaj Mandir Sheesh Mahal** (hall of mirrors) with its ivory-inlaid bed, inviting swing-seat, silver chairs, and polished wooden chests and cupboards seems ready and waiting for its master.

The **fort museum** has a valuable collection of illuminated Sanskrit and Persian manuscripts, and miniature paintings. Art experts rate the extremely elegant and sensitive Bikaner miniatures second only to those of the Mughal school. Outstanding examples of Rajasthani jewelry, enamelware, gold and silver boxes, trays, water jars, ceremonial vessels, *hookahs*, costumes, and carpets are displayed here. Historic weapons and armor include jeweled swords inscribed with the names of famous Mughal emperors or great Rajput warriors, jade and enamel hilted daggers, pistols and muskets inlaid with ivory, gold, or silver. The huge double-edged sword of Rajkumar Padam Singh is always pointed out with great pride. With this sword, which few able-bodied men can lift, Padam Singh left a dent on the sandstone pillar of Agra's Diwan-i-Aam (Hall of Public Audience) when he cut down his broth-

er's murderer in front of the Mughal Emperor Aurangzeb. These weapons, and the legends linked with them, give visitors an inkling of the magnificent madness that inspired and sustained these Rajputs throughout their turbulent history.

You can also examine Mughal *farmans* (written orders), British treaties, decorations, medals, and other heirlooms belonging to legendary figures. The gold insignia of rank presented to Bikaner's rulers by various Mughal emperors, their gold howdahs, palanquins lined with rare brocades, and ceremonial war drums are also displayed here.

Besides being formidable fighters, the Rathors of Bikaner were sophisticated scholars and art patrons. The walls of the 17th-century **Karan Mahal** are so skilfully painted with gold leaf and jewel tones that it seems like outrageously expensive *pietra dura* inlay. The walls are not even marble, but lime plaster polished to perfection with shells. The 18th-century **Phool Mahal** is decorated with elaborate mirrorwork, while the airy **Chandra Mahal** in which the *maharanis* lived has bas-

relief friezes of Hindu gods and goddesses over every arched entrance. Hunting and polo scenes cover galleries in the male apartments. The dazzling **Anup Mahal**, where Bikaner's kings received kinsmen and clan chiefs, is ornamented with scarlet and gold Persian motifs repeated in the specially woven carpet. The seldom-visited chamber under the bright blue clock tower has a quaint combination of "wallfellows"—erotic Rajput paintings, Chinese wallpaper, and Dutch tiles. Together they echo the hybrid Eurasian style sweeping the subcontinent at the heyday of the British Raj.

Lalgadh Palace: Aesthetically, few palaces in India match Bikaner's Lalgadh. Set in the open countryside outside the city, this perfect blend of oriental fantasy and European luxury was designed 90 years ago by Sir Swinton Jacob for Maharaja Ganga Singh, a great modernizer, soldier, and one of the signatories to the Versailles Treaty. Before the Second World War began, Maharaja Ganga Singh wrote to the Secretary of State for India, the Viceroy, and brother princes, advocating the merger of the princely states with a free, federal India.

Statues of Queen Victoria and King Edward VII greet visitors in Lalgadh's entrance hall. This rambling palace is built round an open garden court overlooked by the *zenana* (ladies' apartments) windows. Local craftsmen carved its cupolas, umbrella domes, balconies, balustrades, pillars, windows and walls with such skill that solid sandstone took on the look of delicate lace.

A cloister of peacock arches surrounds the stately marble courtyard of the **Lazmi Bilas**. The main drawing room, library, billiard room, card room, smoking room, and guest suites are located here. All have Belgian or Bohemian crystal chandeliers reflected in huge mirrors over the fireplaces; and carpets repeating the intricate ceiling carvings or moldings. The marble corridors connecting the whole palace are lined with hunting trophies, lithographs, and bronzes. Until recently, a fabulous collection of oil paintings, Indian miniatures, Chinese jade, porcelain, hand-embroidered silk screens, Japanese eggshell enamel vases, ornamental *ormolu* clocks, antique silver,

lamps, bronzes, marbles, and cut-glass ornaments filled this palace. Maintenance problems created by the abolition of privy purses and lack of staff have led to the dispersal of this collection gathered over centuries. But the **Shiv Bilas** dining room (seating capacity:400) with its hunting trophies and wildlife paintings remains unchanged. And autographed photographs of European, Asian, and Indian royalty in crested silver frames still stand where they used to, in a reception hall near the ADC Room.

Peacocks roam freely through Lalgadh's grounds, boldly venturing into verandas and posing on domes. Pigeons, parrots, blue jays, doves, bright bee-eaters, and colorful humming birds thrive here. Once goldfish and silver carp filled the lily pools, and fountains played amidst the lawns. Today, even drinking water is a problem in this drought-prone region, so gardens are difficult to maintain. Lalgadh's present owner, Maharaja Karni Singhji, a famous Olympic shooter, scholar, parliamentarian, and painter, has turned parts of his palace into a hotel. He has also added India's only private trap and skeet shooting range to Lalgadh's existing sporting facilities, where he takes great pride in training aspiring shooting champions.

Manuscript Library, Archives & Museum: The **Anup Sanskrit Library** housed at Lalgadh has one of the world's largest collections of original Sanskrit manuscripts on every conceivable subject. When *Maharaja* Anup Singh of Bikaner captured Golconda and Bijapur in 1687 at the head of Aurangzeb's army, he saved these priceless manuscripts, parchments, inscribed copper plates, and gold and silver plaques engraved with entire Indian epics like the *Ramayana* and *Mahabharata*, or philosophical treatises like the Gita. Research scholars from all over the world come to consult these Sanskrit texts; and to study the historical records, documents, letters, Mughal *farmans*, and hand-painted picture albums stored at the **Rajasthan State Archives**. The **Bikaner Museum** has an excellent collection of sculpture, seals, domestic implements, toys, and clay pots from pre-Aryan archaeological finds. It also has a large collection of coins, marble, stone, and terra cotta

statues, handicrafts, and metalwork from every period of Indian history. There are colorful Jain, Rajput, and Mughal miniature paintings. A scale model of the former *maharaja's* Edwardian special train is a popular exhibit. But the real collector's items are the perfectly carved sandalwood cities, caravans and portraits fitted into almond shells, walnuts, and dry beans, because this is now a lost art.

Modern Township: The **Public Park** and **zoo** lie between the medieval city and the modern township dotted with dignified sandstone buildings, offices, colleges, schools, hospitals, and military barracks. Shady trees line wide roads around comfortable bungalows set in large gardens. All this, plus Bikaner's railways, tube wells, powerhouses, excellent club, railway workshop, wool mills, glass manufacturing and carpet weaving centers, sheep-and cattle-breeding farms, orphanages and rehabilitation centers for deaf, dumb, and blind people, were all built by its dynamic ruler, Maharaja Ganga Singh, whose equestrian statue faces the fort as you enter the Public Park. This large park dotted with fountains, victory towers, shady kiosks, tress, and fishponds is a welcome spot in this dusty city. Here people who have business with the law courts, government offices, police headquarters, and banks so sensibly located under one roof, take a rest, or picnic on the lawns. Children play among the swings and slides throughout the day. Many come to see the animals and birds housed in comfortable enclosures scattered round the park. Pigeons, doves, mynas and sparrows perch near old folk who hold daily meetings on park benches after their morning walks.

Devi Kund Sagar: Beyond the radio station stand the marble and sandstone *chhatris* (cenotaphs) of Bikaner's rulers. Memorials carved with suns symbolize a prince's resting place. Lotus flowers commemorate princesses. Marble footprints beneath warriors on horseback denote spots sanctified by satis like Rani Deep Kanwar. To these, local people bring offerings of coconuts, incense, lamps, and flowers. Otherwise, no one disturbs the peace of Devi Kund Sagar, as the place is called.

These cenotaphs are grouped round

At rest

a large artifical tank. An 18th-century king built a walled enclosure to protect his father's memorial. It was foretold that all the coming rulers of Bikaner would be cremated in this small enclosure over which the *maharaja* had set guards. And, strangely enough, with the cenotaph of the last ruling *maharaja*, Sadul Singhji, built in 1950, the enclosure is full.

Gajner: Just 20 miles (32 km) west from Bikaner, Gajner has a quality of repose quite out of keeping with the bustling imperial sandgrouse shoots to which former *maharajas* invited viceroys, visiting royalty, and brother princes. The lake reflecting a fairytale pink sandstone palace and lush gardens contrasts so effectively with the surrounding scrubland, where black buck, chital, sambar, chinkara, nilgai and wild boar, and Indian bustard abound, that you wonder if it's all real, or a desert mirage. From the paved terrace, main garden, and bedroom windows you see an almost endless procession of jungle animals coming down to the lake for a drink.

Gajner offers hotel accommodation and meals. Honeymooners can even book the delightful little secluded Shabnam Cottage perched on a hillock overlooking the lake, built by Maharaja Sadul Singhji. Gajner's lake attracts millions of migratory birds in winter, when its owner, Dr Karni Singh, still holds houseparties, bringing international celebrities, close relations, and family friends together for shooting grouse, duck, and wild boar. But he has strongly opposed deer hunting, and created a deer park and wildlife reserve at Gajner. A jeep ride through this protected area brings you face to face with browsing black buck and nilgai, lazing sambars, and leaping gazelles, rabbits, partridges, and tiny quail.

From Gajner it's an easy drive to **Kolayat**, an ancient pilgrimage center where Kapil Muni of Vedic fame shed his body under a peepul tree. Kolayat is a collection of delightful marble temples, sandstone pavilions, and 32 *ghats* (bathing places) built round a huge man-made lake which never goes dry even in the worst drought. Here you see *sadhus*, *fakirs*, and boon seekers taking a dip, people picnicking under awnings, and monkeys swinging from old banyan trees. Kolayat has a timeless atmosphere reinforced by the surrounding desert, where you see nothing but vast emptiness, hear nothing but the wind.

People interested in agriculture and archaeology often undertake the 175-mile (280 km) trip to **Ganganagar** and **Kalibangan**. After witnessing the miseries of the great 1899 famine, the 19-year-old Maharaja Ganga Singh vowed to end starvation by building a canal in his state. The British pussyfooted, refusing water rights from the Satluj river in Punjab and financial aid. But Ganga Singh persevered and raised a loan of nearly £5 million for his irrigation scheme. The Ganga Canal, begun in 1921, was completed in 1927. One of the longest concrete-lined canals in the world, it has changed the desert's face around Ganganagar. Bumper crops of wheat, sugarcane, cotton, mustard and citrus fruit have generated industry, and a building boom.

Factories and mills today dot the skyline round **Kalibangan**, where extensive remains of the oldest known Indian civilization have been found. More than three thousand years before Christ, civilizations developed simul-

ʀying grain eside ʌnumangarh ort.

173

taneously in the river valleys of the Nile, Euphrates, Yangtse, and Indus. Archaeologists call the Harappa and Mohenjodaro cultures the Indus valley civilization, after the sites of two great cities excavated on the banks of the Ravi and Indus. Kalibangan, the third city, lies along the old Saraswati river, which is going dry. The Indus valley script has not yet been deciphered, so very little is known about this civilization and its people.

Kalibangan is almost as large as Harappa and Mohenjodaro, and designed on the same plan. Historians have established that Kalibangan formed part of a flourishing urban civilization protected by a large centralized state stretching from Baluchistan to Sind and modern Rajasthan. The excavations show that Kalibangan too had a well-defined citadel like Harappa and Mohenjodaro, which was used for both religious and government purposes. The streets are regular and well planned. Even the bricks, dating back 5,000 years, are uniform in size, like the weights and measures found in all these cities. The houses, often two stories high, are mostly built round square courtyards. They all have bathrooms provided with drains which flowed into covered sewers under the main streets. This impressive sewage system of the Indus people is as good as the much later Roman system, and must have been maintained by some sort of municipal organization. The special attention paid by the people living at Kalibangan to water supply, social hygiene and public baths shows that, like the later Hindus, they had a strong belief in the purificatory effects of water from a ritual point of view.

Kalibangan had trade links with distant places, as the silver, gold jewelry, turquoise, lapiz lazuli and jade dug up show. Copper and bronze images, implements, and domestic vessels; cotton and linen cloth; superb stone and metal seals depicting bulls, rhinoceroses, tigers, lions, buffaloes, elephants and goats; and interesting terra cotta figurines of men and women wearing elaborate headdress have been found here. Charming models of monkeys and squirrels, little toy carts, cattle with moving heads, and terra cotta whistles shaped like birds unearthed at Kalibangan show that these people cherished their children.

The flat metal swords, knives, spearheads and axes are not strong because they lack the reinforced central rib of such weapons found in Egypt and Mesopotamia, but the saws found have undulating teeth, which suggests that they were good carpenters, though their woodwork has perished.

Phallic symbols, proto-Shiva and Mother Goddess seals and figures unearthed prove that the Aryans who overran the Indus valley adopted elements of Harappa, Mohenjodaro, and Kalibangan religion, and these earlier cults were fused with Hinduism. But no one knows who these Indus valley people were, for the skeletons found include the Mediterranean, Proto-Australoid and Mongolian type.

Karni Mata Temple: Nineteen miles (30 km) south of Bikaner stands a unique temple. On his way from Jodhpur to carve out a kingdom for himself, Bika camped at Deshnok village, home of the miracle-working Karni Mata, considered an incarnation of Goddess Durga. She blessed Bika, prophesying his victory. Since then she has been worshiped as the titular deity by the Bikaner dynasty, though the Rathor family goddess remains Naganecchya Devi. **Karniji's Temple** at Deshnok derives its fame from the legion of rats which have territorial rights here, rather than from its miraculous shrine. The entrance is through a beautifully carved marble arch which leads to a black and white marble courtyard topped by wire mesh to protect the rats from eagles, crows and hawks. The sanctuary itself has superb silver doors embossed with images of gods and goddesses. One panel features Karni Mata standing on a footstool holding a *trishul* (trident), surrounded by rats. Visitors are cautioned not to injure these sacred rats, called *Kabas*. Whoever does so, however innocently, must present a gold or silver replica to the temple, or suffer misfortune. These harmless creatures scurry around, or surround the huge metal bowls full of sweetmeats, milk and grain donated by devotees. It is considered highly auspicious to see a white *kaba* near the vermilion-splashed image of Karni Mata.

Few natural sights equal the brilliance of a desert sunset, or the tranquilizing effect of moonlight-drenched sand dunes stretching into infinity.

Protected rats feed from bowls of sweetmeat and grain donated by devotees, Karni Mata Temple, Deshnok.

JAISALMER: DESERT CITADEL

Origin, Myth and History: About 800 years ago, a Rajput prince, on whose uneasy head rested an usurper's crown, sought counsel of a hermit who lived in a cave near a spring on top of a rocky hill. The prince was Jaisal, of the Bhatti clan; the hermit was Eesul, an oracle; the hill was Tricuta, a triple-peaked rock, and the outcome of that meeting was the foundation of Jaisalmer, the Rock of Jaisal, in 1156.

Prince Jaisal had been appointed regent to his young nephew on the death of his brother at Lodurva, capital of the Bhatti Rajputs. He had betrayed that trust and seized power in his own right, but was uncertain of commanding the loyalty of his vassal princes. Fearing an uprising, he wished to move his capital to a less vulnerable site than Lodurva. Having heard of the prophetic powers of the hermit, he decided to consult him.

The meeting proved fateful, for Eesul related a compelling myth about Tricuta, the place of his hermitage. Centuries ago, Lord Krishna himself had predicted that, in time to come, a distant descendant of his Lunar clan would rule from Tricuta. This fired Jaisal's imagination, for the Bhattis claim descent from the Chandravansh or Lunar clan, and he determined to build his new capital on Tricuta. He was not discouraged by the oracle's warning that the fort he built would be sacked two-and-a-half times!

The history of Jaisalmer is as turbulent as the character of its bandit chiefs would lead one to expect. Ferociously independent, inordinately proud of a tenuous "divine" lineage; brave, even foolhardy in battle and often treacherous as allies, the Bhatti Rajputs were the most feared of all desert marauders. When they were on the rampage, the gates of neighboring fortresses were closed and the cowering citizens barred their doors and windows against these "wolf-packs of the wastes." Their major opponents were the powerful Rathor clans of Jodhpur and Bikaner and endless ding-dong battles were waged for the possession of a petty fort, or meager waterhole. Cattle-stealing was a major pastime, along with fal-

conry and the hunt. The major source of income was the forced levies on the great caravans that traveled the ancient Spice Route on their way to imperial Delhi.

With the coming of the Muslims in the 13th and 14th centuries, the nature of the conflicts changed. The new enemy was not given to playing war-games according to a chivalric, if bizarre, code of conduct. The outsiders were here to found an empire and to propound Islam, a fanatically held faith. However, since Jaisalmer was situated deep in the desert, it escaped direct Muslim conquest. The Rawals, as the rulers were styled, agreed to pay an annual tribute to the Delhi Sultans in order to preserve a circumscribed independence.

Unfortunately, the Bhatti rulers could not always control their unruly vassal chiefs. The dire prophesy of Eesul, that the fort would be sacked, came about by their own rash actions.

The sieges of Jaisalmer are the subject of traditional ballads about Bhatti heroes. They are still sung at fairs and festivals by the hereditary bards, the *bhaats* and *charans*, and are the only record of the clan in medieval times. Although elaborately embellished with fabulous deeds of valor, they form the oral history of the period and have been an inspiration to the people during difficult times.

According to the ballads, the first siege occurred during the reign of Alla-ud-din Khilji (1295 A.D.–1315 A.D.), provoked by a foolhardy raid on the royal baggage caravan. For seven long years, the besieging army tried to starve out the defenders. Finally, they breached the ramparts, and the Bhattis, facing certain defeat, proclaimed the terrible rite of *johar*. Once the women and children had perished by sword or fire, the men, clad in ceremonial saffron and opium-intoxicated, opened the gates and rushed out to meet a heroic death.

The second sack followed a daring raid on Sultan Ferozeshah's camp at Anasagar Lake, near Ajmer. Jaisalmer was once again overrun and the dread *johar* repeated.

The half-sack of the prophesy came much later, in the 16th century. A friendly Pathan chieftain persuaded the Rawals to permit the begums of his harem to pay a courtesy call on the

receding
ages:
aisalmer
ort with city
the
reground.
eft, morning
arket
eneath
ty walls.

179

Rajput *ranis* but actually filled the palanquins with armed soldiers, who attacked the palace guards. In a moment of panic, Rawal Lunakaran slew several of the princesses of his family, to prevent them being carried off by the intruders. As it happened, the Pathans were beaten off.

Once the Great Mughals established their empire, relations between the imperial court and Jaisalmer stabilized. Several princes of the family served as commanders of the Mughal forces and Bhatti contingents fought in the Mughal army. Royal princesses were married to Mughal rulers and a Bhatti consort of the Emperor Jahangir was the mother of his eldest son. Unfortunately, this prince so distressed his mother by his incessant intrigues and rebellions against his royal father, that the Rajput queen, true to the stern code she had been brought up in, killed herself to atone for her son's infidelity.

With the opening of Bombay port in the 18th century, the hazardous overland Spice Route lost its importance, and Jaisalmer its main link with the outside world. Gradually the remote desert outpost dwindled in fortune and, in the days of the "Raj," Jaisalmer, was the least known of the Rajputana principalities. It was the last to sign the Instrument of Agreement with the British, drawn up by Colonel James Tod, the Political Agent—possibly the first Britisher to set foot in the legendary stronghold of Jaisalmer. Today, the fort is the center of the largest district in Rajasthan. Soon, the waters of the Rajasthan Canal will make the desert bloom around it. For anyone who wishes to understand the true spirit of historic Rajasthan, Jaisalmer is a rich source of sights and impressions.

Desert Citadel:

> *Horse of wood*
> *Legs of stone*
> *A frame of iron*
> *Get you to Jaisalmer,*
> *alone.*

The old quatrain no longer holds true. Jaisalmer now is easily accessible both by rail and road. And, no doubt, it will soon boast an airport.

An overnight journey takes you by meter-gage train from Jodhpur. Starting at night, it chugs into its destination early in the morning, in time for

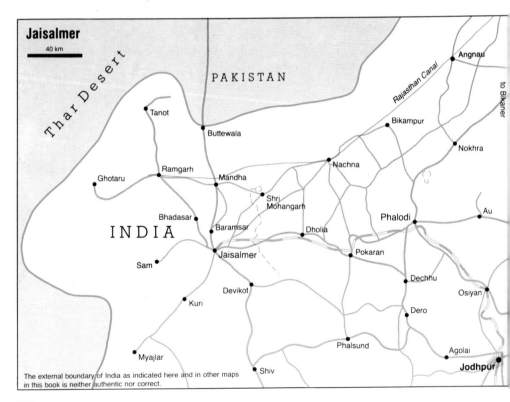

The external boundary of India as indicated here and in other maps in this book is neither authentic nor correct.

180

breakfast at the **Tourist Bungalow** or wherever else you may have arranged to stay. But to sleep all night is to deprive yourself of the rare experience of the Thar. So, unless it is essential for your schedule, take to the road.

Two major highways connect Jaisalmer with important centers in Rajasthan. The slightly shorter and usual approach is the excellent one from Jodhpur (180 miles/288 km). The other, longer and less frequented, starts from Bikaner and is the more dramatic journey, since it goes through stretches of stark desert. It joins the Jodhpur highway at Pokharan, after which a single road runs on to Jaisalmer.

Whether you take the high road or the low, start early, because there are a few unusual and off-the-beaten-track diversions to make at Pokharan, for the more adventurous. Carry drinking water and snacks.

The Thar is part of the great global desert-belt. The second Mughal, Emperor Humayun, while a fugitive (1540 A.D.), made his way through it to Persia. It was while he was still crossing the Thar that Humayun's son, Akbar, later to become the greatest of the Great Mughals, was born at Amarkot, now in Pakistan.

The desert ambience can be quite overwhelming, with endless oceans of sand broken by dunes, scrub and shattered scarps of the Aravalli range. The gray sand shades into rosy tones and then, beyond Pokharan, takes on an increasingly golden tinge. This is the famous Jurassic sandstone of which Jaisalmer is built—**Sonar Kila**, a Golden Fort, growing out of a rock of brandy-topaz and set in an undulating sea of ocher sand. Glimpsed first at sunset, the triangular rock looks like a huge, crouching beast ready to spring at any intruder.

Jaisalmer is a true citadel—the entire living area is within the curtain-wall, the main bastion and royal palaces being further protected by huge ramparts, pierced by enormous gates, protected by guardhouses.

Tricuta is the highest rock-hill in the vast plain. The flat-topped triangle rises in a gradual slope. The **Palace** stands at the highest point of the incline and is contained within double ramparts almost 325 feet (100 meters) above the marketplace. Thus, the royal

Jaisalmer's Fort dominates Gadisar Lake.

apartments could be shut off in case of need, such as a palace revolt.

One enters, through **Ganesh Pol**, the Elephant Gate, from the main market, then up a steep incline paved with large flag-stones past **Suraj Pol**, the Sun Gate. The winding path is wide enough to have permitted four fully armed warriors to ride abreast. Gigantic walls of dry masonry soar above, emphasizing the brooding air of impregnable power.

The silver **Imperial Umbrella**, symbol of protection, rises on **Megh Durbar**, the Cloud Tower, while nearby, is another tower used as a sentinel's lookout, from which flutters a red flag emblazoned with a golden sun, on a tall standard.

Bhointa Pol, the Turn Gate, stands square on a sharp curve. Its name has been corrupted to **Bhoota Pol**, the Haunted Gate, as it has been the scene of many a bloody fight. Nearby is a temple to the Goddess Bhavani, a warlike aspect of the mother deity. As protectress of the warrior Bhattis, it is to her that the Rajputs offered *puja* (worship) before going into battle and their chilling battle-cry "Jai Bhavani!"

echoed through the citadel.

Alongside is a smaller shrine to the benign elephant-headed god, Ganesh, remover of obstacles. No doubt, he got his share of petitions from the departing soldiers, for their safe return.

Finally, **Hava Pol**, the Wind Gate, stands sentinel to the royal palaces and leads to the main enclosure, the Court of Public Audience. It is a spacious square, where the Rawal could hear petitions, review troops, or entertain visiting royalty to spectacular shows during festivals or marriages. It was also here that *johar* took place.

As you face the palace, to the left is a noble flight of marble steps, at the head of which is an imposing white marble throne for the monarch. By its side is a disused covered well, **Jaisal's Well**, which is said to have been built over a spring visited by Lord Krishna.

Returning down the staircase, to the right is a **Kali Temple**, dedicated to the goddess of destruction. Here, sacrifices were offered during the Dassehra festival and the ancient horse-worship rite, *arsha puja* was performed.

Jawahar Mahal, the Jeweled Palace, has only one wing open to the public.

Left, ornate Jaisalmer balconies. Right, Patwon ki Haveli.

Here a young prince of the royal house, having to adapt to a democratic age, has opened a guest-house for travelers.

Manik Chowk: It is a quite a relief to return to the main market-square, with its noise and bustle, after the silent and ominous 12th century fort. Yet, even here the past still beckons, although the ghosts are more friendly than the bloodthirsty specters of Bhoota Pol. While looking at the picturesque village, women with baskets of fresh vegetables before them, or dodging between boys trundling handcarts and the rambling sacred bulls, these images blur into the ancient mart, where swaggering merchants from Africa, West Asia and Iran once brought their swords and scimitars from Damascus, their grapes and nuts from Afghanistan, the famed wines of Shiraz and the high-stepping horses of Balkh, to barter for the spices, birds and animals, the rare gems, rich brocades and fine muslins of India.

Only the water-trough in one corner of Manik Chowk seems to have remained unchanged, with camels, cattle and donkeys queuing for a drink with exemplary patience.

The Havelis: The art of the *silavats* (stone carvers) of Jaisalmer is justly famous. It attained its peak of excellence during the 18th and 19th centuries, rivaling the quality of the carved marble of the Taj Mahal at Agra. The honey tones of the yellow sandstone lend a softer glow to the elaborate facades of the desert *havelis* and are easier on the eye then the dazzle of the reflecting white marble.

Patwon-ki-haveli (House of the Brocade Merchants) is the largest and most elaborate of the famous havelis of Jaisalmer. It stands in a cul-de-sac with an imposing gate spanning the entrance to the lane, protecting this prestigious private residence from prying eyes. *Patwas* are merchants trading in rich brocades, gold and silver embroidery, sequins and ribbons. This family expanded their business to include opium, banking and revenue-collecting. In the late 18th century Guman Chand Patwa had a chain of 300 centers extending from Afghanistan to China. His five sons began building this mansion in 1800. It actually consists of five separate suites, linked together. It took 50 years to complete. For a while, fearing it would

be requisitioned, the family turned it into a Sanskrit school for boys. Fortunately it has been rescued from that ink-stained fate and is now a protected monument, as is the entire citadel.

Nathmalji-ki-haveli (The Mansion of Nathmalji), the last of the great havelis was built in the late 19th century. Nathmalji was the Prime Minister of the state at that time, and his family still lives in the haveli. Its facade was carved by two brothers, master-craftsmen of such consummate talent that, in a land of anonymous artists, their names are still remembered: Hathu and Lallu.

Salim Singh's Haveli: Salim Singh Mohta was a tyrannical Prime Minister of Jaisalmer in the 18th century. His mansion is distinguished by two features: the upper story, in cantilever style, supported by carved brackets, and the unique saxe-blue cupolas that adorn its roof.

Badal Mahal and Tazia Tower: Beyond the entrance gate to Tricuta stands the present home of the former rulers of Jaisalmer, **Badal Mahal** (Cloud Palace), from which rises the delicate, pagoda-like tower, the **Tazia tower**, its chief claim to architectural fame. *Tazias* are the fragile, split-bamboo and elaborately decorated paper and tinsel models of Taj-like mausoleums made by Shia Muslims during the period of Muharram, to commemorate the martyrdom of Hassan and Hussain, the Prophet's grandsons. The *silavats* of Jaisalmer, being Shia Muslims, decided to migrate to Pakistan when it was established in 1947. Before leaving their desert home, they expressed their love for their homeland and their ruler by building this tower in the shape of a *tazia* and presenting it to the ruler.

Jain Temples (12th-15th century): An extensive group of Jain temples stands within the fort complex. They were built from donations by the wealthy Marwari merchants. The finest are the Rishabdevji, the Sambhavnath, and the Ashtapadi Mandir.

Entrance to the **Rishabdevji Temple** is through an intricately carved *toran* (scrolled archway) where shoes, cameras and all leather articles must be shed. A porch whose pillars are carved with entwined creepers and flowers, all in yellow stone, leads to the main *mandap* (hall) with columns sporting graceful *apsaras* (heavenly nymphs), *kinnaras* and *gandharvas*, (celestial dancers and musicians) facing the central image of Rishabdevji. But one's eye is caught by an arresting group of images of Jain *tirthankaras* (saints), sitting in meditation in a circle, to the right of the hall. Some of the images are large, quite three feet (one meter) in height; others are half that size. Some are of white marble, others of red or black stone. All have jeweled third eyes that sparkle. There is a charming quaintness about these silent, meditating figures but they are also, in their quiet way, impressive.

Sambhavnath Temple leads off from the left of Rishabdevji. It is a subsidiary shrine, smaller and simpler in design. A basement is reputed to house a library of fabulous sacred manuscripts. It is rumored that an underground tunnel led from this subterranean chamber all the way to Lodurva, the former capital, from where these treasures were secretly conveyed when the migration to Jaisalmer took place.

Ashtapadi Mandir can be entered by a cloistered passage linking it with Sambhavji Temple. It has beautiful images of Hindu deities on the outer pillars and walls of the *mandap*. This religious syncretism is an indication of the remarkable religious tolerance of the age, and is a distinguishing feature of Jain sacred architecture. Since they were granted freedom of worship under Hindu rulers, they reciprocated by incorporating Hindu deities on their temple walls. The donors of the *mandir*, seated on elephants, guard its entrance.

A short walk beyond Tazia tower is **Gadsi-sar**, an artificial lake that was an important source of water in the past. A natural decline was enlarged to catch every drop of rain and, in a season of drought, Gadsi-sar was the mainstay of Jaisalmer. The Rawal would come to the lake himself to ensure fair distribution and to share in the tribulations of his people.

Many years ago, Telia, a well-known courtesan and singer of renown from a neighboring area, became the paramour of a Bhatti prince. In a gesture to her lover, Telia donated the handsome gateway and *ghats* (steps) that lead down to Gadsi-sar. The princesses

Pabusa village, West Rajasthan.

of the royal house were outraged by her effrontery and refused to use the gate. They even threatened to pull it down. So the wily Telia installed an image of Lord Satya Narain (Krishna) in the upper chamber and had it consecrated as a temple!

Today, the homes of Jaisalmer have the amenity of piped water, but Gadsisar remains a useful and pleasurable reminder of the past, and of the generosity of a clever and lovely lady.

The City: Ample time should be given to wander through Jaisalmer's narrow lanes and to visit the small silversmiths' shops, the stalls selling leathercraft goods, or the colorful traditional shawls and blankets. The homes of the common citizens of the fort are as picturesque as the splendid mansions of the elite. The flat-roofed, white houses, with bands of ocher and brown around lintels and folk paintings and geometric patterns on walls and floors, look like three-dimensional cubist masterpieces come alive.

Around Jaisalmer: Not far from the town is **Bhattiani Sati-rani** (Shrine of the Martyred Bhatti Queen). The awesome rite of *sati*, it must be understood, according to the mores of those times, rendered a woman immortal, i.e. by becoming—not committing—*sati* she attained *moksha*, release from the cycle of rebirth. Jaisalmer has its share of monuments sacred to the memory of such *satis*.

By far the most important and romantic of these is this shrine to a young Bhatti queen known as *Mahasati* (the great *sati*), since she immolated herself, not on her husband's pyre, but on that of her *dewar*, younger brother-in-law, who was suspected of being her lover. Even now, her shrine is a place of pilgrimage for hundreds of star-crossed lovers, who come to pray for her favors and blessings for happy endings to their love-stories.

A curious feature of Sati-rani's shrine is that, while she was a Hindu, the keepers of her shrine are Muslims. They belong to the hereditary caste of Manganiyars, who for eight centuries have been known as the finest musicmakers of the Thar. Not only do they look after the shrine, they also sing hymns of praise to the *sati* and the ballads of her tragic tale, thus transforming her love-story into an immor-

tal saga.

On a rocky eminence on the road that leads into Jaisalmer, stand the **Royal Cenotaphs** (Chhatris) of the Rawals in **Barra Bagh** (Big Garden) where the rulers were cremated. A pillared and canopied *chhatri*, often of white marble, marks the site of each cremation. Despite the bas-relief tablets depicting the ruler along with his consort-*satis*, a garden of *chhatris* does not have the lugubrious atmosphere of a graveyard. Barra Bagh is no exception and this is the best place from which to watch the spectacular desert sunset, and to photograph the fort.

Lodurva, the former capital of the Bhatti rulers, is still an important place of Jain pilgrimage. It is just 10 miles (16 km) northwest of Jaisalmer. The ancient township lies in ruins about the temples and the seasonal river Kak is usually dry. But thereby hangs a tale.

On the banks of the Kak, in a legendary era, the beautiful Princess Moomal lived in a fabulous palace. The Prince of Amarkot, Mahendru, riding by, heard her sing, fell in love with her, and became her lover. The lovers were parted by Mahendru's jealous wives. Moomal, disguised as an itinerant singer, made her way to far-off Amarkot to seek her beloved, only to die of fatigue and a broken heart at the gates of his fort, where Mahendru found her. And that is why the river Kak refuses to flow!

The Desert: Ride to the dunes of Samm on camel-back. Only then will you get some idea of the pace and space of desert life. Gaily caparisoned riding animals can be hired by the day. By jeep, the outing would require just a couple of hours.

The dunes at Samm are treacherous. They look smooth and firm, and the golden sands run like silk through your fingers, but you can sink to your knees in a second, as they are loosely packed. Often, a sudden wind can blow a dune up into a moving funnel to deposit it yards away. Cattle have been known to flounder to their death in such shifting sands.

The camel-drovers (*Raikas*) are the best guides. The *Raika* is a handsome, romantic figure, and in local legends and folk-songs, he is referred to as the messenger of love or the bringer of tidings, good or bad; a sort of old-fashioned news-vendor.

Raikas travel with their animals over vast distances and know every pasture and waterhole in their region. They can trace a lost camel by its hoof-prints, while the beasts recognize and respond to the call of their drovers.

Another worthwhile diversion from Pokharan, en route to Jaisalmer, is the shrine to the medieval saint, Ramdevra. The **temple** stands on a low hill and is open to all, as Ramdevra is worshiped by persons of all castes and creeds. At the annual **Ramdevra Fair**, (August–September) the dextrous *Tera-Tali* performers are the biggest draw. They are acrobatic dancers, both men and women, who execute feats with cymbals, swords and *divas* (oil-lamps), to the resounding rhythm of drums. The traditional offerings at the shrine are horses of clay, cloth, wood or paper. Some are larger-than-life-size; others small enough to fit in the palm.

The Jaisalmer Winter Festival, is held annually in January and brings together musicians, dancers, puppeteers and many other performers, including fire-walkers and sword-swallowers, from all over the desert region.

If Jaisalmer whets your appetite for desert life, take the National Highway to **Barmer**. On the way, 10 miles (16 km) out of Jaisalmer, is **Aakal**, the Fossil Park, proof of the geologic cataclysms that have taken place in the Thar. Here, 180 million years ago, stood a forest of giant deciduous trees, whose trunks, petrified into fossils, litter a bare hillside of mica and red and yellow stone. The fossil trunks have had to be protected by iron grids as "unbelievers" were apt to hack off bits and pieces for building houses!

Barmer, growing in importance as a border outpost, has the air of a dusty garrison town. But if you are there in January, enquire about the great **Tilwara Cattle Fair** on the banks of the salt-water river Luni. Tilwara has a temple dedicated to the warrior-saint Mallinath, and the fair is held on the dry river-bed, where every night, they say, the saint rides his ghostly steed across the sands. You may not see the ghost-rider but you may certainly hear the heavy rhythm of his horse's hooves. Tilwara Fair is the largest cattle-mart held in Rajasthan. Horses, bullocks and camels are brought here for sale.

DESERT NATIONAL PARK

Twenty-eight miles (45 km) to the southwest of Jaisalmer the Desert National Park covers 1220 sq. miles (3162 sq. km) of scrub, thorn forest, desert and dunes. The range of both flora and fauna is, to many, surprisingly large for a desert area. The unique ecosystem reflects the successful adaptation by a range of mammals, birds, insects and flowers to a harsh climate with temperature ranges from below freezing to over 130° F (55° C).

The rolling landscape of sand-dunes and scrub-covered hills is often breathtakingly beautiful. The active dunes of Sam contrast with the 180 million-year-old wood fossils at Akal 10 miles (17 km) from Jaisalmer which indicate that his now arid area must have once been hot, humid and luxuriant.

The scant vegetation and the animals dependent on it are in turn dependent on whatever water is available. Waterholes are therefore the ideal spots from which to watch

Chinkara,
the smallest
Indian
antelope.

animals and birds.

The small, active desert **fox** is an important predator keeping a natural check on the population of desert **rats** and **gerbils**. The fox, although normally shy, is often seen in the Miazalor area, especially in the winter, basking in the sun. The **wolf** is perhaps the main predator and the jackal is found on the periphery of the park.

Many of the villages on the edge of the park are Bishnoi and the areas around these settlements are natural sanctuaries where the strong religious beliefs of the Bishnois ensure protection to all living creatures. Groups of **blackbuck**, **chinkara** and **nilgai** are found around the villages and now thrive in the park's areas of sparse, arid grassland. The blackbuck is a true antelope of the open grasslands, living in large herds of 50 to 60 animals (mainly fawans and doe). The chinkara of Indian gazelle is spread throughout the park, in the sandy areas as well as the scrub grasslands, in small groups or as individuals.

Some smaller mammals have adapted to the desert environment by burrowing like the gerbil, by living in colonies or by being nocturnal, like the **crested porcupine**.

The desert birdlife is extensive, ranging from a large number of birds of prey to **sandgrouse**, **doves**, **quails**, **partridges**, **shrikes**, **flycatchers**, **bee-eaters**, **warblers** and **desert coursers**. The most remarkable bird of the desert is the **Great Indian Bustard**, weighing up to 30 pounds (14 kg) and standing up to 18 inches (45 cm). A reluctant flyer, the bustard lives on an omnivorous diet of locusts, grasshoppers, seeds, berries, lizards and even snakes. Habitat destruction and hunting threatened this majestic bird but its population in the Desert National Park alone is now estimated to be over 1,000. The **Houbara bustard** is also found in the park. Of the three resident species of sandgrouse, the **Indian sandgrouse** is impressive with its routine of arriving in small groups to join large turbulent flocks in the early morning to drink at the same place each day. The **pintail sandgrouse** is a winter visitor.

The many insect and reptile species evident throughout the park form important links in the desert food chains. The 43 species of reptile include lizards, chameleons, and snakes.

187

JODHPUR

It is said that when the defeated Maharaja Jaswant Singh fled the battlefield of the victorious Mughal princes Aurangzeb and Murad in 1658, his proud wife refused to accept this sully to Rajput honor. Slamming the fort gate in his face, she sent him back to redeem the good name of the Jodhpur house.

Legend, perhaps, but made credible even now by the tall and proud Jodhpur men who, with their lovingly curled, caricature-big mustaches, jostle on camel, cart, rickshaw and bicycle through the sandy lanes of this delightful, slow-paced city set on the edge of the Thar Desert.

Jodhpur, former capital of Marwar state, retains much of its medieval character. Beginning in 1549, when the city was called Jodhagarh, the Rathor clan of Rajputs fought and ruled from the virtually impregnable fort until their territory covered some 35,000 sq. miles (91,000 sq. km), making it the largest Rajput state.

According to Rathor tradition, the clan traces its origins back to the Hindu god, Rama, hero of the epic *Ramayana*, and thence to the sun. So the Rathors belong to the Suryavansha (solar race) branch of the Kshatriyas, the warrior caste of Hindus. Later, breaking into historical reality, in 470 A.D. Nayal Pal conquered the kingdom of Kanauj, near modern Kanpur in Uttar Pradesh. The Rathor capital for seven centuries, Kanauj fell in 1193 to the Afghan invaders led by Muhammad Ghori.

The fleeing ruler, Jai Chand, drowned in the Ganga. But his son or grandson, Siahji, had better luck. Moving west into the Thar Desert, he achieved glory in battle for the local Solanki prince, whose sister he won as reward. He later set himself up as an independent ruler around the wealthy trading center of Pali, just south of Jodhpur. His descendants flourished, battled often, won often, and in 1381 Rao Chanda ousted the Parihars from Mandore which then became the Rathor seat of government.

Rathor fortunes then turned. Rao Chanda's son and heir, Rainmal, won

praise for his capture of Ajmer and was then entrusted with the care of his orphaned nephew, destined to inherit the Mewar throne of Chittor. Rainmal may well have had his eyes on this fine, hilltop fort. But court intrigue and treachery stopped him. In 1438 he was doped with opium, and finally shot dead. This triggered bitter feuds, ending with Mewar and Marwar becoming separate states.

Rathor legend continues in various versions. One is that Jodha, one of Rainmal's 24 sons, fled Chittor and finally, 15 years later, recaptured Mandore in 1453. Five years later he was acknowledged as ruler. A holy man sensibly advised him to move his capital to hilltop safety.

It was an obvious and irresistible site. The building of Meherangarh, or Majestic Fort—a structure so massive it seems to grow out of the cliff—was begun. And Jodhpur's glory was born.

Jodhpur City: Today Jodhpur, with its 320,000 inhabitants, is the second-largest city of Rajasthan. It still fulfills its historical role as the area's main trading center for wood, cattle, camels, cotton, salt, hides and agricultural crops.

Although the **old city** was founded by Rao Jodha, its walls with seven gates and countless bastions and towers were built by Rao Maldeo in the 16th century when Jodhpur was a booming trading town. Poised on both the international east-west trading route between Central Asia and China and on the strategic Delhi-Gujarat route, the Marwari traders amassed fortunes from the passing camel caravans whose exotic loads might include elephants' teeth, copper, silks, sandalwood, dried fruit, camphor, spices and opium.

In the maze of old lanes focused on **Sardar Bazaar** and its **Clock Tower** of 1912 are several former palaces, some *havelis* and a dozen temples. Many have richly carved facades, such as the **Tulati Mahal**, a palace built by Jaswant Singh which is now a hospital. And many of Jodhpur's traditional craftsmen thrive here, too. With a little help from a taxi driver or the keeper of a large shop, they are easy to find and fascinating to watch at work.

In a dimly-lit room, a man uses his fingers and feet to turn a wooden box before coloring it green, red and mustard yellow with lacquer. In another shop, a young boy skilfully makes gaily-striped lacquer bangles, turning out one a minute. Nearby, in **Mochi** (Cobbler) **Bazaar**, a regular tap-tapping betrays a cobbler. Further west, the nimble-fingered Muslim women and children confined to their houses around Jalori and Siwanchi Gates (or in Bambamola district) create delicate, multi-colored *bandhani* (tie-and-dye) patterns on cotton. Other craftsmen make glass bangles, felt goods and leather water-bottles. Some carve marble and ivory, or make painted wooden horses. Still others emboss silver, weave handloom textiles or make carpets.

Then, there are the famous puppet-makers of Jodhpur who re-enact the deeds of such heroes as Amai Singh Rathor of Nagaur. Puppeteering is an ancient entertainment, some say the origin of classic Indian drama. The *kathputliwala* (puppeteer) makes his own two-string, three-foot-high marionettes, giving them carved wooden heads and fancy costumes. And as he makes them perform, he speaks through bamboo or leather to give his voice a distinctive shrillness, while his wife plays a drum and elaborates the story—usually about the Rajputs' favorites: love, war and honor. Indeed, such is the place of *kathputli* that there is a special ceremony marking the "death" of a puppet. When, after many generations of use, the puppet is worn out, it is floated down a holy river, accompanied by prayers. The longer it remains afloat, the higher the gods are judging its life.

Modern Jodhpur: Spilling out from the walled city is the more modern side of Jodhpur. To the east lie the **Umaid Gardens**, with zoo, library, and the **Government Museum** founded by Sardar Singh in 1909. Its moth-eaten birds, various unlabeled but fascinating sculptures, old weapons and early models of aeroplanes make it a time-capsule museum in itself. On the other hand, the nearby **Rajasthan Academy of Music** is valiantly trying to tape the state's rich but threatened musical heritage. The grand **State High Court** is near here. And, to the south, lie the Air Force, Engineering and Medical Colleges and the University (established 1965).

As for polo, you can catch some in

Monsoon skies over Mehrangarh Fort.

action at the **Polo Grounds** which are on the airport road. Polo, pigsticking and tennis were the favorite sports of the more recent Rajasthani royals. And Jodhpur has produced some of the most outstanding Indian polo players, including Rao Raja Hanut Singh.

Palace Fortress: The gentle atmosphere of Jodhpur today belies a stormy, sometimes glorious, past. The best way to trace its history is to make a leisurely visit to the aptly-named **Meherangarh** (Majestic) **Fort** (three miles/ five km), taking a taxi from town up through Nagauri Gate to **Jai Pol** (Victory Gate). As with other great Rajput forts, its general inspiration came from Raja Man Singh's stupendous 15th-century fort at Gwalior. But, as the historian Percy Brown observed, "for grandeur of conception and elegance of detail, this palace is unsurpassed (*Indian Architecture*)."

Such was the threat of skilled Rajput warring in 1459 that Rao Jodha and his successors built an almost impregnable fort on already superb natural defenses. The bold bluff soars 393 feet (121 m) above the flat surrounding plains, commanding views for some 80 miles (120 km)—in post-monsoon clarity the towers of Khumbhalgarh Fort to the south can be seen. The fort itself is guarded by seven gates piercing walls which are 68 feet (21 m) wide and 117 ft (36 m) high in places. When complete, in ghoulish tradition, its architect, Bambhi Rajra, was said to have been buried alive with its defense secrets.

Jai Pol is a late addition to the fort. Maharaja Man Singh built it after he successfully repelled the combined forces of Jaipur and Bikaner in 1808. Above it is the water pump which finally ended the daily slog of carrying drinkable water from **Gulab** (Rose) **Sagar** at the bottom of the steep hill. For the water of both lake and well inside the fort is brackish. The story goes that when a hermit's cave was included in the fort buildings, he was so angry that he cursed the water for ever.

Inside the gate, Man Singh also built the wall on the right. Yet another legend says he did this after a trusted Muslim employee was buried outside the fort walls. His spirit returned to complain to his master who solved the

problem by building an extra wall.

Passing the Jaipuri's cannon-ball pits on the left side of the original outer wall, **Fateh Pol** is the first of the fort's seven protective gates proper. With Hindu sturdiness, it is built with a flat lintel supported on corbels between twin bastions. But after an acute angle turn, which would slow down any enemy, the road runs up through the elegantly arched **Gopal**, **Bhairon** and (after one lost gate) **Dodkangra Pols**.

The sixth gate, **Amirita Pol**, built by Rao Maldeo, is a sharp turn to the left. Inside it, on the left, is **Rao Jodhaji's Falsa**, or Jodha's barrier. Wooden logs were fixed into holes in the stone slabs. Jodha's friends and foes entered here only to be confronted with the strongest gate of all, **Loha** (Iron) **Pol**. Again, it is built immediately after a bend so the enemy could not charge it, and reinforced with iron spikes against elephants. With such defenses, Rao Jodha brought most of Mewar, Nagaur, Sambha and Ajmer under his rule before his death in 1489.

Of Rao Jodha's 14 sons, the second, called Suja but known as the "cavalier prince" was to die in true Rajput style, attempting to rescue 140 Rathor maidens who were being carried off by the Pathans from a fair at Pipli. The sixth and ablest, Bika, founded Bikaner, while others founded Idar, Kishangarh, Ratlam, Jhabua, Sailana, Sitamau and Alirazpur. All eight looked to their Jodhpur ruler as head of the Rathor clan.

Loha Pol was later further strengthened by Rao Maldeo (ruled 1532-73), who expanded the Marwar kingdom to reach up to Sind in the north, Hissar in the east and Gujarat in the west. However, in 1544 he met his match at the battle of Khanua, narrowly failing to beat Sher Shah Suri who had ousted the Mughal Humayun from the imperial throne in Delhi.

For two years, Jodhpur was under Sher Shah's control. But won back, Marwar's territory, power and independence reached their zenith. Maldeo had even out-powered Rana Sanga of Chittor. And he could refuse to help the ousted Humayun, fleeing Sher Shah. But the tables turned with the Mughal restoration when Akbar came to the throne. Enraged by this snub to his father, he besieged the Rathor ruler

Stained glass reflected in table top.

who eventually made peace by sending his son, Udai Singh, to the Delhi court.

However, on Udai Singh's succession, the new ruler changed the policy towards the Mughals. He gave his sister Jodhi Bai in marriage to Akbar and his daughter Man Bai to Prince Salim, who later became Emperor Jahangir. Jodhi Bai must have possessed considerable charm. She persuaded Akbar to return all of Jodhpur's territory (except Ajmer) to her brother, to give him extra land and to bestow upon him the title of *raja* (king), calling him King of the Desert.

Another Rajput clan had allied with the Mughals. Jodhpur flourished, while its rulers shone on the battlefield, conquering lands and quelling rebellions for the ruling Mughal emperors.

When Raja Gaj Singh put down Jahangir's son's rebellion he was made Viceroy of the Deccan and Marwar horses were exempted from being branded with the imperial insignia. But it was his second son, Jaswant Singh (ruled 1638-78), who was created *maharaja* (great king) and who had the most remarkable career. First, he led Shah Jahan's army against his rebelling sons in 1658. The battle lost, he quickly switched sides and joined Aurangzeb. Not long after, he turned again and plundered Aurangzeb's army. And somehow he later managed to become viceroy of Gujarat, then of the Deccan.

But Jaswant Singh's wife was less forgiving. When he returned home a defeated man, his proud Rajput queen slammed the gates of Loha Pol in his face. And just inside them, on the wall, the *sati* hands with their bejeweled wrists attest to the valor of these royal Rajput women. *Sati* was the Hindu custom of a widow's death by self-immolation. On the death of her husband, a woman would leave home for the last time, dipping her hand in red pigment and laying it flat on the doorpost or lintel, a moving testimony of loyalty.

Nowhere was *sati* more important and nowhere did it persist as long as it did in princely Rajasthan. For a prince's success in life was measured by the number of women who committed *sati* on his death. And for Jaswant Singh's successor, Ajit Singh, six queens and 58 concubines joined his funeral pyre

Graceful arches, Mehrangarh Fort.

in 1731. Later, for many years, the 1829 British law prohibiting *sati* made little impact. Indeed, in proud Jodhpur, the last recorded royal *sati* was in 1953.

Finally, **Suraj** (Sun) **Pol**, the entrance to the fort's palaces. And to serenade you from fierce battlements into a fairyland of sumptuous domestic sophistication, musicians of the Mirashi caste strike up their traditional tunes.

The Palaces: The various buildings constructed by Jodha and his successors now serve as the **Meherangarh Museum**. Royal retainers still tend their master's possessions which are arranged in the former public and private rooms and in the *zenana*.

Up the narrow stairs from Suraj Pol find the courtyard of the **Moti Mahal** (Pearl Palace), enclosed by *jali* (lattice) work of gossamer fineness and beauty. It was Sur Singh (ruled 1581-95) who built it. Here the marble **Sringar Chowki** (Coronation Seat), with peacock armrests and gilded elephants, is kept. Apart from Jodha, every ruler of Jodhpur has been crowned on it.

Royal palanquins fill the nearby **Palki Room**, including a massive gold-polished one that was booty from Gujarat and needed a dozen men to carry it. A fine gift from Emperor Shah Jahan to Jaswant Singh sits in the **Elephant Howdah Room**—a silver howdah which he presented together with an elephant to put it on and a hundred horses. And every royal birth is recorded in the **Jhanki Mahal**, a room from which ladies could watch events going on below. Here, the royal cradle of the latest maharaja is an ingenious mechanical machine whose guardian angels rock the crib, despite the 300 maids who served the palace. It was gifted by the electricians union of Jodhpur, "with profound loyalty," reinforced by a portrait of the young lad's ruling father.

Ministers and nobles would discuss state affairs in the **Chandan Mahal**. A.H. Muller's 1893 mural shows a bearded man clad in white riding a horse and baking some bread at the end of a spear. This illustrates the story of Jodhpur's great hero, Durga Das, celebrated by poets and bards. It recounts how, after Jaswant Singh's death in 1678, the orthodox Muslim Aurangzeb wreaked his revenge. He

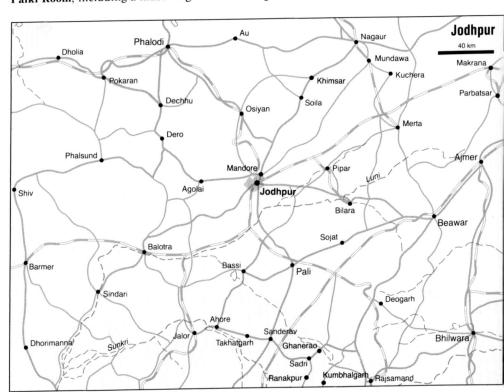

196

sacked Jodhpur, plundered the large towns of Marwar, destroyed temples, demanded conversion to Islam and implemented the *jizya* tax on non-Muslims that Akbar had abolished back in 1564. Meanwhile, Durga Das smuggled Jaswant Singh's posthumously-born son, Ajit, out of Delhi. After 30 years of guerilla warfare, hardship and wandering—the subject of the mural—Durga Das courageously re-took Jodhpur and Ajit Singh took up his rightful throne.

Jodhpur, Jaipur and Udaipur now finally buried their mutual enmity and formed a triple alliance to throw off the Muslim yoke. Under this fragile security, Jodhpur's internal history entered a rather stormy period that compares with that of the Roman Nero family.

Meanwhile, external Rajput affairs plunged, too. Despite the alliance, the innate Rajput inability to unite led to constant inter-clan warfare. And from all sides the Marathas, Pathans, Pindaris and British fought over the disintegrating Mughal Empire and its Rajput allies.

Eventually, in 1818, after almost a century of internal and external war, Jodhpur signed a treaty with the East India Company for "defensive alliance, perpetual friendship, protection and subordinate co-operation." Rathor honor was put to shame.

In the **Darbar Takhat**, or Throne Room, one of the last *durbars* (public audience or meeting) was held in 1819. The octagonal *gadi* (throne) was another of Shah Jahan's gifts. Chairs on the right were for nobles, in descending rank. Those on the left were marked for representatives of villages—Alniwas, Riyan, Bhadrjun, etc. And lattice windows behind the *gadi* permitted the women to witness the *durbar* and, via messengers, contribute their voice to discussions.

Now to the *zenana*, the sealed area where the women lived in apartments and on sprawling roof terraces around the communal **Rang Mahal**. Here, at the spring festival of Holi, the king and his ladies would flirt and play, squirting one another with colored waters and tossing clouds of crimson and ocher powders.

Miniatures: Umaid Vilas now houses a fine collection of Rajput miniature paintings, well worth a good look. In the secular subjects, especially the fine portraits, the prevailing influences of the delicate Mughal and Deccani court styles reflect the Jodhpur alliance with the emperors. In the devotional paintings, the more robust Rajput style asserts itself, with strong lines, bright colors and simple designs. But as Mughal power waned, this bold style took over entirely, as is clear in the big, jolly portrait of Maharaja Thakhat Singh (ruled 1843-73) out riding camels with his courtesans.

Other portraits show off the tower-like, voluminous turbans—the biggest in Rajasthan—that were fashionable with Jodhpur rulers during the late 18th and early 19th centuries. But their jodhpurs, those comfortable riding trousers with baggy upper sections that the British adopted from here, are usually hidden beneath a coat.

After a peek at the adjoining room built for *puja* and now called the **Mirror Room**, Thakhat Singh's bedroom is upstairs. Decorated just before his reign, its walls are coated with paintings, its lacquered ceiling is hung with baubles, and its furnishings include a giant, bed-like swing.

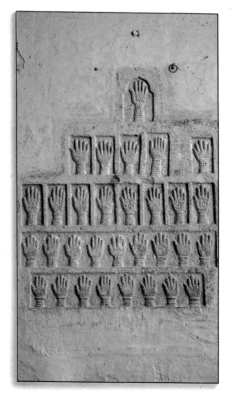

Sati stone, marks the spot of self-immolation by women whose husbands died in battle.

Next, a remarkable collection of musical instruments: a stringed *Sindhi sarang*, a vast *Chang drum*, and a huge conical horn called a *karna*, used at court and in the battlefield. Royal costumes of extraordinary extravagance fill **Ajit Vilas**. The pearl shoes of Raja Gaj Singh's favorite concubine, Anara Begum, are here.

Upstairs, the airy **Phool Mahal** (Flower Palace), was built by Abhai Singh as his *Darbar-e-Khas* (Private Audience Hall). Former rulers look down from the elaborately painted and gilded ceiling. *Ragamala* paintings, which illustrate musical modes and occasions, decorate the walls between gold cartouches. A pictorial royal family tree helps visitors sort out who's who. And above a couch-like *gadi* hangs the Jodhpur coat of arms.

Downstairs, in the **Tent Room**, is one of Jodhpur's proudest pieces of booty: a portable cloth palace. This is a huge royal Mughal tent made of red silk velvet covered with floral designs embroidered with gold thread. It was made for Shah Jahan as his mobile audience hall, where he would sit on his velvet *gadi* in the inner colonnaded chamber and receive visitors. Aurangzeb inherited the tent. But when that turncoat Jaswant Singh attacked him for the second time, the tent was part of his loot.

Lastly, there is **Maan Vilas** housing the appropriately fine Rathor armory. Here are the tools that brought such honor and wealth to these skilled warriors. Special craftsmen made each weapon and lived inside the fort. *Sikligars* (swordsmiths) might cover a hilt with delicate inlay of calligraphy or stud it with precious jewels, giving the blade a leaf-shape or making it double-edged, curved or pointed. Then there were *dhabdars* (armorers) to protect man, horse and elephant. Axes came in all shapes, and shields were made of anything from bamboo or steel to crocodile skin or rhino hide.

And a selection of Jodhpur's bigger defense weapons stands on the **ramparts**. Some of the cannons are the spoils of Gaj Singh's warring in Jalore, others of Abhai's triumphs in Gujarat. Nearby, the image of the goddess Chamunda Devi, worshiped by the Rathors since Jodha's time, sits in her temple. The view from the ramparts is

Steam locomotives still operate on Rajasthan's metergauge lines.

stunning. And from below, soft music and chatter waft up from the town.

On the road down from the fort, the splash of blinding white marble on the left is **Jaswant Thada**, Maharaja Jaswant Singh II's *chhatri* (cenotaph) built in 1899—all previous rulers have their *chhatris* at Mandore. As with the Taj Mahal, the marble is from Makrana. Inside, the faithful still come to petition the portrait of Jaswant. Outside, *chhatris* of the next four Rathor rulers adjoin it, including that of Umaid whose outsized palace sits heavily on Chittor Hill to the east of the city.

Following two pretty disastrous rulers, Jaswant Singh (ruled 1878-95) ushered in a golden age for Jodhpur. According to rumor, Jodhpur treasure and wealth was sixth in the Indian league—following Hyderabad, Jaipur, Kashmir, Gwalior and Baroda. So Jaswant could not only be photographed in 1890 dripping in egg-sized pearls and precious stones; he could also invest in his state. For he was an energetic and successful ruler. He cleaned up crime and suppressed the dacoits, began building railways, started much-needed irrigation projects,

A street in old Jodhpur.

and generally vastly improved the economy of Marwar with regular revenue and organized customs tariffs. As the *Imperial Gazetteer* noted in 1908: "In every department, wise and progressive policy was pursued"—praise assisted by his fervent loyalty to the British.

In all this—especially the loyalty—he was helped and encouraged by Pratap Singh (1845-1922), a remarkable man whose strong personality dominated the Jodhpur court from the 1870s to the 1920s, during which he was thrice regent.

Palace-building as Famine Relief: It is unlikely the *Gazetteer* would have praised Maharaja Umaid Singh or his advisors as it had Jaswant and Sir Pratap. For in 1929, aged 27, his solution to long-term famine was to employ 3,000 citizens a day for 16 years to build himself the playtime palace par excellence, completed on the eve of Indian independence. This latest 347-room royal dwelling is so huge that the former royals now spread themselves airily over a third of it, run the official rooms as a museum, and leave a mere 57 suites and various dining and leisure rooms to be a hotel.

From its inception, **Umaid Bhawan Palace** is a catalog of wild extremes. Astrologers dictated the hilly and arid site. So a railway was built to bring the sandstone up, teams of donkeys trudged up with earth, rock was blasted to make room for tree roots, and very deep wells were bored.

Next, the building. H.V.Lanchester, a British architect of civic buildings who admired the *Beaux-Arts* Movement and Lutyens' Viceregal Lodge (now Rashtrapati Bhavan) in New Delhi, designed it. It is his *tour de force*. Within a rigidly symmetrical plan full of courtyards, he somehow managed to cater for strict *purdah*, the latest princely European fashions, the Indian royal taste for gilt, his own interest in craftsmanship, and every whim of both Indian and British lifestyle on a small and grand scale. And the somber, domed building is enlivened by Hindu details. His concession was size: the palace plan measures 212 yards by 111 yards (195 meters by 103 meters). It is one of the largest private homes in the world, and one of the finest buildings of the 1930s.

Thus, glorious *Beaux-Arts* doors are the entrance to the part that is now a hotel, still guarded by tall Jodhpuris glowing in their orange turbans. In the first hall, sweeping marble staircases decorated with stuffed leopards lead to suites with art deco mirrors and Belgian crystal. A double dome with a whispering gallery covers the second hall, while an indoor swimming pool lies beneath it. Beyond, the terrace overlooks the restored garden; cerise and mauve blossoms blind in the desert brightness. And in what is now the **museum section** (with fine clocks and more fine miniature paintings and arms), the Polish artist S. Norblin painted scenes from the Hindu epic, the *Mahabharata* on the walls of the **Oriental Room**.

Umaid watched his giant toy being built from his favorite home, **Raika-bagh Palace** at the bottom of Chittor Hill—it now houses government offices. Here, he could live in sumptuous splendor on the first floor while 400 of his beloved horses lived in almost equal comfort beneath him.

Sadly, Umaid had little time to enjoy his new private paradise with billiard room, cinema, eight kitchens and a

Mughal tent now in the fort museum.

ballroom to seat 300. In 1944 he moved in. Early in 1947, during a hunting trip to Mount Abu, he died of a burst appendix aged 43.

Further tragedy struck. His son, Hanwant Singh, inherited the title at 28. Like Umaid, he loved modern toys. His game was flying. He developed Jodhpur as a premier aircraft center in the east. In 1952, Hanwant stood as an Independent in the elections of the newly independent Indian democracy. Voting had taken place when he flew into some telegraph wires and died instantly. Two days later, the vote-count revealed he had won a sweeping victory with a majority of 10,000.

Democracy and feudalism have continued to walk happily hand in hand in Jodhpur. On Hanwant's death, his four-year-old son was crowned on the marble **Sringar Chowki** at the fort at sunrise. A *tilak* was placed on his forehead. He performed the *nazir* ceremony of exchanging coins.

Trips out of Town: After the charm of Jodhpur city, the majesty of its fort and the extravagance of Umaid Bhawan, it is worth making a foray into the desert—there's more than just sand.

There are some remarkable *chhatris*, temples and forts, and a surprisingly rich variety of wildlife. Drop in on a local village where a friendly welcome is assured. This desert land gets very hot: it is best to start early, taking a good supply of drinks.

Mahamandir (one mile/two km), or Great Temple, lies on the northeastern outskirts of Jodhpur. This small temple town was founded by Maharaja Man Singh, who was a strong devotee of the Nath sect of Shaivas. His guru was Deva Nath, for whom he built the Mahamandir in 1812 after his escape from Jhalore. Inside, a forest of pillars supports the temple roof. Murals of aspects of yoga cover the walls.

Man Singh combined Rajput warring with serious cultural and religious pursuits. As a scholar, he studied Sanskrit, Urdu, Persian and much more. He was a considerable poet and generously patronized other poets, heaping state money, court honors and some 62 villages on his favorites.

The lakeside palace at **Balsamand** (four miles/seven km), further north on the same road, is now a public park and a bird sanctuary. But it was built as a

little royal oasis, a pleasure-ground where welcome fresh air wafted off the lake and across the lush green gardens. It is said that Balak Rao Parihar of Mandore cut out the lake in 1159, making it the oldest artificial lake in Rajasthan. Maharaja Sur Singh enlarged the lake and built himself a summer palace, which seems to have been later enlarged and modified first by Jaswant Singh II, then Umaid Singh.

Just north of here, through a narrow pass between high cliffs, lies the former capital of Jodhpur, **Mandore** (five miles/nine km). Originally called Mandaya Pura, the city was the capital of the Parihar Rajputs from the sixth century until their defeat by Rao Chanda in 1381. Rao Chanda married a Parihar princess, had 14 sons and established Mandore as the Rathor seat of government until 1459. From the ancient fort set on craggy hills above the fertile gorge the Rathors warded off attacks by the Khaljis and Tuglaqs and other Delhi sultanates.

Mandore's glory are the **six dewals**, the domed royal *chhatris* of the Rathors which stand in a line on the right of

the lush, shady, landscaped gardens. Each is built on the spot where the ruler was cremated, joined on his pyre by various wives and concubines whom Tod perceptively described as "all that made life agreeable or poisoned its enjoyment."

Starting with Rao Maldeo's fairly modest *chhatri*, the monuments to Sur Singh, Udhai Singh, Guj Singh, Jaswant Singh and Ajit Singh rise in increasing height, grandeur and quality, neatly mirroring the rise in Marwar's fortunes. Their architecture mixes Buddhist and Shaiva styles. But the rich and fine decoration carved into the hard, brown stone is entirely Jain. Whereas Jaswant's is rather ponderous, Ajit's achieves a rare elegance: a Shaiva-style pyramidal temple with columned interiors.

Across the garden is the **Hall of Heroes**, where 16 life-sized figures were carved out of the rock during the reigns of Ajit and Abhai (1707-49) or possibly earlier. The heroes are either appropriate Hindu deities or local Rajputs, each one fully armed, mounted on horse-back and gaily painted. There is Chamunda, a form of the goddess of destruction; Kali another destructive goddess, riding her tiger and crushing a demon; and Nath, the Rathor's spiritual leader, holding a *churri* (rod) to guide his devotees.

Among the warriors is Pabuji on his famous black mare, Kesa Kali (Black Caesar), who so moved the historian Tod that he scratched his name here and even admitted to the graffiti in his *Annals*. The heroic deeds of Pabuji, an ally of Rao Jodha, are a favorite subject of *bhopas* (wandering bards). Next but one to Pabuji is Hurba Sankla, who helped Jodha win back Mandore from Chittor's clutches in 1453 and who is celebrated with the **Veerpuri Mela** (fair) every August.

The larger hall next door is the **Shrine of 30 Crore** (300 million) **Gods**. An optimistic title, but the interior is indeed crammed with huge, painted statues of Hindu gods.

Nearby are remains of **Abhai Singh's stone palace**, where he would have come to feast off the famous Jodhpur pomegranates and to enjoy his garden with its cooling fountains and water-channels, the air perfumed by sweet-smelling jasmine.

Ruins of the ancient city litter the

The Hall of Heroes, Mandore.

rocky plateau above—materials were re-used for the *chhatris* and the new **Jodhpur fort**. On the way up, there is a **monument to Nahur Rao**, last of the Parihars. Through what remains of massive walls and square bastions, there are traces of the Parihar gateway, arch and fort. There is also an eighth-century **Gupta temple**.

Beyond the walls lie the *chhatris* of four earlier Rathor rulers, of which the carving on Rao Ganga's (died about 1532) is especially fine. Back in the gardens, some 60 *chhatris* of royal *ranis* lie quietly up a steep winding path and across the reservoir.

Peacock Island: A more ambitious trip north, but thoroughly rewarding for architecture addicts, goes on to **Osiyan** (40 miles/65 km). This small, peacock-infested island of greenery in the desert sand was once a great trading center. Since Jains were the prosperous traders who formed the backbone of the local economy, the Hindu rulers showed them religious tolerance, permitting them to build lavish, often marble, temples which became repositories of historical and cultural manuscripts. The 16 fine **Brahmin and Jain** temples of the eighth to 12th centuries testify to the city's former wealth under its Parihar rulers.

The first group, on the town outskirts, are the earlier temples. These 11 represent the opening phases of medieval temple architecture in Rajasthan. Standing on high terraces, each has a porch, hall and sanctum. The halls are mostly open, balustrades replacing walls to give more light, And the whole group is richly and elaborately decorated. Vase-and-foliage capitals top the columns. And four or five bands of decoration rise up from river-goddesses to surround doorways and sanctum surroundings. Percy Brown wrote enthusiastically that here "we find portrayed, by symbol and image, whole volumes of folklore and mythology for those who can see but cannot read (*Indian Architecture*)."

The largest is **Mahavira**, a Jain temple set up on a terrace and dedicated to their last Tirthankara. The sanctum was built during the rule of the Parihar Rajput, Vatsaraja (783-793). After 10th-century renovations, the graceful *torana* (gateway), with carvings of nymphs and the *sikhara* (bee-

hive-shaped tower) were both added the following century. Behind **Surya** (Sun) **temple**, with two fluted pillars at its entrance, steps by a pool lead down to the ruins of what was possibly a summer palace.

The later **Mahashamardi temple**, known locally as **Pipla Devi**, has a big assembly hall and a row of the nine personified planets adorn the lintel. It is also worth looking at the two temples dedicated to Vishnu and the three eighth-century temples dedicated to Harihara. The 12th-century **Sachiya Mata temple**, well decorated inside and outside, is the focus of the second group which stand on a hill just east of Osiyan, reached through a sandstone arch carved with celestial nymphs.

If the desert has worked its magic, travel another 37 miles (60 km) to **Khimsar**, whose fort is now a hotel. As expected in this area, its history is all in the family. Rao Jodha's fifth son, Karam Singh was the local *thakur* (ruler). He named his fortified *thikana* (ruler's home) Fateh Mahal after a Sufi saint who was buried there. Today, Karam Singh's descendants live in an 18th-century addition to the fort.

Isolated in a time-wrap, Khimsar's romance is heightened by a sunset drive into the desert, returning into the safety of the guarded gates before darkness falls.

Desert City: From Khimsar, **Nagaur** is a 25-mile (40-km) hop (it is 85 miles/135 km from Jodhpur). This ancient, heavily fortified, desert city is now the headquarters of Nagaur District, an area famous for its fine bullocks. Indeed, it is well worth coinciding your visit with the huge cattle fairs when there are four days of races and competitions for camels, cocks, horses and bullocks, with plenty of colorful Rajasthani dancing and singing. Named after local heroes, the **Ramdeoji Fair** is in February, the **Tejaji Fair** in August.

According to legend, Nagaur is named after the Naga Rajputs. But its turbulent history see-sawed between Hindu and Muslim ownership. The old town is surrounded by a tall, thick wall, with sturdy battlements which have been repaired with bits of demolished mosques—hence the occasional Arabic or Persian inscription. The fine decoration on the high gateway is

A *minar* is all that survives of an old mosque, Nargar.

probably by the same artisans who worked on Ajmer mosques in the mid-13th century. A cluster of royal Hindu *chhatris* stand outside it.

Inside, the two most interesting buildings are Muslim. One is **Akbar's five-domed mosque**, his shrine for a disciple of Khwaja Muin-ud-din Chishti, the Sufi saint who came to India in 1192 and died at Ajmer. The other is **Shams Masjid**, named after the 13th-century Governor Shams Khan.

The remarkable **fort** sits on a hill in the city, further protected by double walls of massive proportions: the outer one 25 feet (eight meters) high, the inner one 50 feet (16 meters) high and of a thickness tapering from 30 feet (nine meters) at the base to 12 feet (four meters) at the top. Inside, Akbar built the 17-jet fountains; Shah Jahan built the mosque; and both Muslims and Hindus claim their saints lived in the cave. But the **palaces**, once set in lush formal gardens, are its delight. Delicate murals of cyprus trees and peacock feathers, occasionally framing a dancer or flower, decorate the exterior walls. And there are more paintings inside.

About 15 miles (25 km) east of Nagaur lies **Manglud**. Its ancient temple has a Sanskrit inscription recording its repair in 604 A.D., one of the oldest inscriptions in Rajasthan.

Many of the villages in this area—and around Khimsar—are lived in by the fascinating *Bisnoi* community. All Bisnois follow the 21 (bis-noi) tenets laid down by the 15th-century Guru Jambeshwar. They fervently believe in the sanctity of animal and plant life, so all animals live near their villages without fear. When a Bisnoi dies, he is sometimes buried in the sitting position and often placed at the threshold of the house or adjoining cattleshed. But a Bisnoi believes he will later be reincarnated as a deer—hence the herds often seen near their villages.

Bisnoi villages are immaculate, daily scrubbed by the brightly-clad women who are weighed down with jewelry and festooned with bangles right up the length of their arms. By contrast, their tall men dress entirely in white, their large turbans loosely swathed around dark-skinned, weathered faces.

Camels draw water from extremely deep wells.

MOUNT ABU: PILGRIM CENTER

To discover a tropical hill-resort in the middle of the Rajasthan desert would appear impossible. Yet this is exactly what **Mount Abu** is. The broken ridges of the Aravalli hills attain the highest point at **Guru Shikhar**, the Saints Pinnacle, in the southwestern corner of Rajasthan, bordering the State of Gujarat. This range is separated from the main chain of the Aravallis by a valley about 15 miles (24 km) wide. In this vale are grown the fruits and vegetables that feed the surrounding region.

As one drives from Udaipur towards Abu, it is incredible how fertile the area appears. From **Sirohi**, once a formidable Deora-Chauhan stronghold, now a neglected stopover, the fields on either side glow with vigorous splendor. During the monsoon, one passes heaped piles of vivid scarlet chilies, golden pumpkins, warm red tomatoes, purple brinjals waiting to be transported by trucks to nearby cities. Gujarat is the main gainer rather than the more distant, less accessible, Rajasthan markets.

Sirohi was once an important center of Rajput power. The Chauhans, after their defeat by the Afghans in the 12th century, fled southwest. Settling in Kota-Bundi, they were called the Hada Chauhans, while another branch, the Deora Chauhans made Sirohi their main center. All branches of the Chauhan clan owed allegiance to the Sisodias of Mewar (the Royal House of Udaipur).

One still catches a glimpse of former glory in Sirohi such as a beautiful white temple gleaming on a hilltop with an endless stretch of clean whitewashed steps climbing the steep incline. If you have the stamina to go up, the effort will be rewarded by a remarkable view of the surrounding countryside. From Sirohi, you will also notice the curious type of local cattle; small, compact, strong and with long, sharp and straight horns. These are often painted in bright colors and natty little bulls are decorated with necklaces of beads and cowrie shells. These animals are said to be very intelligent and can be trained to do all sorts of tricks. One often comes across bulls who are the companions of mendicant fortune-tellers who entertain the crowds at fairs and festivals with their "holy bulls" who can tell the fortune of standers-by, shaking or nodding their heads in answer to questions.

As you climb up the winding road to Mount Abu, the tropical splendor of the hills is overwhelming. They are covered by forests with a wide variety of trees. Each curve of the road brings into view silk-cotton and bottle-brush, mango, bamboo, eucalyptus, wild pomegranate, coral, date-palm and lime. Flame of the forest (the famous pallas of the ancient poems), gulmohur, jacaranda, amaltash and oleander paint the woods with their variegated hues. Flowering shrubs crowd the jungle, creating the effect of a gigantic wild garden planned by a master landscape gardener.

No wonder Abu was selected as the site for one of the most sacred mystic rites in legendary times, the *yagna* of the *Agnikund* or the sacrifice of the fire-pit. This ceremony was to have a profound effect on the whole basic structure of Hindu society and its

effects can be seen in current social life up to today.

The *yagna* was an initiation ceremony. Such rites of passage qualify those who participate to be accepted into the social fold.

After the fall of the great Gupta Empire, northwest India was in a state of chaos. The ancient fighting caste, the Kshatriyas, had been decimated by the endless hordes that entered India via the Hindu Kush: Huns, Gujars, Hellenes, Persians, Scythians, who mixed, married and settled in petty kingdoms. These fighting clans, through an elaborate, mystical sacrificial ceremony, and purification through an ordeal by fire, at a Concord of Brahmins, held at Gaumukh in Abu, were now proclaimed Kshatriyas and accepted as the fighting caste, the fireborn or *agnikula* Rajputs. They were the Paramars, Chauhans, Pratiharas and Solankis. Even today these castes claim a mystic origin and a direct Kshatriya link with the ancient Aryans. This had an important impact on the history of the region. No longer considered as marauding foreigners, these clans went on to set up flourishing kingdoms; the Chauhans in Delhi-Ajmer; the Paramars in Central India, where the remains of their beautiful temples can still be seen in Madhya Pradesh; the Pratiharas were the direct forerunners of the later Rajput rulers who held power up to the time of the independence of India in 1947.

Abu is also a center of Jain pilgrimage and here is found one of the greatest achievements of the temple-builders' art: the **Dilwara temples**. Never has carving in marble achieved such subtlety and complexity or such delicacy and intricate detail. It is almost beyond belief that stone could be manipulated with such skill and dexterity, or that so many variations on a theme could be encompassed on a single pillar or a frieze. In a way, Dilwara is almost too much. It can overwhelm and even satiate. But it cannot be missed.

Gaumukh Temple lies about 2.5 miles (four km) below Abu on a bridle path. A small shrine to Vishnu has images of his incarnations as the divine Rama and Krishna. A natural spring flows through a cow's head which gives the shrine its name. This is the scene of

Mount Abu developed a a summer resort from the 1840s.

the ancient *agnikund* from which the Rajput clans, *Agnikula*, are said to have sprung. Pilgrims haunt this sacred shrine and carry home the holy water of the spring.

Achalgarh: This fort is about five miles (eight km) out of Abu along a motorable road up to Uria. From here the ascent is made on foot through steeply rising woods (palanquins available for those not wishing to walk). There are several temples on the way, many in a ruined state, and only the ramparts and broken walls of the original fort, built by Rana Kumbha of Mewar (14th century) remain. Kumbha was one of the great rulers of the state responsible for making Mewar the leading Rajput kingdom. Unfortunately he was murdered by his son and the fight that followed split the House of Mewar. The first large temple is dedicated to *Achaliswar Mahadev* or Lord Shiva and was built in 1412.

Dilwara Jain Temples: Barely two miles (three km) north of Abu are temples set on a hill in the midst of a grove of old mango trees. These are Jain shrines. The temples are open between noon and six in the evening. A small entrance fee and camera fee is charged. Shoes and leather objects must be left outside.

The main temples are not very large and are covered by domes rather than the more usual pyramidal *shikaras*.

Adinath Temple (1031): The older of the two main shrines is dedicated to the first of the Jain *tirthankaras* (saints). It was built by Vimala, a minister of state. Constructed entirely of pure white marble, this temple is in some ways the more pleasing of the two. It is less ornate and so the fine carving is more easily appreciated. The outer porch has a pavilion to the right in which the donors were shown mounted on elephants, but these have been badly mutilated.

The entrance opposite leads one to the main shrine. Once inside, one is entirely overwhelmed by the art of the *silavats* or stone carvers. Elaborate *makaratoranas* or scroll arches decorate the hall, the pillars of which are entirely covered with fine carvings of nymphs and musicians. The inner sanctum contains a figure of Adinath (the first of the *tirthankaras*) in the posture of meditation. The door lintel

he high
round and
ool climate
ave made
bu a
opular
oliday
esort.

and jambs are encrusted with carved figures. The domed ceiling of the hall has a flower-pendant encircled by large female figures in dancing postures. All round the shrine runs a covered cloister, its pillars also carved, its ceiling divided into innumerable sections, each again cut and carved in different patterns. Along the corridor are niches housing statues of the *tirthankaras* and each niche again has delicate carved figures and designs on its facing. There are 52 such niches.

Neminath Temple (1230): Built by two brothers, Tejapala and Vastupala who also built the famous temple at Girnar, Gujarat, this shrine, dedicated to the 22nd *tirthankara* is a fabulous work of art. There is a profusion of carving on its convoluted scroll arches, its covered pillars, of which no two are carved alike; the elaborate scenes carved in bas-relief on the corridor ceilings, the stalactite-like pendant from the main central dome, and the magnificent hall of donors at the farther end are especially fine. The craftsmanship overwhelms and stuns.

The Hall of Donors: Behind the central shrine, in some ways the most interesting and unusual feature of this temple, in a long hall are several figures mounted on elephants, some of black marble. Behind the mounted figures are niches, each containing two or three figures, almost life size, of a donor and his wife, or with two women. The exquisite carvings show the fine texture of the muslin drapery and the delicate designs of the shadow and drawn-thread work.

There is a **museum** at Abu set in a pleasant garden which is worth a visit.

Nakki Lake: A focal point for visitors to Abu is a lovely little artificial lake ringed round by hills and overhung by the enormous **Toad's Rock**. Boating and exploring the lake's little islets is a favorite recreation. The rulers of most Rajput states built summer villas round the lake; some of these are now guest houses or hotels. Nakki Lake is said to have been dug by the gods with their nails, hence its name, as *nakki* means nails.

Sunset Point: There are many beautiful walks round the hills. The best mountain view is to be had from Sunset Point southwest of Nakki Lake, where the sun sets between two craggy

Nakki lake.

peaks. Steps lead to a high terrace which offers a magnificent view of the sunset. Monsoon sunsets are the most dramatic.

Trevor's Tank: A part of the forest around Abu has been turned into a wildlife sanctuary. The road winds through steep hills, thickly wooded and alive with peacocks, pheasants, partridges and other birds. In a sudden opening the hills encircle a deep pool, built by a British engineer named Trevor. A small but pretty forest lodge stands on the far bank. An open terrace was built by a former ruler and, in the past, shoots were arranged and picnics held by the royal hosts. Birdwatchers will find this a wonderful place. Mushrooms can also be found.

While returning from Mount Abu, pause at **Abu Road** at the bottom of the incline. This is a medieval town that has retained its old-world character. Essentially a stopover for the sacred sites at Mount Abu, Abu Road is where the pilgrims gather. They pause to pick up offerings, or to look for inexpensive lodgings, or just to rest before completing the long and arduous pilgrimage to the holy shrines, often made on foot.

The winding lanes in the bazars are lined with shops heaped with colored powders. Here you can get the pure vermilion *sindhoor* or *kumkum* that adorns the forehead and hair parting of Indian women. There are flower stalls selling sweet-smelling jasmine garlands and posies of marigolds. Incense of many kinds, oil-lamps and beautiful marble images are also favorite offerings. Here you can pick up smooth polished stones of jasper, agate, cornelian, amethyst and necklaces or bracelets of semi-precious stones at a very reasonable price. Carved ivory or bone statues, bowls and ornaments, scarves and skirts, printed or embroidered with mirror-work, make attractive gifts.

Since Abu is a sacred city and an important Jain center, most people there are strict vegetarians. One can get delicious vegetarian food at the better hotels and guesthouses and it is best to stay with this. As much of the food is highly spiced with chilies, ask for lightly spiced dishes.

Mount Abu is a convenient stop between south-western Rajasthan and Gujarat to the south. It is also linked with Jodhpur and Udaipur.

UDAIPUR: MEWAR, LAND OF LEGEND

Royal House of Mewar: Legend has it that the Sisodias of Mewar are descended from the Sun God through Lav, the son of Lord Rama whose life story is told in India's great epic, the *Ramayana*. They came from the borders of Kashmir and by the second Century B.C. they had moved south to what is now Gujarat, founding, as they went, several cities along the coast, one of which was called Vallabhi.

The chronicles of the bards tell us that in the sixth century Vallabhi was sacked by strangers from the west. The Queen of Vallabhi, Pushpavati, who was on a pilgrimage offering prayers for her unborn child, heard of the destruction of Vallabhi and the death of her husband while traveling through the Aravalli hills in the north. Despairing, she took refuge in a cave, and there gave birth to a son whom she called Guhil, or "cave born." Then, entrusting her child to a maidservant, the queen ordered a funeral pyre lit, and walked into it to join her dead husband's soul.

Guhil, or Guhadatta, was befriended by the Bhils, tribal aborigines who had lived in the Aravalli hills since well before 2000 B.C. Amongst the Bhils, Guhadatta grew in power, and became a chieftain. His progeny came to be known as *Guhilots*.

In the seventh century the Guhilots moved north, and down to the plains of Mewar, changing their name to Sisodia, after a village they encountered on the way. The descendants of Guhadatta were the great Ranas, Rawals and Maharanas of Mewar, builders of forts and palaces, whose exploits in peace and war are unmatched in valor and chivalry.

By the time of India's independence, the royal line of Mewar had ruled for 75 generations, 1,400 years; the oldest of Rajasthan's ancient dynasties.

The Founding of Udaipur: In 1567, the capital of Mewar, Chittor, was sacked for the third time by the armies of the Mughal Emperor Akbar; Rana Udai Singh II withdrew into the hills and ravines of the Aravalli. One morning, the rana was out by Lake Pichola hunting. While mounted and on the move he performed the difficult feat of spearing a fast-moving rabbit. Then, a short distance away, he saw a sage, meditating. The rana dutifully paid his respects to the holy man.

"Where, O Revered One," the rana asked the sage, having recounted the fall of Chittor, "should I build my next capital city?"

And the sage answered, as sages will, "Why, right here of course, where your destiny has brought you to ask such a question."

And that's what Udai Singh did.

Udaipur Today: The spirit of **Udaipur**, someone has said, gazes toward Chittor, as at a lost and distant horizon. For it is from the misfortunes of that fort that this city of pleasure was born. Luxurious Udaipur is an interesting counterpoint to stark Chittor. While the fort stands rugged, battle-scarred, blending with the scrubby country, atop a stark plateau, Udaipur nestles like a gem in a valley surrounded by the green Aravalli hills, reflected smooth and white in the clear blue of Lake Pichola.

The old city within the fortifications is built on tiny hills. Narrow medieval roads and lanes wind and bend, with a small temple at each turning, making the city one of the most charming in all Rajasthan. Interspersed among the old dwellings, temples and palaces which speak to you of a royal, aristocratic past is the new and the modern—shops, houses, markets and down-to-earth bus-stands.

The **City Palace**, once entirely the home of Mewar's rulers, is today largely a museum run by the Maharana Mewar Foundation. It actually consists of four major and several minor palaces forming a single breathtaking facade overlooking the Pichola lake. Built by successive kings, every addition was so flawlessly integrated in style and feeling with the existing structures, as to make the whole seem one.

From the outside, the palace resembles nothing so much as a formidable Rajput fort with sheer impregnable walls rising high out of the water, broken only near the top by an exuberance of domes, arches, cupolas, turrets and crenellations.

The approach to the palace is through the **Hathi Pol** (Elephant Gate) to the north on the main street of the city, leading to the **Tripolia** or triple gate of marble arches, right at the spot at which Rana Udai Singh II speared his hare five centuries ago.

Above the Tripolia is **Hawa Mahal**, built in the 19th century, a facade of windows from behind which the women of the palace could watch the world outside. Beyond the Tripolia is the **Bada Chowk**, the Big Square, in which in the past, a hundred elephants, the rana's infantry, cavalry and artillery were massed for inspection before battle.

The **Toran Pol** on the south side of Bada Chowk leads into the palace buildings, and if you look to its right, high on the wall you will see the sun emblem of Mewar. Below this emblem is the **Padgadi-Hathni**, where in the past, visitors to the royal house dismounted from the backs of richly caparisoned elephants.

Entering the palace now, there is a profusion of courtyards, rooms, galleries—themselves so decorated and embellished as to be museum pieces housing artifacts connected with the history of Mewar and its rulers.

The **Shrine of Dhuni Mata** is the oldest part of the city palace, in fact the oldest building in Udaipur, built on the spot at which Rana Udai Singh met the meditating sage. It is a simple room containing pictures of the four major Hindu deities of Mewar: Sri Charbhujaji, Sri Eklingji, Sri Nathji (or Krishna), and Amba Mata.

The **Raj Angan** or Royal Courtyard in which the shrine of Dhuni Mata stands has rooms leading off it which house part of the **Museum of Rana Pratap** which was once in the Victoria Hall.

Rana Pratap (ruled 1572-97) was one of the great warrior kings of Mewar. He lived in troubled times: Emperor Akbar, the Great Mughal, was expanding his domains, irresistibly, across the subcontinent. He had already sacked the Mewar stronghold, Chittor, driving Pratap's father, Rana Udai Singh II, out towards a new life in the new capital, Udaipur. Rana Pratap was imbued with stories of the lost greatness of Mewar and obsessed with a desire to recover its territories, and the fort of Chittor, the soul of Mewar.

The indomitable Pratap threw himself against the might of the Mughal

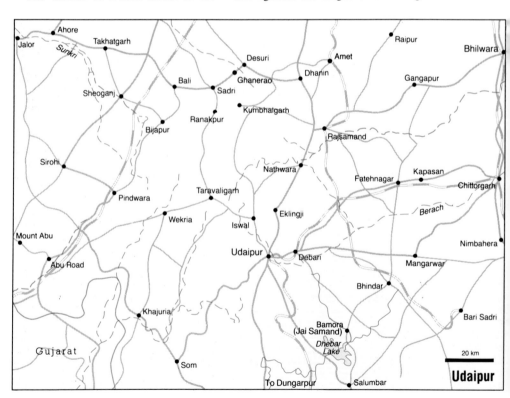

armies again and again, losing the battle of Haldighati, losing every fort, including Kumbalgarh, retreating to the hills and ravines of the Aravallis where sometimes his family hadn't enough to eat. In these years of adversity, they were sustained by loyal Bhil tribesmen, whose ancestors had, centuries earlier, supported the rana's ancestor, Guhadatta.

Rana Pratap was one of the two Rajput kings who refused to accept Mughal suzerainty or compromise with Akbar: no daughter of Mewar was ever given to a Mughal emperor or prince in marriage. The other Rajput ruler similarly to hold out against the Mughals was the king of Bundi. Akbar allowed both states to survive and the next generation of rulers had to accept reality and sign treaties with the Mughals.

Eventually, Pratap freed Udaipur and much of Mewar from the Mughal grip but he failed to win his heart's desire: Chittor.

In the museum in the City Palace are paintings depicting incidents in the life of Rana Pratap. His armor and weapons and other memorabilia are also on display.

Dil Kushal, a room created in the 17th century by Rana Karan Singh, has walls lined with mirrors interspersed with miniature paintings.

On the walls surrounding **Mor Chowk**, a courtyard in **Priyatama Vilas** built in the late-19th century by Maharana Sajjan Singh, are intricately crafted peacocks in fine mosaic relief, which delight the eye.

Bhim Vilas has a famous sun window, **Suraj Gokhala**, installed by Maharana Bhim Singh in the late-18th century.

The **Bada** (big) **Mahal** is also called the Garden Palace, for here in the center, raised 90 feet (27 meters) is a breathtakingly beautiful garden. It stands on a hill in the middle of the palace complex, making the rooms around it appear to be on the top floor of the palace. They are actually ground floor rooms built around the periphery of the natural rock topped by the garden with trees growing around a central pool.

Krishna Vilas: In 1805, the kings of Jodhpur and Jaipur were on the offensive against Mewar where Maharana

Shiv Niwas, part of the City Palace complex, now a deluxe hotel.

Bhim Singh was then ruling. Both the rulers indicated that they would settle for the lovely 16-year-old Sisodia princess, Krishna Kumari. The king of Mewar was in a quandary: he could refuse neither; he could accept neither, for appeasing one would set the other against him. When Krishna Kumari heard of her father's dilemma, she resolved it—by poisoning herself. Her heartbroken mother died soon after, and the maharana soothed his grief by building Krishna Vilas which today holds some of the most beautiful miniature paintings to be seen in Rajasthan.

Manek Mahal (Ruby Palace) houses an exhibition of glass and porcelain, including the **Chini Chitrashala**, a collection of Chinese porcelain.

Khush Mahal (Palace of Pleasure) was built by Sajjan Singh in 1874.

Zenan Mahal: South of the City Palace Museum and east of the magnificent gardens of Chandra Chowk is the Palace of the Queens. The building was begun in the early-17th century. In 1974, Zenana Mahal was opened to the public as a museum.

We enter Zenana Mahal through the **Zenana Dyodhi**, appropriately named the "devious gate," as it guards Mahal's entrance. Through this gate you pass into **Rang Bhawan** where gold and silver ornaments, heirlooms, and other state treasures are on display. On the right are shrines to Lord Krishna and Princess Mira Bai, Rana Sanga's daughter-in-law, a renowned mystic poet and saint.

Rang Bhawan opens into **Laxmi Chowk** (square) which is flanked by the domed apartments of the queen and her guests. The queen's apartments are decorated with murals of Lord Krishna at play amongst the milkmaids.

There is exquisite glass inlay work in the **Osara**, the place of ceremony, in the eastern wing of Zenana Mahal.

In the center of Laxmi Chowk is a pillared pavilion with a magnificent fretwork peacock spreading its tail. Flanking him are two not-quite-so-magnificent fretwork peahens. Inside the pavilion are housed musical instruments—a brass trumpet, cymbals, a drum captured from the Mughal emperor, Babur.

On the first floor of the structure around Laxmi Chowk is a succession

Local tourists add color to the City Palace.

220

of rooms housing miniatures of the Mewar school, showing the minutiae of daily life in the Mewar court, a subject peculiar to the Mewar school. And here too you can see some fine old photographs of the British political residents and viceroys. One of the alcoves off these rooms is set up in memory of Colonel James Tod, the devoted historian of Rajasthan, and Resident Representative of the British Crown from 1818 to 1822.

The **Fateh-Prakash**, the newest of the city palaces, is next to Zenana Mahal, but, being the current residence of the maharana, it is not open to the public.

Beyond Zenana Mahal and the exquisite garden of Chandra Chowk, or Moon Square, past another square to the east, is the **Durbar Hall** of which Lord Minto, the British viceroy, laid the foundation stone in the reign of Maharana Fateh Singh, a proud and conservative man, constantly at odds with the British in defense of his rights and privileges as a ruling prince. He was virtually dethroned by the British and the *gadi* passed to Maharana Bhupal Singh who led Mewar into the Indian Union in 1947. On the formation of the state of Rajasthan in 1949, the Government of India honored Maharana Bhupal Singh by making him Maharaj Pramukh (the premier maharaja) of Rajasthan.

Shambu Niwas, adjacent to the Durbar Hall, was built in the mid-19th century. It is not open to the public. Nor are the older apartments of the saint, Kanwarji Bhaiji, east of the Durbar Hall, where *puja* ceremonies are still performed as they have been through the generations. The former royal guest house nearby, **Shiv Niwas**, has, however, recently been turned into one of the most luxurious hotels in Udaipur.

Jagdish Mandir: Close by the main gate of the City Palace, high on a hill is a temple complex dedicated to Jagannath, an aspect of Lord Vishnu. It was built by Maharana Jagat Singh in 1651. Thirty-two steps lead up to it from the main road. The central temple in the group is heavily ornamented with excellent carvings. In its main shrine is an enormous black stone image of Jagannath. At the entrance, in an enclosed shrine of its own, is a fine bronze figure of Garuda (a mythical

eft, Shiv
iwas.
ight, a
che for God
anesh, City
alace.

221

bird), the *vahana* or vehicle of Lord Vishnu.

In the reign of Maharana Raj Singh, the Mughal Emperor Aurangzeb defeated the combined armies of Mewar and Marwar. While the maharana and his men attempted to defend Udaipur, making guerrilla raids on Aurangzeb's army from the surrounding hills, Naroo Bharat, a simple bard, gathered a small force to defend the Jagdish Temple. He fell to the Mughal sword, and the temple was destroyed. A cenotaph adjacent to the temple commemorates the heroism of Naroo Bharat.

Udaipur Today: It is through the streets of today, the markets and the bazaars, that the traveler must wander if he is to get the feel of the city as a whole. The **Bara Bazaar** is close behind the palace, and under the ramparts to the east is **Bapu Bazaar**, a fascinating place.

Here, you will find carpenters in side alleys making wooden toys in the traditional manner: there are military bands dressed in the uniform of another era, birds and animals in the lovely lines established by tradition, elaborately decorated with mirrors,

beads and tinsel in the style of Mewar. Here are puppet makers painting huge eyes alongside the long Rajput nose of wooden puppets, dressing them in time-honored styles of dress. Puppet shows reenact ancient sages of heroism and romance.

In these bazaars you can see craftsmen decorating silver and copper pots and plates; and jewelers engaged in the craft of *meenakari* (enamel inlay on gold or silver). Here you can buy old coins and images of gods, and watch women making *bandhini* (tie-and-dye) fabrics and *pichwai* paintings in styles which haven't changed for generations.

Sajjan Niwas lies a little farther south, still within the old city walls. In its grounds is **Gulab Bagh** (Rose Garden) laid out by Maharana Sajjan Singh in the late-19th century. The grounds cover 100 acres (40 hectares) with spacious lawns, a zoo, and Victoria Hall (now called Saraswati Bhawan) which was opened in 1890 by the British viceroy, Lord Landsdowne, to commemorate the 1887 Diamond Jubilee of Queen Victoria. Saraswati Bhawan is now a library.

Farther south, toward Lake Pichola,

Lakeside houses in the shadow of the City Palace.

is **Machchalaya Magra** (Whale Hill), so called because it resembles nothing so much as a contented whale beached on the sands, sunning itself. It rises about 2,500 feet (760 m)above sea level and extends right to the lake. The view from this hill, over the city and lake, is magnificent.

From **Eklingji Hill** south of **Doodh Talai** (Pond of Milk), the ramparts of the old city wall ramble down the hills to the east and north, skirting the banks of Lake Pichola.

Lake Pichola: This lake takes its name from the small village of Picholi on its west bank. A *Banjara* (grain transporter), back in the 15th century, found that the bullocks carrying his load could not ford the stream there, so he built a raised path across it. The path acted as a dam, and a lake began to form behind it. By the time Rana Udai Singh II came to this region, Pichola Lake was quite large. Rana Udai Singh strengthened the dam, **Badi Paal** (Big Dam), and greatly enlarged the lake as a defence measure.

Pichola Lake consists today of a complex of the original Pichola, Amar Sagar, Rang Sagar, Swaroop Sagar

north of it, and Doodh Talai toward the south, which is currently dry land covered by a garden. Later maharanas strengthened the dam further. The lake is about 3.5 square miles (eight square km) in area. In the lake are several islands. On two of them, the maharanas of Udaipur constructed pleasure palaces, one of which, **Jag Niwas**, is today the Lake Palace Hotel.

Jag Mandir: It is said Maharana Karan Singh built this island retreat for the family of his friend Prince Khurram, who later became the Emperor Shah Jahan. Huge seamless stone slabs of translucent thinness were used. Cupolas; a lofty dome; spacious courtyards guarded by elephants in stone; majestic palms; beautiful rooms embellished with inlaid stones—onyx, jade, cornelian, jasper, agate; and paintings—these are but a few of the splendors of the palace.

As a mark of his gratitude, and a symbol of brotherhood, Prince Khurram exchanged turbans with Maharana Karan. This turban is preserved, still in its original folds, in the City Palace at Udaipur.

The palace was named after Mahar-

The Lake Palace by moonlight.

ana Jagat Singh, the son of Maharana Karan Singh, who made several additions to it and later built Jag Niwas as well. Today, the western part of the palace is a charming rest house, with a swimming pool. For bird-watching value alone it is worth a visit.

Jag Niwas, the Lake Palace Hotel: Legend has it that, as a youth, Prince Jagat Singh once asked his father's permission to take a group of friends and hangers-on with him to Jag Mandir for a bit of fun. The old maharana refused, saying that for fun and frolic Jagat Singh could go build his own palace on the lake. Stung, the prince did just that; he built a most magnificent pleasure palace on a rocky island nearby—a sort of posthumous retort to his crusty father.

The Jag Niwas Palace and its grounds, covering an area of four acres (1.6 hectares), is an airy stucco complex floored with marble and has graceful granite columns. The gardens, fountains and lavishly decorated rooms are a refreshing retreat in a fairy-tale setting.

Arsi Vilas: This small island near Jag Mandir was never built on. It is a sanctuary for water-fowl and other birds.

Nathani ka Chabutra: A small platform rising out of the water near the Jag near Jag Mandir Palace has an interesting history. A professional tight rope-walker of the Nat caste, was promised half the kingdom of Mewar, by a somewhat drunken maharana, if she could walk the tightrope from a village on the west bank of Lake Pichola to the City Palace on the east bank. The confident Nathani gladly accepted the challenge and, toes curled around a tightrope strung for the occasion, gracefully balanced her way over the lake until she had almost reached Jag Mandir—at which point, a canny minister imbued with a strong practical streak, had the rope cut. The girl fell into the lake and drowned. The kingdom of Mewar was safe. But a *chabutra*, a small marble platform, was raised in memory of this acrobat.

North of the Old City: Lake Fateh Sagar, lying north of Pichola, past Lake Rang Sagar and Lake Swaroop Sagar, was excavated in the late-17th century by Maharana Jai Singh.

Nehru Park: Out in Lake Fateh Sagar

Udaipur has its own style of wall painting.

is an island. In 1937, intending to create work for his people to alleviate famine conditions, Maharana Bhupal Singh initiated work on the foundations of a water palace. However, the famine passed, and work on the new palace was discontinued. The island was left to birds and animals, reptiles and swamps, for the next 35 years. Recently, the state government of Rajasthan has converted it into a park named after India's first Prime Minister, Jawaharlal Nehru. Visitors reach it from the **Municipal Rock Garden** on the eastern bank by boat.

Bharatiya Lok Kala Mandal: A little farther north is the center for Rajasthan's folk culture. Created in 1952, the institution has been recording Rajasthani folklore and folk music, collecting folk arts, staging plays, collecting tribal art, and supporting the ancient Rajasthani art of puppetry.

On **Moti Magri** (Hill of Pearls), in a garden named after Bhama Shah, the Prime Minister of Rana Pratap, is an 11-foot-(3.3 meter) tall bronze statue of Rana Pratap astride his horse, Chetak. You enter the garden through a fort-like gate facing Lake Fateh Sagar. The road winds steeply up Moti Magri, past the **Bhama Shah Garden** which is laid out in Japanese style. The view from the top of the hill is well worth the climb.

Sahelion-ki-Bari (Garden of the Maids of Honor) was originally constructed in the early-18th century by Maharana Sangram Singh, using the waters of the Fateh Sagar to feed the pools. It had been the scene of many royal parties for centuries and is now a favorite spot with townfolk and tourists alike.

Sajjan Garh Palace was constructed by Maharana Sajjan Singh in the late-18th century. It is three miles (five km) west of Udaipur, high on a hill called Bansdara and visible from miles around. It stands 2,468 feet (750 meters) above sea level.

From the palace, there is a breathtaking view for miles around: hills, lakes, rivers, fields, forests and palaces. During the monsoon, clouds shroud the palace, making it seem distant, ghostly, romantic, full of mystery. It is said a nine-storied astronomical observatory was planned here, but Maharana Sajjan Singh died when he was 25 years

Wayside dentist.

old, when only one story was completed.

Khas Odi Hunting Lodge: To the left, off the Sajjan Garh road, in the hills on the west side of lake Pichola, is a hunting lodge called Khas Odi or Shikarbadi. This lodge features frequently in Mewar miniatures and is worth a visit. In the center of the building is a square pit where boars, tigers, and leopards were pitted against each other, spectators cheering from the surrounding wall. You can stay the night in this peaceful lodge (by arrangement with the Lake Palace Hotel), listening to the sounds of the night—the crickets, nightjars and owls.

Haridasji-ki-Magri is a large, walled enclosure on a wooded hill close to the hunting lodge where wild boar and deer roam free—in captivity.

No account of the spirit of the people of Mewar, of the land, all that has been built upon it, can be fully comprehended unless one has visited **Chittor** and listened to the legends of those who once inhabited this mountain-top fort. This fascinating town is treated in a separate article.

Nahar Magri (Tiger Hill): On the way to Chittor from Udaipur, almost exactly opposite the turn off for the airport, pennants fly over a small white shrine, the *dhuni* (place of worship) of ascetics. Here, Bappa Rawal, the founder of Mewar, stopped to receive the blessings of the goddess Durga, in the form of a tiger skin presented to him by the solitary old prophetess who kept the holy fire burning there.

Ahar Village and Museum: Two miles (three km) east of Udaipur, on a small hillock called **Dhimkot**, archaeologists have discovered a town belonging to a period between the chalcolithic age and Kushan era (c. 150 A.D.). In ancient times, it was called **Tambawati Nagri**. Here, bones of fish, deer and birds, and pieces of pottery have been found, dating back to 4000 B.C. Wells and drainage indicate town planning of some maturity. There is a museum near the site.

Before Bappa Rawal wrested Chittor from his Mori uncle, Ahar was the capital of the ruling house. Every time Chittor fell to an enemy, and until Udaipur was built, Ahar sheltered the Rana's kinsmen and forces.

Cenotaphs of Kings: The rulers of

Aravalli landscape.

226

Mewar were traditionally cremated with their wives near a tank called the **Gangabhar Kund** on the banks of the river Ahar which flows out of lake Fateh Sagar. Cenotaphs or *chhatris* to the ranas are grouped within an enclosure, each grandson completing the memorial to his grandfather. Every cenotaph contains an image of Shiva, and a single upright stone on which are carved the figures of the rana and his wives. Nineteen ranas have their cenotaphs here. The Gangabhar Kund is considered to be as holy as the Ganga.

Shi Eklingji Temple: Fourteen miles (22 km) northeast of Udaipur is the village of **Kailashpuri** which is known for its 108 temples surrounded by a high fortified wall. The whole complex is known as Shi Eklingji Temple and has been a holy site associated with Lord Shiva since ancient times. The present structures, however, date from the 16th century.

Bappa Rawal spent much of his childhood at Kailashpuri in the hermitage of a sage called Harita Rishi from whom he received religious instruction. The sage invested his favorite pupil with the insignia of royalty and bestowed upon him the title *Dewan* (regent) *of Eklingji*, which succeeding Mewar kings carried with pride.

The main temple is said to be on the very spot at which Harita Rishi and Bappa Rawal conversed. It is built of granite and marble and has a large, ornate *mandap* (pillared hall) under a huge pyramidal roof. There is a four-faced image of Lord Shiva in black marble in the inner sanctuary. Outside, opposite the west-facing face of Shiva, is a statue of the bull Nandi, the mount of Shiva.

The temple was damaged by the Sultan of Gujarat in 1433, restored by Rana Kumbha, and again destroyed by Aurangzeb in the late-17th century.

Lakulish Temple stands within the precincts of the Eklingji complex. It was built in 971 A.D. by a ruler of Nagda. It is the only temple of the Lakulish sect in India and has only recently been discovered.

Nagda: Close to Kailashpuri, down a rough country road, is Nagda, once a Solanki stronghold, and now a major railway junction and industrial center. It is believed to have been established

Saas-Bahu
emple,
Nagda.

by Nagaditya, the fourth Mewar king, a descendant of the Guhadatta who was born in a cave in the Aravalli mountains after the sack of Vallabhi. There are several temples dating from the fourth century A.D., ancient rock edicts, stone inscriptions, and simple prehistoric shrines at which the Bhils still worship during the Mahashivratri festival in February.

All that is now left of those times at Nagda are the temples of **Saas-Bahu** and **Adbhutji**. The former dates back to the 11th century and is famed for its beautiful carvings. **Saas-Bahu**, literally means "mother-in-law and daughter-in-law." Adbhutji is an old Jain temple named after a somewhat odd statue of a Jain saint seated within. *Adbhut* means, quite literally, "peculiar."

Nathdwara: Thirty miles (48 km) north of Udaipur, past Kailashpuri and the Eklingji temple is a town once known as Sihar. Now it is called Nathdwara, and is a *dhaam*, one of the principal places of pilgrimage in Rajasthan.

In the 17th century, when Emperor Aurangzeb prohibited idol worship, devout Hindus in Mathura, the home of Lord Krishna, fearful that their sacred statues might be smashed, decided to remove them to a safer location. The Maharana of Mewar, Raj Singh I, offered sanctuary to the idol of Nathji and it was loaded reverently on to a chariot and sent on its way to Mewar accompanied by its *goswami* (priest). At Sihar, a wheel of the chariot sank deep into the mud, and it could not be moved despite repeated efforts. This was interpreted as a sign that the image wanted to dwell at that place. So there it dwelt. A temple was built for the idol, and the village came to be known as Nathdwara, "Home of Nathji" or Krishna. Today, it is a celebrated spot for Vaishnava pilgrims.

Temple rules forbid entry by non-Hindus. However, the town is still worth a visit. The streets are narrow, cobbled, and wind up the hill to the temple. Little shops sell all manner of goods: ivory carvings, paintings, meenakari jewelry, and sweets that are sent to relatives abroad after they have been blessed by the deity. Here, in this town, you can see *pichwais* being painted.

Kankroli and Rajasamund: Forty miles

Cattle fairs are important local events.

PICHWAIS OF NATHDWARA

Nathdwara, a sleepy, dusty, small town set on a hill some 30 miles (50 km) from Udaipur, is—quite literally by accident—the scene of the flowering of one of the most lush, verdant and vibrant art forms in the Indian cultural tradition, *pichwai* painting.

The Vallabh Sampradhya sect was founded by a Telugu Brahmin, Sri Vallabhacharya (1479-1531).

Fleeing from Govardhan in the late 16th century to escape the persecution of the puritanical Mughal Emperor, Aurangzeb, who had proscribed the worship of Krishna throughout his empire, the Vallabhacharis were hoping to reach the benevolent sanctuary of Udaipur, capital of the kingdom of Mewar. Some distance away from their destination, the wheels of the chariot carrying the holy image got stuck in a rut and could not be dug out. Taking this as divine intervention, the Vallabhacharis built their new shrine on the spot. The hitherto unknown village of

Sirah became known as Nathdwara, home of Srinathji, Lord Krishna.

Behind the sculpted image of Krishna or Srinathji, elaborately bedecked and bejeweled, hang huge decorative cloth curtains— *pichwais* (meaning "that which hangs behind")—literally backdrops setting the mood and mystic significance of each ritualized scene. There are 24 iconographic renderings of the Krishna legend traditionally portrayed in the Nathdwara *pichwais*. Each is linked with a particular festival or holy day, e.g. *Gokulashtami* will have Krishna playing the flute to the assembled *gopas, gopis* and their cows; *Dana Ekadashi*, the taking of the toll or *daan* from the *gopis* and breaking of pots.

The *pichwais* were traditionally done in a variety of media: brocaded, block-printed, embroidered, or worked in gold. In Nathdwara, however, a rich tradition of painted *pichwais* grew.

Done on handspun cloth, sized with starch, and painted in vegetable and mineral colors, also mixed with starch (giving the *pichwai* its characteristic strong smell), the *pichwais* have a stylized, rather static format, with frozen figures set in an idyllic landscape of brilliant green trees and midnight-blue skies in which sun, moon, stars, forked lightning, all shine together amid fluffy white clouds; peacocks, parrots and monkeys riot in flowering fields, and swans and storks, fish and turtle swim in lotus-strewn, silver waters. In this verdant paradise, so unlike the bleak, beige Rajasthani landscape, Krishna, the blue eyed boy-god, Radha and the *gopis* play, dance and make love; an eternal pictorial allegory of the soul's yearning for union with the divine.

Today, the *pichwai* tradition goes on and it is not only devotees of Srinathji who buy the cloth scrolls painted by 20th-century descendants of Raja Raj Singh's original court painters. The *pichwai* has become a tourist souvenir, and the love and devotion that went into its creation has been overtaken by commercial avarice and the export boom. Factory-made fabric paints have taken the place of indigo, cochineal, lapiz and orpiment, and stiff, muddy, mass-produced versions are available for sale everywhere, from air-conditioned hotel lobbies to pavement corners.

(65 km) from Udaipur, and a few north of Nathdwara, is Kankroli on the banks of the lake Rajasamund. The temple here resembles in many ways that which stands at Nathdwara, and the idol, Dwarkadhish, Lord Krishna, was installed by Maharana Raj Singh I in 1676.

An additional attraction in the area is the exquisite **Nauchowki**, pillared edifices by the lake's edge, paved with marble. Emperor Aurangzeb wanted to marry Princess Charumati of Kishangarh. The princess appealed to the Maharana of Mewar, Raj Singh I, to help her, and the maharana gallantly married the princess himself. To commemorate this act, Maharani Charumati built a set of white marble steps on the embankment of Lake Rajasamund. Maharana Sajjan Singh in the late-19th century built a palace on the embankment, and laid out the beautiful gardens around it.

The **mansion of Dayal Shah**, a famous Jain prime minister, is truly worth visiting. The sculptures here equal those at Mount Abu in grace. There is an inscription of 1,017 verses in Sanskrit in one of the edifices recounting the history of Mewar. These were inscribed on 27 slabs in 1675. This is the longest literary work inscribed on stone so far known.

Haldighati: The Battle of Haldighati, often called the Thermopylae of Rajasthan, is celebrated in murals and paintings at Udaipur's City Palace. But you may want to visit the battlefield itself–17 miles (27 km) north of this city. It falls well within reach on a trip to Eklingji to the northeast or to Kumbhalgarh to the northwest. The battlefield comprises a narrow pass which runs south to northeast and ends in a plain where the main battle took place. The color of the earth is yellow, like that of *haldi* (turmeric), giving the battlefield its name.

Having learnt the lesson of Chittor and unwilling to be besieged at Kumbhalgarh, Rana Pratap Singh met the armies of the mighty Mughal Emperor Akbar at the height of the Indian summer of June 1576 on this open field. Ranged behind the rana were the Raja of Gwalior, Pathans from the northwest frontier, and Bhil archers and infantry under their leader, Punj. Three times, the intrepid Pratap had to

The ever popular *chilum*.

be rescued as the royal umbrella over his head made him the main target. Eventually, one of the Mewar nobles, Jhala Man, took the umbrella, drawing the attacks away from the rana. Wounded and unattended, Rana Pratap was carried off the battlefield by his loyal horse, Chetak. The horse died of its own wounds, but only after he had seen his master out of danger. A cenotaph stands at the spot at which great-hearted Chetak died. And a more contemporary tribute is a daily train from Delhi to Udaipur named after Rana Pratap's war horse—the Chetak Express.

Of the 22,000 Rajputs ranged against the Mughals, only 8,000 finally fled the battlefield.

Shi Charbhujaji: Twenty miles (30 km) west of Kankroli, to the northwest of Udaipur, is the temple of Shi Charbhujaji built by Rana Mokal in the early 15th century. A grand fair is held here every year, attracting thousands of pilgrims from all over Rajasthan, Gujarat, and neighboring Madhya Pradesh.

Kumbhalgarh: Off a difficult rutted road from Charbhujaji is the fort of Kumbhalgarh. Its very inaccessibility ensured its security as a refuge for Mewar's rulers in times of strife. It was built by the scholarly Rana Kumbha in the mid-15th century. It stands on the site of a more ancient fortress said to have been built by Samprati, a Jain prince, in the second century A.D.

An aerial view shows a fortified city on top of a rocky peak of the Aravalli hills, 3,500 feet (1,100 meters) above sea level, and 700 feet (200 meters) above the closest pass. Enclosed within its crenellated ramparts spreading over eight miles (12 km) are palaces, temples, humble dwellings, fields, water sources, farms and kitchen gardens— everything needed to withstand a long siege.

Kumbhalgarh fell only once in its history, and that to the armies of Emperor Akbar, combined with those of the Rajas of Amber and Marwar. And this siege succeeded because the Mughals contaminated the water supply of the fort.

Kumbhalgarh can only be reached by jeep, but once there, you are rewarded by the counterpoint of lovely, domed palaces with beautiful suites,

A latter-day addition to a traditional folk dance.

231

the temples of Nilkanth, Mahadeo and Kumbhaswami, and the inevitable, lovely cenotaphs, with a view over the rugged scrubby countryside which has seen the battles and blood of many lifetimes.

Ranakpur: The Jain community has a history closely interwined with that of the Hindus of Mewar. Many officials at the Mewar court were Jains, such as the prime minister, Asa Shah. The ranas in turn patronized Jain temples and saints. Rana Kumbha gave a large tract of land to the Jains in the 15th century in a valley deep in the Aravallis where the most magnificent Jain temples in India are to be seen.

Ranakpur stands about 60 miles (100 km) from Udaipur. It is reached by road through Ghasar and Charbhuja, or from Mount Abu via Sirohi.

The Jains built their temples either on hilltops as at Mount Abu and Dilwara, or in deep secluded valleys as at Ranakpur. The central temple in this complex is called **Chaumukha** (four-faced). It is dedicated to the Jain *tirthankara* (revealer of truth) Adinath. It is the most complex and extensive of Jain temples in India, covering over 40,000 sq feet (3,600 sq meters). It has 29 halls containing 1,444 pillars, not one like the other, and each covered with intricate, delicate carvings. The temple is built on a high plinth, encircled by lofty boundary walls with graceful turrets. The temple has two stories which rise in parts to a third.

Seen from the outside and above, there are five spires, each covering ashrine below, the largest covering the central shrine housing the white marble image of Chaumukha. Surrounding the spires are cupolas, each forming the roof of a pillared hall.

The temple has three entrances with double-storied portals, each leading through columned courts into the main halls—a seeming confusion of halls, pillars and courtyards radiating from the central shrine with a hundred pillars.

Some distance away, nestling in the valley, is a sun temple which is polygonal in shape and embellished with a running band of solar deities seated in racing chariots. Farther away are two more temples dedicated to the Jain deities, Neminathji and Paraswadathji, built earlier in the 14th century.

A Jain temple in a forested area.

Rishabdeo: In this village, also called Dhuler, 25 miles (40 km) south of Udaipur, is the celebrated 15th century temple of Lord Rishaddeoji, a reincarnatioin of Mahavira Jain, the founder of the faith. Here, in a charming temple, an image of this Jain saint, three feet high, sits, carved in black marble. On special occasions the image is clothed with the *angia* (a garment studded with precious stones worth severed hundred thousand rupees) presented to the temple by Maharana Fateh Singh.

This Jain saint is also considered a reincarnation of Lord Vishnu, so the idol is worshiped by Vaishnava Hindus, Jains and Bhils with equal reverence. The Bhils call Rishabdeoji, *Kala Baba* (Black Master), as the idol is black.

Galiakot: 168 miles (268 km) south of Udaipur is an ancient town known for its famous mausoleum of the Saint Fakruddin Shaheed of Bohra Muslims. A thousand years ago, a Hindu king, Sidhraj and two of his ministers, Tarmal and Bharmal embraced Islam. Saint Fakruddin was the son of Bharmal. He traveled up from the coast to the Bagar region south of Mewar, preaching the message of Muhammad. He died at the hand of an assassin and a mausoleum marks the site of his burial. Thousands of Bohra Muslims from all over the world come to Galiakot especially at the time of the *urs* on the 27th day of Moharram, to pay their respects to Saint Fakruddin. Bhils in the area also greatly revere him.

Dungarpur: Early in the 13th century, there was serious disruption in the house of Mewar. Samant Singh, the eldest son of Mewar, was cheated of his inheritance by a first cousin. In disgust, he migrated south to Bagar to make his place amongst the Bhils and other Rajput clans. In time, Samant Singh's heirs came to rule all Bagar. Rana Dungar Singh happening upon a rock 7,000 feet (2,100 m) high and five miles (eight km) in diameter, built upon it the city of Dungarpur.

The Dungarpur Sisodias, unlike split-offs in most Rajput clans, did not long remain hostile to the main line at Chittor. They fought alongside the ranas against the invaders from the northwest, giving their full assistance

to Rana Sangra against Babur during the battle of Kanwa. They did, however, later accept Mughal suzerainty, unlike the main Mewar line which resisted until the last, and the princely state of Dungarpur ultimately yielded suzerainty to the British East India Company in 1818.

Dungarpur is certainly off the beaten track for the average tourist, lying as it does in a remote region accessible only via poor roads along rocky ridges, not the most comfortable of climbs for any vehicle. However, if you have an interest in perfectly preserved medieval palaces and wall paintings, you can do no better than to make the effort to get to Dungarpur, south of Udaipur. For here are two palaces which will certainly reward every effort you might make to get there.

The **Juna** (old) **Palace** is built quite obviously along the lines of a fort. Above the sturdy outer walls there is a jumble of turrets, cupolas, terraces, crenellated watchtowers and ramparts with slits for archers and for pouring boiling oil, all designed to withstand a long siege. The whole interior of the palace, as with many Rajput palaces, bursts with color and design in delightful contrast to the severity of the fortifications. The lime plaster walls are polished to resemble marble and covered with mirrorwork, frescoes and Chinese tiles.

All the works of art are very well preserved because they lay inaccessible for many years with no invaders to despoil or deface them.

Udai Vilas, in contrast, is set on a promontory jutting out over a lake. It is reached after a long drive through a jungle filled with wildlife, in itself an enjoyable experience. The area around here is rich in granite of the most remarkable colors, most especially a gray-green variety.

In the center of Udai Vilas palace (which is built of this extraordinary granite) is a courtyard and a pavilion, the most elaborate extravaganza of Rajput architecture in existence. The pillars at the lower level are covered with friezes. Over these are arches supporting curved brackets, twisted pillars, windows around a room of cool marble for women, and an encrustation of balustrades and airy balconies.

Udai Sagar, was excavated by Udai Singh II in the middle of the 16th century in an area of great natural beauty east of, and slightly south of Udaipur, soon after he began work on that city. It is 2.5 miles (four km) long and two miles wide.

It is to Udai Sagar that Rana Pratap of Mewar invited Raja Mansingh of Amber, emissary from the Emperor Akbar, for a picnic. Man Singh's aunt, Maharani Jodh Bai was Akbar's queen and mother of his heir, Prince Salim. Rana Pratap disapproved of this alliance of convenience, as he viewed it, and therefore did not attend the picnic himself, sending his son to deputize for him. To compound the insult, he later got the picnic spot ostentatiously washed with water from the holy Ganga to cleanse it of the defilement it had suffered from the presence of a Mughal lackey.

Ambika Durga Temple: About 90 miles (56 km) southeast of Udaipur, on a regular bus route, is the temple of Ambika Durga in the village of Jagat. It was built in 960 A.D. and is dedicated to the various aspects of the goddess Durga, the protector. *Apsaras* (heavenly nymphs), and *sur-sundaris* (beautiful women) too have been lovingly sculptured in great detail. Several of the sculptures from the temple dating from the 10th to the 16th century can now be seen in the Udaipur Museum.

Jaisamudra Lake: In 1685, Maharana Jai Singh dammed the river Gomti, thereby creating the Jaisamudra Lake, 32 miles (51 km) southeast of Udaipur. It is a little less than nine miles (14 km) long and six miles (10 km) wide and lies in an area of astonishing natural beauty, ringed by hills.

Along the lake's long embankment stand six cenotaphs with delicate carvings of elephants surrounding a small temple dedicated to Lord Shiva.

Chavand: Twelve miles (19 km) west of Jaisamudra lake, in wild country in which the Bhils have always lived, is the village of Chavand where Rana Pratap lived for the last 10 years of his life. He built himself a small palace here and a temple to the goddess Chavandji. In 1597, while hunting a tiger, he suffered an internal injury, and died. Here, in memory of this famous, brave king, who in the true Rajput spirit bowed his head to no man, is a cenotaph—a legend commemorated in stone.

"Taking aim"— detail from wall panel, Dungarpur.

CHITTOR, HOME OF THE BRAVE

About 72 miles (115 km) east of Udaipur, stands Chittor. With its formidable fortifications, Chittor is one of the most fiercely contested seats of power in India.

Bappa Rawal, the legendary founder of the Sisodia dynasty, received Chittor in the middle of the eighth century, as part of the last Solanki princess's dowry. It crowns a seven-mile-long hill, covering 700 acres (280 hectares), with its fortifications, temples, towers and palaces.

From the eighth to the 16th century, Bappa Rawal's descendants ruled over an important kingdom called Mewar stretching from Gujarat to Ajmer. But during these eight centuries the seemingly impregnable Chittor was surrounded, overrun, and sacked three times.

Sacks of Chittor: In 1303 Allauddin Khalji, Sultan of Delhi, intrigued by tales of the matchless beauty of Padmini, Rani of Chittor, of her wit and charm, decided to verify this himself. His armies surrounded Chittor, and the sultan sent a message to Rana Rattan Singh, Padmini's husband, to say that he would spare the city if he could meet its famous queen. The compromise finally reached was that the sultan could look upon Padmini's reflection if he came unarmed into the fort. Accordingly, the sultan went up the hill and glimpsed a reflection of the beautiful Padmini standing by a lotus pool. He thanked his host who courteously escorted Allauddin down to the outer gate—where the sultan's men waited in ambush to take the rana hostage.

There was consternation in Chittor until Padmini devised a plan. A messenger informed the sultan that the rani would come to him. Dozens of curtained palanquins set off down the hill, each carried by six humble bearers. Once inside the Sultan's camp, four well-armed Rajput warriors leaped out of each palanquin and each lowly palanquin bearer drew a sword. In the ensuing battle, Rana Rattan Singh was rescued—but 7,000 Rajput warriors died.

The sultan now attacked Chittor with renewed vigor. Having lost 7,000 of its best warriors, Chittor could not hold out. Surrender was unthinkable. The rani and her entire entourage of women, the wives of generals and soldiers, sent their children into hiding with loyal retainers. They then dressed in their wedding finery, said their farewells, and singing ancient hymns, boldly entered the massive community funeral pyre in the **Mahasati Chowk** and performed *johar*.

The men, watching with expressionless faces, then donned saffron robes, smeared the holy ashes of their women on their foreheads, flung open the gates of the fort and thundered down the hill into the enemy ranks, to fight to the death.

The second sack or *shaka* (sacrifice) of Chittor, by which Rajputs still swear when pledging their word, occurred in 1535, when Sultan Bhadur Shan of Gujarat attacked the fort long since retrieved from the khaljis.

The ruler of Chittor at the time was a 16-year-old prince, Vikramaditya. He was spirited away at dead of night by loyal retainers (the Sisodia line, in any event, had to be continued). His mother, Queen Karnavati, herself led the flower of Rajput chivalry into battle. But the Mewar troops were hopelessly outnumbered.

Rana Sanga's younger son, Udai Singh, saved from the assassin's sword by his valiant nurse Panna at the cost of the life of her own son regained control of Chittor, but only briefly. The last rana to rule there was no match for Akbar, the Mughal emperor.

In 1567, Akbar attacked Chittor. One hundred and fifty feet (40 meters) below the ramparts, at the southern end of the fort, is a hillock called **Mohar Magri** (Hill of Gold Coins) which was raised, the story goes, by Akbar. Because the work was so dangerous, the emperor is said to have paid one *mohar* for each basketful of earth placed on the mound. This raised the hillock to a height sufficient for the Mughal cannons to fire into the fort.

The Road to Chittorgarh: The road up to the fort zigzags steeply for about a mile and passes through seven huge *pols* or gates which are actually a series of strong points, each with watchtowers and great iron-spiked doors. Near **Bhairon Pol** is a cenotaph, a *chhatri* (pillared, open-domed structure), a

239

memorial to Jaimal and his cousin Phatta who fell during the third sack of Chittor. Udai Singh II (who later founded Udaipur) had left Jaimal, a lad of 16 in charge while he went out on guerrilla sorties against Mughal supply lines. Jamil was wounded when inspecting the ramparts. Unwilling to be left to die in bed, he was carried into battle on the shoulders of his cousin Kalia. Linked together thus, they died fighting by Bhairon Pol.

By **Ram Pol** is a memorial to Phatta of Kailwa, who took charge of the fort after the death of Jaimal. Phatta, too, was 16, and had just been married. His father had already fallen defending Chittor. Now Phatta's mother urged him to don the saffron robe and die for Chittor. To free her son from every care, Phatta's mother armed his young bride with a lance and, picking up a sword herself, advanced against the Mughal might. The two women fell within Phatta's sight.

The next day, the women of Chittor committed *johar*, and the saffron-robed men led by Phatt thundered down from the mighty fortress to die fighting.

Thereafter, on each anniversary of this third *shaka*, the Maharanas of Mewar gathered at the Mahasati Chowk in the fort to offer prayers for the souls of those who gave their lives in defense of Chittor.

The Great Builder: The Palace of Rana Kumbha is the first large palace to be seen inside the fort itself. The original was said to have been built by Rana Hamir on regaining the fort after the first sack of Chittor. Chittor remained the true seat of Sisodia power for two centuries after its recovery, reaching its zenith under Rana Kumbha. This was also the golden age of art and architecture in Mewar. For Rana Kumbha was a great builder, not only a musician and poet. He is one of the best-loved warrior kings of Mewar.

To commemorate his victory against the combined might of Sultan Mahmud of neighboring Malwa and Sultan Ahmad Shah of Gujarat, Rana Kumbha erected the **Vijay Stambh** a mile to the west of the palace. It is 120 feet (36.5 meters) high, and has nine stories served by a winding stairway. It is built of limestone and is covered from top to bottom with carvings depicting the social life of the time.

There is another pillar in Chittor called the **Kirti Stambh** dedicated to Sri Adinath Rishabdeo, the first Jain *tirthankara* (enlighted soul). There are several small Jain temples in Chittor. Some Buddhist artifacts dating back to the Maurya dynasty are also to be found.

Rana Hamir also built the **Kalika Mata temple** towards the south end of the fort. It is the oldest there, the original dedicated to the Sun God having been built by Bappa Rawal in the eighth century. It was destroyed during the first sack of Chittor and, regaining the fort. Rana Hamir put in an image of Kalika, the patron goddess of Chittor, to replace that of the Sun God.

The **House of Chunda** stands near the Kalika Mata temple.

Through the southern gate of the Mahasati Chowk a lonely flight of steps winds down to the **Gaumukh** (Cow's Mouth) **reservoir**. Here, through the mouths of cows carved on the rock face, the waters of an underground spring flow into the reservoir on to a sacred *Shivalinga* placed below. The underground passage leading from

Tower of Victory.

Kumbha's palace comes out on the north bank of the reservoir, inside a small Jain temple called the **Paraspath Temple**.

Further south, a road branches off to the southeast, to a compound containing two temples. The **Kumbha Shyam Temple** was built by Rana Kumbha in 1448, and dedicated to the Varaha (boar) incarnation of Lord Vishnu. The smaller temple in the compound is that of the famous devotee of Lord Krishna and the great mystic princess poet, Mira Bai, Rana Sanga's daughter-in-law.

In front of Mira Bai's temple at Chittor is a *chhatri* in memory of Mira Bai's guru, the saint Rai Das of Banaras. In its dome is carved a circle of five human bodies with one head, symbolizing the belief that all castes, Brahmin, Kshatriya, Vaishya, Sudra, even outcastes, can reach God.

An 18th-century reconstruction of Padmini's palace can be seen at Chittor by the pool in which her image was reflected for viewing by Sultan Allauddin Khalji.

Panna, the Diamond of Mewar: In 1536, a year after the second sack of Chittor, Rana Vikramaditya was assassinated by Banbir, a pretender to the throne. Banbir then went after the rana's younger brother, Udai Singh II, who had been left in the care of the nursemaid, Panna, by his mother Karnavati before she performed *sati*.

Bari, the court barber, stole into the ladies' apartments where the young prince lay asleep, to warn Panna Bai of Banbir's evil plot. Panna Bai did not hesitate; she placed the young prince in a basket and handed him to Bari, telling him to wait for her outside the fort, and put her own son in the prince's bed, not a moment before Banbir crashed into the room and demanded the prince. Panna Bai, trembling, pointed to her own child sleeping in the prince's bed. Banbir grabbed the child, swung him high, and disembowelled him with a slash of his sword.

Panna Bai wandered for some time from chieftain to chieftain seeking a protector for her charge. She came finally to Kumbhalgarh where the governor, Asa Shah, a Jain, took Udai Singh under his wing and, when Udai was 15, restored him to Chittor and the throne of Mewar.

IN AND
AROUND KOTA

The city of **Kota** (previously spelt Kotah) is situated at the center of the southeastern region of Rajasthan, a region widely known as Hadaoti (Hadavati), the land of the Hadas. The Hadas are a major branch of the great Chauhan clan of the Agnikula (fire dynasty) Rajputs. They had settled in the hilly terrain of Mewar near Bijolian at Bambaoda in the 12th century A.D. and soon extended their rule, conquering Bundi in 1241 and Kota in 1264 (some writers date both these events exactly 100 years later). Originally, all this formed the Hada state of Bundi with Kota as the *jaghir* (land grant) of the eldest prince of Bundi. Kota later became a separate state in 1624. The domain of the Hadas of Bundi and Kota extended from the hills of Bundi in the west to the Malwa plateau in the east, with a similar expanse north to south. The state of Jhalawar was formed in 1838, out of Kota territory.

Hadaoti is an expanse of fertile plain having rich black-cotton soil. It is watered by several rivers, giving it a verdant look. The largest and the only perennial river of Rajasthan, the Chambal (Charmanyavati), rises in the south and flows through this territory to join the Jamuna in the north. It is a very ancient river which finds mention in the Upanishads and this is evident also from the great 60-mile-(96-km-) long gorge it has cut through the rock in its relentless flow through the millennia. It has several tributaries, the chief ones being the Kali Sind, the Parvan and the Parvati. The Aravalli Hills, which are the most ancient folded mountain range in India, rise near Abu in the south of Rajasthan and one arm crosses Bundi in a south to north direction, while another cuts across Kota from the southwest to the northwest, roughly dividing the plains of Hadaoti from the Malwa Plateau. These hills and the surrounding areas were once thickly forested and teemed with wildlife, including tiger for which Hadaoti was famous. Scenes of hunting in Hadaoti have been captured in the beautiful miniature paintings of the Kota Kalam (school). Unfortu-

Preceding pages: Gagron Fort. Below, wall painting, Kota Fort.

244

nately, most of these jungles have been badly denuded in the course of the last 30 years and there is hardly any animal wildlife left outside the present game sanctuaries.

The climate of this area is very similar to that of the Indo-Gangetic plain, with hot dry summers and delightfully cold winters. The monsoon here is, however, quite unlike and very distinct from the oppressive humid climate of the North Indian plains. Hadaoti receives an average of 35 inches (87.5 cm) of rainfall, which keeps it cool, and gentle breezes ward off the stifling humidity. Good rainfall has made this area the traditional granary of Rajasthan and it also offers good pasturage in times of drought and famine for the livestock from the arid zones of Rajasthan.

Hadaoti has been the abode of early man, as is clearly evident from several well-preserved Upper Paleolithic period cave paintings dating back to 20,000 B.C. Legend links it to the epic periods of the *Ramayana* and *Mahabharata*. Being a fertile and prosperous area, it was the ancient battleground between invading tribes like the Hoons (Huns)

and the Sakas (Scythians) and the entrenched empires of ancient India like that of the Imperial Guptas and of Harsha Vardhana. During the medieval period, Hadaoti attracted the attention of practically every powerful monarch of Delhi, for this region was one of the keys to the gates of the rich kingdoms of Gujarat and Malwa. Numerous passages of arms, battles and sieges have left an imprint on this land. Nevertheless, scores of beautiful temples and countless treasures in sculpted stone are spread over miles in the wilderness; spectacular fortresses and grim strongholds, beautiful palaces and delicate pavilions—all testify to a basic stability and continuity of tradition despite political and military up-heavals.

Kota City: The building of medieval Kota began in 1264 (some say, 1364), when Rajkumar Jait Singh of Bundi slew in battle the Bhil chieftain, Koteya. He raised the first battlements of the *garh* (fort) over the slain chieftain's severed head, treating it as a foundation "stone." Today, the **Sailar Ghazi Gate** stands at this spot. As the fort complex grew, a small settlement out-

A view of Kota town.

side the walls also started growing and it was called Kota after the dead tribal chieftain. The independent princely state of Kota became a reality in 1624, when Rao Madho Singh, the second son of Rao Rattan of Bundi, was made the ruler by the Mughal Emperor Jahangir, an act which was formalized by Emperor Shah Jahan in 1631. Soon Kota outgrew its parent state of Bundi to become bigger in area, richer in revenue and more powerful. It also developed into an artistic, cultural, and religious center.

In 1947, Kota was a town of 60,000 people, the capital city of the state bearing the same name, with graceful palaces and public buildings, with a modern administration, civic amenities and utilities. The population swelled soon after, first with the refugee influx from the Punjab and Sind and later by the growth of industry. Industrialization was possible because of Kota's excellent geographical location. It is situated on the right bank of the Chambal river which provides an abundant supply of water; electricity is generated at the hydro, atomic and thermal power stations sited on the river. It has a rich agricultural hinterland and has ample vacant land available for the growth and spread of industry. Besides, it is on the main broad-gage route of the Western railway between Delhi and Bombay and is within easy reach of Jaipur, Ajmer, Udaipur, Indore, Bhopal and Gwalior by road. There is an air service between Delhi and Kota too. All this makes Kota a premier center of industry, trade and commerce in Rajasthan.

The town has the usual colorful bazaar but its speciality, known throughout India, is the famous *Kota doria sari*, locally known as *masooria* because the original weavers were brought here from the Mysore region in the 17th century by the rulers of Kota who campaigned in the Deccan with the Mughal armies.

Palace-fort: The foremost tourist attraction in Kota is the *garh*. This large complex, also called the **City Palace**, is built in a predominantly Rajput style of architecture. Each successive ruler has added something to it. The *garh* was the fulcrum of all activities in former times, being not only the resi-

Kota Fort from the Chambal river.

dence of the king but also the seat of power, housing the court, the treasury and other offices of state, the arsenal, stables, stores, ateliers, kitchens, a large garrison of troops and hordes of servants. The presiding deity of the House of Kota, the idol of the Lord Shri Brijnathji, and other family deities, also reside here. All ceremonials, functions and *pujas* were held here—and some continue to be held here even today.

In keeping with the times, this property is now administered by the Rao Madho Singh Museum Trust which has a rich collection of art and artifacts showing the cultural heritage of the House of Kota and Hadaoti. Some of the finest examples of the famous *Kota Kalam* can be seen among the wall paintings in the palace and the miniature paintings in the *mahals* (apartments) and in the **Art Gallery**. The museum has a rich collection of paintings, old photographs, arms and armor, *objets d'art*, banners and flags, regalia and a wildlife gallery. There is a small **Government Museum** housed in the **Hawa Mahal** of the *garh* which has an excellent collection of stone idols

and architectural fragments collected from the far corners of the former Kota State.

The entrance to the *garh* is by the **Naya Darwaza** (New Gate) built around 1900. It is flanked by the **Hawa Mahal** and leads to **Jaleb Chowk** (Big Square) where parades used to be held and processions assembled. To the east of the *chowk* is the **Nakkarkhana Darwaza** (Kettledrum Gate) with the shrine of Koteya outside it, and the **Jantar Burj** (Zodiac Bastion). To the west of the *chowk* stand the **Kunwar-bade-ka-Mahal** (Crown Prince's Palace) and the **Bada Mahal** (Big Palace) and the **Hathia Pol** (Elephant Gate) which is typical of Hadaoti in design.

The delicate stonework, the fluted canopies and some fine elephant-shaped brackets supporting carved balustrades give the palace "an air of light elegance." Inside the glittering **Raj Mahal** is the *Raj Gaddi* (throne) on which the kings of Kota were anointed and sat during *durbars* (audiences). The mahal is embellished by medieval gold and glass work on friezes on the walls and silver and mirror work on the ceilings. It has some fine 18th-century

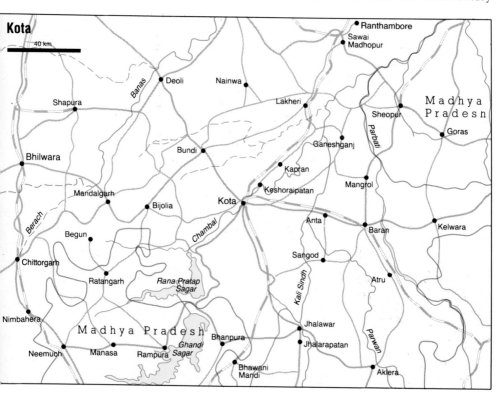

wall paintings in blue-green hues depicting mainly the Krishna Leela theme, a few hunting scenes, beautiful damsels and portraits of all the Kota rulers.

Across the Raj Mahal courtyard is the old **Akhade-ka-Mahal** (Wrestling Palace) in which are displayed the regalia and paraphernalia of state and other articles. Next to it are the various galleries housing the arms and armor, old photographs, miniature paintings and specimens of wildlife. On the first floor is the small room of Arjun Mahal which has bright and cheerfully colored wall paintings in mint-fresh tints, though done in the 19th century. The breezy **Bara Dari** where private parties were held by the ruler and the **Bhim Mahal** which was used as the *Diwani-Khas* (private audience chamber) are also on the first floor. Right on top is **Bada Mahal**, the private living quarters of the king. A large open veranda in front has a rich melange of paintings of various schools and periods set in the glass on the walls, beautiful white marble friezes and an ornate 17th-century ceiling. Inside the main living chamber there

are more wall paintings and some very early (1680) Kota Kalam miniatures. A small, beautiful balcony facing the east, called **Sooraj Gokh** has rich gold and glass and crystal work. The **Chhattra Mahal** has still more wall paintings, with a rare painted ceiling. The imposing pink sandstone latticed **Zenana Mahal** and **Alsi Mahal** were built by Maharao Umed Singh II in the early 1900s. The **Dilkhushal Bagh** (Garden of Heart's Delight) below has a grand white marble *chhatri* (pavilion).

Traditional Kota: The old town was encircled and defended on three sides by a moat and massive fortified crenellated walls, built in two successive rings. They were first erected by Rao Ram Singh in the late 1690s and later enlarged and improved upon by Zalim Singh, the Diwan of Kota around 1790–1800. On the western side, the Chambal river forms a natural barrier.

Kishore Sagar, the picturesque artificial lake in the middle of the town, popularly known as **Bada Talao**, was built in 1346 by Rajkumar Dheer Deh of Bundi. The small island palace, **Jagmandir**, was built around 1740 by the Maharani Brij Kunwar of Kota

Hathia Pol, Kota Fort.

248

who was a princess of Mewar. Below it are the **Chhattar Bilas Gardens** which are beautiful in spring with the **Brij Bilas Palace** and the **Sarbagh** (Park of Royal Chhatris or Cenotaphs) on either side. Some of the *chhatris* are magnificent, with beautiful carved friezes and elephant figures.

Of the many **temples** located in the town, the most famous are those of Mathureshji, belonging to the middle 18th century and of Neelkanth Mahadeo belonging to the 10th century. There are two striking temples with beautiful carvings, just outside the City Palace.

Inside the town, near the Sabzi Mandi (vegetable market) are the tombs of two Pathan brothers, Kesar Khan and Dokhar Khan, who had seized Kota for a brief interlude between 1531 and 1551. Their yoke was thrown off by the famous Rao Surjan of Bundi after a bloody battle. Adjacent to the public gardens is the British cemetery where lie interred some of the officers killed in the Great Revolt ("Mutiny") of 1857.

Amongst Kota's many beautiful buildings, the pride of place, after the *garh*, goes to the **Umed Bhawan Palace** built in 1905, which is the new residence of the Maharaos of Kota. It was designed by Sir Swinton Jacob who designed palaces for other Rajput rulers too. Next comes **Brijraj Bhawan Palace**, formerly the British Residency, built around 1840 on the bank of the river commanding a beautiful view. It became the State Guest House in 1900 and numerous VIPs have stayed there.

The **Herbert College** (Government College) built in local, white stone, the **Crossthwait Institute**, the **Curzon Wylie Memorial** (Mahatma Gandhi Hall) and the **Bailey Clock Tower** are some of the other buildings noted for their beauty. There are some interesting statues; one is a red sandstone, lifesize statue of Colonel James Tod's favorite horse which died here around 1820.

A bronze statue of Maharao Umed Singh II (1889–1940) stands in the **Umed Park**. Beside the river are the new **Chambal Gardens** with a pool. The river once used to teem with crocodiles and gharial but, by 1960, they had almost all been exterminated by widespread netting and ruthless killing. Efforts are now being made to revive

al Mandir.

249

these dwindling populations.

Next to this garden is **Amar Niwas**, a pleasure-palace built on the bank of the river, with old Hanuman and Surya temples near-by. The **Bitheria Kund** (tank) with its 18th-century Shivalinga (phallic symbol of Shiva) and a rare idol of **Panch-mukhi Ganesha** is one of the popular picnic spots of Kota.

Before leaving Kota for nearby sites, for those so inclined, a restful boat-ride on the Chambal would be rewarding.

Near Kota: Six miles (10 km) east of Kota, towards the industrial area, lies the **Kansuan Temple** (Karneshwar Mahadeo). It has a stone inscription dating to 740 A.D. which says that it was built by Raja Shivgana Maurya. Beyond Kansuan, another four miles (six km) away is **Umed Ganj**, a pleasure garden with a pavilion near a lake built by Maharao Umed Singh I (1771–1819). Until the early 1950s, there was a dense forest around it and many types of game were to be seen here but, alas, this is no longer so. Another two miles (three km) further lie the ancient temples of **Dadh Devi** set in a surviving grove of old trees. **Kaithoon** village, the weaving center for the famous Kota *doria* sari is close by. It also has perhaps the only temple in India dedicated to Vibhishan, the brother of the legendary but evil Ravana, of the epic *Ramayana*.

At **Borkandi**, seven miles (11 km) east of Kota, on the road to Gwalior, stands a bridge built by the British in 1818, commonly known as **Tod's Bridge**.

To the west, across the river, four miles away, is the pretty lake and palace of **Abhera**, and just below the bund is the shrine of Karni Mata set amidst a pretty garden. Towards the north, seven miles (11 km) down the river, is the temple village of **Keshorai Patan**. The imposing temple of Keshorai was built by Rao Raja Chattar Sal of Bundi in 1653. There are other ancient temples and statues around here with two stone inscriptions dating to 35 A.D. and 93 A.D.

On the road to Jhalawar, on **National Highway 12**, 14 miles (22 km) south of Kota is the small village of **Alnia**. Across the railway line, beyond the cable factory, is an island in the small Alnia stream where there is a group of rock shelters with paintings dating to the Upper Paleolithic age which

are still in good condition. The whole area is a delightful spot with forest all around.

Towards the south, on the road to Bardoli and Rawat Bhatta Dam, 14 miles (22 km) away is the lovely big **chasm of Gaipar Nath** (Gavyeshwara Mahadeo) with an old Shiva temple set in a deep gorge, with a spectacular view of the rugged beauty of the forests and the *kerais* or cliffs of the Chambal valley.

Bardoli Temples: (35 miles/156 km southwest of Kota): The road to these beautiful eighth to ninth century temples runs along the Chambal river and enters the southern end of the Darah Wild Game Sanctuary through a lovely, thickly wooded *ghat* (hill) section. This cluster of temples set in a grove has some of the best temple architecture that can be seen in Rajasthan. The main temple is that of Ghateshwara Mahadeo. In front is the *mandap* (hall) with exquisite pillars. The entire temple is beautifully adorned with figurines of *apsaras* (nymphs), amorous figures and the Ganga and Yamuna deities carved with delicate grace. On one side is the temple of Ganesh and on the other is that of Kali. There is also a Trimurti temple. Unfortunately, many of the faces of the idols were disfigured by iconoclastic Muslim armies in medieval times.

There is a smaller group of temples set around a small rectangular pool. The famous statue of **Shesh Shayyi Vishnu**, the reclining Vishnu, now on view at the Government Museum, Kota, was originally from here. The entire courtyard is littered with beautiful carved stone pieces from the remains of other buildings, including a *torana* (gate). Some of the good pieces lie in a store near the temples and can be viewed if you get permission from the Archaeological Survey of India Inspector at Kota.

A couple of miles further on is the big **Rawat Bhatta Dam**, with a bronze equestrian statue of Rana Pratap of Mewar dominating the cliff. There is a pretty garden on top which affords a fine panoramic view of the dam and the Pratap Sagar reservoir, the atomic power station across the lake, the rocky bed of the Chambal where it flows down through the Chulia Falls below the dam, the pile of Bhensrodgarh Fort rising above the fields, and the range of hills and forest encircling the whole valley.

Darah Wildlife Sanctuary:(35 miles/156 km south of Kota): This famous forest area was once the hunting preserve of the Maharaos of Kota. It was a rich abode of flora and fauna, especially the tiger. It is called *Darah* for short, the full name being *Mukundarrah*, after Rao Mukund Singh of Kota. *Darrah* in Persian means *pass* and this strategic pass is the only place between the rivers Chambal and the Kali Sind, a distance of nearly 80 miles (130 km), where an army can pass through. Many battles were fought near here between the Kheenchi and the Hada Rajputs.

Beside the *mahals* are the ruins of the ancient **Bhim Chauri temples**. The name is derived from its link with the legendary Bhimsen of Mahabharata fame, as it is believed he got married here to the *rakshasa* (demon) princess Hidimba. There is a stone inscription dating back to the fifth century A.D. which tells us that Dhruvaswamy, a general of the Imperial Guptas, died here fighting against the Hoons (Huns).

Darah was the finest *Shikargarh* in Kota where organized *shikar* (hunting) took place from the early 1700s up to 1955. These forests and the cliffs with the fierce tiger and other animals have been vividly drawn and painted with rare artistry by the master artists of the Kota Kalam. All these forests and places still stand unchanged. These vast jungles sheltered even wild buffalo and rhino in those days, as is evident from old records. It appears unbelievable now, just as today people find it difficult to believe that game was so plentiful here hardly 30 years ago. There are good jungle roads and the visitor can drive in a jeep into the Darah Valley to view the wildlife and also to sit in old *malas* or *odhis* (shikar towers) and watch the animals. There is a Forest Rest House at Darah.

Jhalawar–Patan–Gagron Fort: (50–60 miles/80–100 km south of Kota): The Jhalawar State was created in 1838 and the old cantonment town of Chaoni Umedpura was named as its capital and renamed Jhalawar. The road to Jhalawar goes past Darah through an extensive belt of limestone-bearing strata where the famous Kota stone is

Processions or weddings r announcing *melas* (fairs) often travel between villages.

251

quarried in great quantity. The stone is widely known for its use as flooring and takes a good polish. Jhalawar has a fairly good **Government Museum**. Four miles away is the town of **Jhalara-Patan** (City of Temple Bells). Colonel James Tod mentions counting 108 temples here. Enclosed within its old walls is the famous 10th century 100-foot-high **Surya Temple**, also known as *Sat Sahelion Ka Mandir* (Seven Sisters Temple). The idol of Surya here is perhaps the finest in India. The temple is also full of other lovely sculptures. Nearby is the beautiful group of temples on the Chandrabhaga stream which rises from a spring. They belong to the sixth to 14th centuries. The **Chandramauleshwar Mahadeo Temple** (also called Sheetleshwar Mahadeo) is a fine example of exquisite temple art, which both Cunningham and Fergusson have described as one of the finest in India. It dates to 689 A.D. according to an inscription found here and now lying in Jhalawar Government Museum. The other temples in this complex are equally outstanding. This whole area was a great flourishing center, perhaps

as early as 500 B.C.

On a low mound between the towns of Patan and Jhalawar is the small fortress of Naulakhi, thus called because it took *naulakh* (or nine hundred thousand) rupees to build it in the late 18th century.

Six miles (10 km) from Jhalawar is the famous **fort of Gagron**. It is perched on a low ridge at the confluence of the rivers Ahu and the Kali Sind whose waters surround it on three sides. On the fourth side there used to be a deep moat completing its defenses. Gagron is one among the rare forts which are both a *vana* and a *jala durg*—i.e. both forest-protected and water-protected. It is surrounded by forests and has behind it the Mukundarrah range of hills. Like all major forts, it has had its share of bloody battles and sieges. It was attacked amongst others, by the Sultans of Delhi but it held out against them. It was conquered and sacked in 1423 by Sultan Hoshang Shah of Malwa. The Rajput ladies preferring death to dishonor and servitude immolated themselves. For the next century and a half there was an almost continuous struggle for its possession till,

Surya Mandir, Jhalara Patan.

finally, in 1561, the fort was annexed by Emperor Akbar and it remained under Mughal rule till 1715, when the fort was granted to and came under the rule of Maharao Bhim Singh I of Kota.

Outside the fort walls is the **Dargah** (shrine) **of Sheikh Hamid-ud-din Mithé Shah**, a Sufi saint who lived here till his death in 1353. The shrine is a place of pilgrimage for both Muslims and Hindus.

Close by, on an island, is the *chhatri* of Peepaji, the great, pious Kheenchi poet king of Gagron, who ruled here from 1360 to 1385. His poems are enshrined in the Guru Granth Saheb of the Sikhs. Guru Nanak, the founder of the Sikh faith, once passed through here and paid his respects at Peepaji's shrine. Gagron, apart from its rich historical past, is a lovely spot, with the blue waters of the Kali Sind, the forest and the fields, and a range of hills with precipitous cliffs.

Across the river lies the infamous 300-foot (90-m) high **Gidh Kerai** (Cliff of the Vultures) where state prisoners sentenced to death were executed by being hurled down on to the rocks below.

Kakuni-Bhimgarh (90 miles/145 km southwest of Kota): For those interested in ancient remains there is a fine group of temples and ruins at Kakuni, approximately eight miles (13 km) from Sarthal (which is about 30 miles/50 km from Jhalawar). There is a huge full-length idol of Ganesh and a beautiful eight century Sehastralingam (phallic symbol).

Many idols, figures and carved stones lie scattered around this place which denote that in its time, it was an important urban center. Across the Parvan river spread the ruins of Bhimgarh Fort, built by Raja Bhim Deo in the same period.

Ramgarh: (60 miles/35 km north of Kota): This is another interesting 10th-century site. The road goes via Anta and then along the Chambal Main Right Wing Canal. Ramgarh lies about four miles (six km) from the canal road near Mangrol. It is a curious, hollow, circular hill sprouting out of the plains. Only one entrance leads into the bowl, with a small, pretty lake situated in the middle. A **Shiva temple** stands near the lake, with many beautiful carved pillars and perhaps the best of the

erotic sculptures to be found in this entire region. The place is known as *Bhand Deora* by the local people. This temple was built by Raja Mallaya Varma of the Meda dynasty. On top of the hill, with some 750 steep steps leading up to it, is the small temple of Kishnai Mata. At the side of the hill, near the entrance, are the ruins of an old palace built in medieval times.

Bundi:(14 miles/22 km west of Kota): As already mentioned, Bundi was conquered in 1241 by Rao Deva Singh from the Meena tribe. This was the first step in the establishment of Hadaoti, when the Hadas moved down from Pathar around Bambaoda which was their former home. Bundi takes its name from the *bindo* or *bando nal*, the narrow passage between the rugged hills. The town of Bundi is settled in the cleft and has a special medieval flavor, quite untouched by time.

Under Rao Bar Singh, the work on the **Taragarh** (Star Fort) crowning the top of the 500-foot (150-m) hill was completed in 1354. There are huge water reservoirs inside the fort hewn out of solid rock, strong battlements and bastions, the biggest one called **Bhim Burj**, on which the famous cannon, **Garbh Ganjam**, is mounted.

The fort commands a marvelous view of the plains of Hadaoti towards the east, with the towers and chimneys of Kota vaguely visible in the haze, the lovely azure waters of Jait Sagar below on one side, the quaintly medieval town of Bundi on the other, and the encircling forests and hills all around.

Below Taragarh, hugging the hill, is the big pile of the **Bundi Palace**. It is one of the purest examples of Rajput architecture. To reach it, a flagged ramp goes up from the town. It is an easy climb. One passes through the **Hazari Pol** where a guard of 1,000 troops used to be quartered and the **Naubat Khana** where ceremonial music was played, and enters the inner courtyard of the palace through the **Hathia Pol**, a tall portal surmounted by stone elephants so typical of Hadaoti. The small square inside is called the **Nauthana-ka-Chowk** where nine steeds of the king used to be stalled. Climbing the steep stairs one reaches the **Rattan Daulat**, the Diwan-i-Aam or public audience chamber, which was built by Rao Raja Rattan Singh (1607-31), one

Bundi town below the Paragarh Fort. The Ci▶ Palace is to the left.

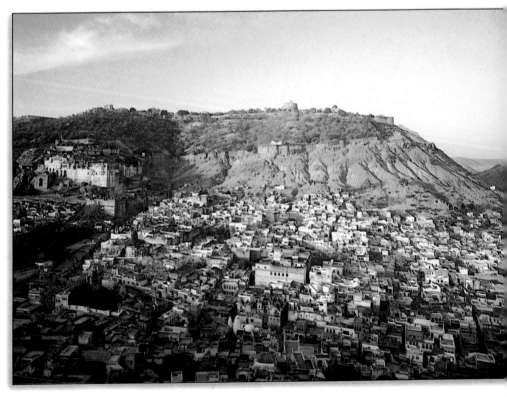

of Bundi's greatest rulers. Here stands a simple white marble *takht* or throne on which the kings were anointed.

The living apartments of the ruler, **Chhattra Mahal**, were built in 1660 by Rao Raja Chattar Sal. Inside, it has beautiful wall paintings of the famous Bundi Kalam. On the other side, across the open courtyard, is the many-pillared **Rattan Mahal** which has four small black stone elephants mounted as capitals on each pillar. Behind this are the **Zenana Mahals**, with the **Badal Mahal** which also has some good wall paintings and typical old Rajput courtyards with shady trees inside. On the other side is the famous **Chittra Shala** built by Rao Raja Umed Singh (1739-70). It is an open quadrangle with cloistered galleries running round it where some of the best of Bundi wall-paintings are to be seen. Depictions of Ras Leela and other mythology, gods and goddesses, processions, court life, and beautiful damsels adorn it. The dominant color is blue-green. Inside, on one side, is a small dark chamber with wall paintings in bright pigments. It can be seen only with the help of a torchlight or a flare. In the Chittra Shala is a small shrine dedicated to the memory of Rao Raja Umed Singh or Shriji Saheb, the saintly ruler of Bundi who abdicated to devote himself to religion and whose wooden sandals are worshiped here. Outside is a small formal Mughal garden overlooking the town.

The rectangular **Naval Sagar**, built by Rao Raja Umed Singh, lies in the middle of the town, between the hills. There is an island temple of Varuna in it which gets submerged when the lake is full.

North of Bundi lies **Jait Sagar** with **Sukh Niwas** (Palace of Bliss) built in 1773 by Rao Raja Bishen Singh. It is situated amidst a pretty garden on top of the *bund*. There are some lovely sculptures in the garden. Rudyard Kipling stayed here and here got inspiration for some of the scenes in *Kim*. At the other end of the lake is the **Sar Bagh** with 66 royal cenotaphs, some most beautifully adorned with statues and marble friezes. **Shikar Burj**, a large shooting tower, stands not too far away, set in deep forest. It was built by Rao Umed Singh who lived here after his abdication.

Adjacent to Shikar Burj are the **Hanuman-ki-Chhatri** and the **temple of Kedareshwar Mahadeo** where Rao Kolhan was cured of leprosy. Perhaps one of the finest pieces of Rajput architecture is **Rani-ki-Baodi**, a step-well built in 1700 by Dowager Rani Nathawatiji, a Solanki princess, mother of Rao Raja Budh Singh. It lies in the town just off the main road as it starts to climb the by-pass. Wide steps lead down to the water under a graceful *torana* (archway) surmounted by a frieze of elephants. The *baodi* was built as a public amenity and the utter neglect in which it lies today is a crying shame. Opposite the well is a small statue of Bundi's most illustrious poet-historian, Suryamal Mishran, who wrote the *Vansh Bhaskar*, a history of the Hadas in the old Dingal language. Another interesting monument is the splendid 64-pillared *chhatri* built by Dhaibhai Devji in 1683 not far from the main road as one enters Bundi from the direction of Kota.

The lovely **Phool Sagar Palace**, is situated six miles (10 km) to the west of Bundi. It was the residence of the last ruler, Maharao Raja Bahadur Singh, M.C. Located between two hills and forests below the bund of the lake, with the waters flowing through the palace, it is a very typical Rajput edifice. Originally, it only had a small pavilion (which still stands) built in 1603 by Phool Lata, a concubine of Rao Raja Bhoj. The rectangular.*kund* or pool was added later by Maharao Raja Ram Singh (1821–89). The palace itself was built in 1945 around this pool and pavilion but retaining the basic essence of the old architecture on the exterior while the interior has all the modern amenities. In decorating the palace, the considerable skills of the Italian POWs, lodged at Deoli 30 miles (50 km) away, were freely engaged.

Bijolian-Bambaoda-Menal-Mandalgarh: (30–50 miles/50–80 km west of Kota): On the main highway to Chittorgarh and Udaipur via Bundi lie three interesting places. The first is **Bijolian**, a great cultural center of the Chauhan kingdom in the 10th century. It has yielded some key stone inscriptions mentioning the full genealogy of the great Chauhan kings and the first historical mention of Delhi, dating back to 1170 A.D. Later it came under Mewar and was a stronghold of a Parmar feudatory. It has some very ancient and beautiful temples, the Shiva and Ganesh temples being of rare beauty. There used to be as many as a hundred temples around this place but now many lie in ruins.

Soon after leaving Bijolian, the road goes past **Menal**, which has another beautiful group of ancient 12th-century temples and ruins of a palace situated at the edge of a deep gorge. Mehal, or *Mahanal* (the great gorge) of ancient times, was a habitation of considerable importance, as is evident from the great ruins. It was the retreat of the great Prithviraj III. One enters the temple of Shiva through a handsome gateway. A big *Nandi* (bull) of stone stands in front of it. The stones of the temples are extensively carved and decorated, showing Lord Shiva and his consort Parvati in different poses, a beautiful frieze of animals, musicians and dancers. There is a breathtaking view of the gorge from the courtyard of the temple.

Opposite the temple complex, across the highway, is a small pretty lake shaded by trees at the edge of a forest.

A few miles along the top of the escarpment, towards the east, the road leads to the ancient temple of **Jognia Mata** and to the nearby old ruins of Bambaoda, the first place where the Hadas took shelter in the 12th century before founding Bundi.

About 20 miles (30 km) away from Menal towards the south, the road branching northeast from the main highway to Udaipur takes one to the old fort of **Mandalgarh**. It was one of the very first of the 35-odd forts built by that great king of Mewar, Rana Kumbha. It guards and protects the heartlands of Mewar. It was occupied by the Mughals in the 1560s and now lies in ruin. It commands a good view from the top of the escarpment.

Sawai Madhopur-Ranthambore National Park: (55 miles/90 km) north of Kota: There is a good road to Sawai Madhopur from Kota via Keshorai Patan, Lakheri and Indargarh where it crosses the Bundi range of the Aravalli Hills and soon reaches Sawai Madhopur.

Indargarh is a small town with a lovely fort climbing the hill behind it. The fort has some good wall paintings but permission to enter needs to be taken in advance from the family who owns it. It was founded in 1605 by

Shiva temple, Bijolian.

Indarsal, a cadet of the Royal House of Bundi and came under Kota State in 1763. Indargarh is also famous for its temple of Bijasan Mata on top of a hill and Kuanwalji (Kamleshwar Mahadeo).

Sawai Madhopur is the well-known entry point to the fort of Ranthambore and also to the well-known National Park known by the same name. It is an important railway junction on the main Delhi–Bombay route and also links Jaipur with a meter-gage line.

The great historic fort of Ranthambore, which rises approximately 800 feet (250 m) from the floor of the forested valley, surrounded by a range of hills, is one of the most ancient and famous in Rajasthan. It is said to have been founded by Raja Jayant in the fifth century. Later, around the eighth century, it became the stronghold of the Yadav kings, from whom it was wrested by the Chauhans in the late 10th century. When Prithviraj III was defeated by Muhammad Ghori in 1192, his son Govinda came here from Ajmer and made it his base.

The fort is sited on a rugged hill running east to west. The hill is flat on top over an area of nearly 350 acres (142 hectares). Massive ramparts, crenellations, mighty gates and bastions have been built all around the hill, rising straight from near-vertical cliffs and rocks. The **Badal Mahal** (Palace of the Clouds) really hangs out in space. There are two recognized ways to ascend to the fort. The northern one is the one used by all now, a steady, paved climb with wide shallow steps going past four fortified gates. The other, the eastern entry, is now locked and not in use. There are several large water reservoirs on top and an underground spring called Patal Ganga which flows throughout the year. The famous 84-columned *chhatri* of king Hamir Deva stands in good shape at the spot where he held audience and entertained. The other palaces, now in ruins, lie spread around. The most famous places today are the ancient temples of Ganesh and of Shiva. Thousands of people worship at the Ganesh temple during Ganesh Chaturthi, when a large *mela* is organized. A postman brings a large sack of wedding invitations to Lord Ganesh's shrine every day, seeking his blessings

agars or mall eservoirs at Nenal (left) nd at Mandalgarh ort (right).

for the unions. There is a spectacular view from the top, with the entire valley, the forests, the hills, the three lakes and pavilions dotting the landscape, spread out below.

Ranthambore is one of the impregnable forts of India which has never been take fairly in battle. It is an important and strategic fort commanding the roads to Malwa and Gujarat from Delhi and is one of the keys to Rajasthan. Many sieges and battles have taken place here during the last 800 years and it has changed masters often. The greatest king to live here and get immortalized in history by his outstanding chivalry, courage and valor was Hamir Deva Chauhan. He gave shelter to fugitive neo-Muslim Mongol commanders of Sultan Allauddin Khalji of Delhi and refused to yield them to the sultan. Soon a large army from Delhi besieged the fort, but it was beaten back. The next time the indefatigable sultan came personally, and, after a prolonged siege, was successful in getting the gates opened only by treachery. The fort thus fell in 1303. The Rajput ladies performed *johar* (self-immolation) and Hamir beheaded himself as a penance and as a sacrifice to Lord Shiva. The fort was sacked and many beautiful buildings destroyed.

Later the great Mughal Emperor Akbar wanted to conquer the fort by force but faced great difficulties in positioning his artillery on top of the adjoining hills. Though heavily bombarded, the fort was ultimately taken over by good diplomacy. Rao Surjan of Bundi, who was the Commander of Ranthambore saw wisdom in negotiating an honorable peace rather than face inglorious defeat and certain death. He surrendered the keys to Akbar in 1569 and secured honorable terms in return. The fort became thereafter a prized Mughal possession.

A most interesting monument to be seen on the road to Jaipur from Sawai Madhopur is the giant monolith elephant. It stands serene in the countryside about eight miles (12 km) out of Uniara near the fortress of Kakor.

Some other places of interest are the great forts of **Shahabad**, **Shergarh** and **Manoharthana** in the Kota area and the ancient Buddhist caves near **Kyasra** in Jhalawar.

Old wooden Gangaur figures, Mandalgarh

RANTHAMBORE NATIONAL PARK

Situated at the junction of the Aravalli and the Vindhya ranges, Ranthambore is one of India's conservation success stories. Since becoming one of the original 11 areas under Project Tiger in 1973, the park has recovered much of its previous natural glory, proving that, with careful management, a once-wooded area which has been reduced to arid scrub can be restored.

In 1973, the then sanctuary of 60 square miles (156 square km) was expanded to 158 square miles (411 square km) with a core area of 65 square miles (169 square km) and later became a national park. In 1984 and adjoining area of 40 square miles (104 square km) to the south became the Sawai Man Singh Sanctuary (named after the last ruling Maharaja of Jaipur).

The blend between nature and history is strong in this park, and like Bandhavgarh National Park in Madhya Pradesh, the fort, the temples, the tanks and other relics are a constant reminder of man's involvement in the area. The fort commanded a large area and up to the late-13th century was the center of a Hindu kingdom. During the 18th century, the area was protected as a hunting area for and by the Maharajas of Jaipur and it is thanks to an extension on this protection that the park exists today.

The fort is the natural focal point of the park with a series of well-established artificial lakes stretching to the north.

Most of the area is covered by typical dry, mixed deciduous forest. The undulating hills have a few bare rockfaces and barren ridges. The area supports a mixed range of birds, mammals and insects. On the gentler hillsides and in the valleys, dhok (*Anogeissus pendula*) is the main tree. The few areas of lush vegetation are around the lakes and have peepul, mango, palas and banyan, creating a thick forest. The huge banyan near Jogi Mahal at the base of the fort is reputedly the second-largest known.

The major predator here is the **tiger** but leopard territories overlap: **leopards** are occasionally seen in areas on the park periphery. **Jackal**, **hyena**, **caracal** and **jungle cat** are also found. In recent years, the tiger population has become increasingly diurnal and there have been many sightings of tigers hunting **sambar** on the banks of the lakes. The greater visibility of this magnificent animal, directly due to careful management, has made the park well-known as one of the easier parks for tiger photography.

Sambar and **chital** are common throughout the park and are found in large concentrations near the lakes along with small groups of **nilgai**. In the scrub and thorn, **chinkara** are often seen. Other animals seen include the **marsh crocodile** (basking on rocks or along the banks of the lakes), **wild boar**, **ratel**, **monitor lizard** and **sloth bear**.

The rich birdlife reflects the range of flora on which it feeds. During the winter months the lakes attract a variety of migrant water birds.

The park entrance is only eight miles (13 km) from Sawai Madhopur station on the main Bombay-Delhi line. A meterguage line connects Sawai Madhopur with Jaipur (100 miles/162 km).

Jogi Mahal.

BHARATPUR, DEEG AND DHOLPUR

Bharatpur: This area occupies an important place in the cultural history of Rajasthan. It was closely associated with the ancient kingdom of *Matsyadesa*. During the fifth and fourth centuries B.C., the region covered by Bharatpur, Dholpur and Karauli formed part of the Sursena Janpada with its capital at Mathura to the northeast. Many late Mauryan (second century B.C.) sculptures and remains of pottery have been found at Noh on the Agra road east of Bharatpur and can be now seen in the local museum.

Unlike most of Rajasthan, this area is populated by Jats, people of the land, who, over much of northwestern India, form the backbone of the agricultural population. They were settled in this region long before either the Rajputs or the Marathas became the dominant powers. In many areas, Jat chieftains made marriage alliances with the new overlords, but they continued to harass the Mughal armies and often revolted against the Rajput princes.

During the late 17th century, a Jat headman from the Sinsinwar clan called Churaman formed a loose force of fellow Jats and began to systematically raid the surrounding countryside, but the Mughal governor in Agra retaliated and in turn destroyed many Jat villages. Under Badan Singh, the Jats regrouped and by 1752 controlled a large area west of the Jamuna river between Delhi and Agra. The Amber (Jaipur) rulers gave Badan Singh the title of Brij-Raj and in 1725 the building of the fort of Deeg with gardens and palaces was started. In 1732 Badan Singh's son and regent, Suraj Mal, began work on the Bharatpur Fort and building continued for the next 60 years.

The **Bharatpur Fort** was, perhaps, among the most formidable in India at that time and in 1805 Lord Lake unsuccessfully laid siege to it for four months and had to retreat after suffering the largest losses experienced by the British in India up until then. Maharaja Ranjit Singh took advantage of this and Bharatpur was the first state in India to sign a treaty of "Permanent Equal Friendship" with the East India Company.

Throughout the 19th century Bharatpur remained at peace and this continued till independence came to the subcontinent. In 1948, four princely states, Alwar, Bharatpur, Dholpur and Karauli, formed the *Matsya Union* with the Maharaja of Dholpur as *Rajpramukh* and in May 1949 the Union joined the new state of Rajasthan.

The local language around Bharatpur is the *Braja Bhasha* dialect of Rajasthani while south, toward Karauli, the *Dang* dialect is more widespread.

Music, Dance and Drama: As with most of Northern India, festivals are celebrated throughout the year and a few have particular local significance. The *Ram-Leela* performances are most impressive and, while principally performed during *Dussehra*, are also sometimes performed on other more local occasions.

Bharatpur is close to the Braj country of Lord Krishna's birth and childhood. The *Ras-Leela* depicting the life of Krishna is performed by professionals drawn from the Rai community. During the *Narsingh Chaturdashi* festival, the dancers and other performers wear masks depicting various gods, saints and demons. The *khyal* form of rural entertainment is popular throughout Rajasthan but the *nautankis* (village actors) of Bharatpur, using a well-built stage and colored backcloths, have developed their own speciality of beating *nagaras* and a form of dancing including high, and often violent, jumps, earning the name *Takhta-Tod*. The stories depicted are usually centered on the lives of Ram and Krishna.

Bharatpur is well located and there is a good road from Jaipur to the west and the 115 miles (150 km) can be covered in about three-and-a-half hours. To the east is Akbar's capital, Fatehpur Sikri (11 miles/18 km) and Agra (32 miles/50 km). To the north, Delhi is only 125 miles (184 km) away. Besides being at the hub of an excellent road network, Bharatpur is a junction on the main Delhi–Bombay railway (with onward connections to Sawai Madhopur and Kota to the south) and the meter-gauge line running east–west between Agra and Jaipur.

The Iron Fort: While most visitors to

Bharatpur now visit the area for the nearby bird sanctuary, the **Lohagarh Fort** is still the focal point of the town. The fort takes its name (*lohagarh*: iron fort) from its supposedly impregnable defenses. Its ingenious design gave it an awesome reputation. Surrounded by two massive earthen ramparts, each encircled by a moat, the mud walls were so thick that all missiles were absorbed and the inner fort remained intact. The moats were 150 feet (45 m) wide in part and up to 50 feet (15 m) deep. Now all that remains is part of the inner mud wall (the original outer wall was leveled in 1826) and the moat surrounding the masonry walls. The outermost wall was originally seven miles (11 km) in circumference and took eight years to complete. A cannon still points defensively to the northeast from a remnant of the mud and rubble wall.

The entrance to the fort from the north is over an ancient brick and stone bridge with pointed arches and through the **Assaldati Gate**. On either side of the gate are fading murals of elephants. This "Gate of Seven Metals" which possibly belonged to the Sisodia Rajputs of Chittorgarh but was removed to Delhi by Allauddin Khilji and, with the south gate more often known as the *Loha Darwaza* (Iron Gate), was brought from Delhi by Maharaja Jawahar Singh in 1764.

The old walled city within the fort forms an irregular oblong and the inner fort contains three palaces and many new (and not very attractive) buildings. Numerous local government offices now occupy part of the fort.

The **palace** within the fort was, like many throughout Rajasthan, built by different generations. Most of the buildings adopted Rajput and Mughal styles but in simplified forms, reflecting the Jat lack of ostentation. Of the three palaces, the central building is the oldest, being built by Badan Singh. Part of it now houses the museum. The **Kamra Palace** to the west, part of which is now with the museum, previously housed the Bharatpur State armory and treasury. To the east is the raja's palace or **Mahal Khas**, including the royal apartments built by Maharaj Balwant Singh (1826–53). The rooms are compact, with stone-latticed windows set in long, arched alcoves. Many **Central portion of Bharatpur Fort.**

walls are still covered with multi-colored, painted designs. On the ground floor is a set of *hamams*, sunken baths for both hot and cold water. These rooms with painted walls and domed roofs are, along with the rest of the royal apartments, in strong contrast to much of this otherwise unadorned fort.

The State Museum: Primarily an archaeological collection, this museum was founded in 1944 by Maharaj Sawai Brijendra Singh. While overshadowed by the older and better known collections of Mathura and Agra, it is certainly worth visiting. It has some extremely interesting sculptures, including a late Gupta Shiva–Parvati from the eighth century, a Jain tirthankara dated c.1020 and a 10th-century Ganesh. Perhaps the most interesting piece is a second-century red sandstone Shivalinga. From the nearby village of Noh are terra-cotta toys from the first-to-third-century Kushan period.

Two other places of interest within the fort are the two bastions. The central tower known as the **Jawahar Burj** was built in 1765 to commemorate a successful assault on Delhi. The coronation ceremony of the maharajas of Bharatpur took place here and nearby is an Iron Pillar about 12 inches (30 cm) in diameter with the names of the rulers from the time of Lord Krishna to the present inscribed on it in Hindi. The other tower, known as **Fateh Burj**, was built to remind the fort's inhabitants of the successful defense of Bharatpur from the British attack in 1805.

Other than the fort and the bird sanctuary, there is little of interest in Bharatpur. A house built by Begum Sumroo was later used as a girls' school. Begum Sumroo played an important and colorful role during the late-18th century when she supplied troops to the Bharatpur rulers under the command of her German mercenary husband, Walter Reirhardt.

The villages of **Noh**, a few miles to the east, and **Mallah** to the south, have both produced interesting archaleological finds, many of which are now in the museum. At Noh a seven-foot-(2.15 m) high *Yaksha* sculpture of the Kushan (first century) period was found, similar to the one in the Mathura museum. About 25 miles (40 km) southeast of

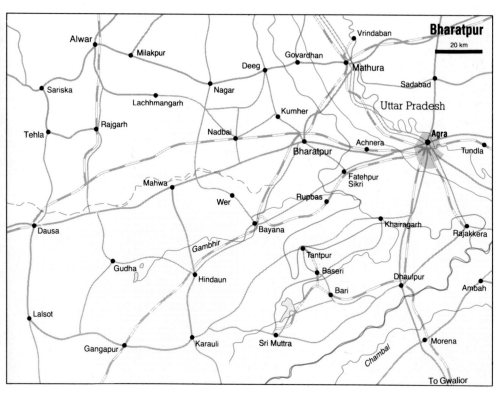

Bharatpur, at **Rupbas** is a 27–foot-(8–m) long sequence of rock-cut images showing "Baldeoji, his consort Reoti, Lakshmi-Narayan and the Pandava hero Yudhishthira with Vishnu." The now ruined, but still attractive, palace and tank at Rupbas was used as a shooting lodge by Akbar on hunting visits from Fatehpur Sikri.

Deeg: The road north of Bharatpur goes via Kumher to Deeg (22 miles/34 km). Kumher was founded by Kumbi Jat of Sinsini and was at one time the second capital of Bharatpur State. Badan Singh in 1722 built the palaces and many of the fortifications which are now impressive ruins to the east of the road. The now small and dusty village was in 1754 the site of an important siege when Suraj Mal withstood a combined Mughal and Maratha army of over 80,000 men. During the siege, one of the opposing generals, Khandeo Rao Holkar, was shot and, with his typical decency and generosity, Suraj Mal later built an impressive *chhatri* (cenotaph) in his memory at the spot where he fell.

Deeg is now a small agricultural town with a busy, dusty market. It is also approachable from either Kosi or Mathura (23 miles/36 km) on the Delhi–Agra highway. Any visitor going by road from Delhi to Bharatpur is well advised to take the slower (and slightly rougher) road via Deeg. When approached from the south, the massive fortifications divert the road. The **fort** forms part of the town's fortifications and massive masonry walls tower up to 85 feet (28 m) above a moat 50 feet (17 m) broad. The fort has 12 bastions, the largest on the north-west corner, known as **Lakla Burj** and still mounted with cannon. The only gate is on the northern side and within the fort today still lie some locally cast guns and a partially ruined, simple *haveli*.

Deeg is justly known for its palaces and gardens begun by Badan Singh and laid out by Suraj Mal following the tradition brought to India by the early Mughals. The palace pavilions and gardens are laid out with an excellent sense of balance. The present area is probably only half what was originally planned with two complementary gardens to be linked by a broad terrace. However, what was built is exciting and well preserved, with the buildings

Gopal Bhawan Deeg.

266

forming a large rectangle enclosing the gardens and two large tanks at the eastern and western ends.

The largest and most impressive building, **Gopal Bhawan**, was built around 1763 and overlooks the **Gopal Sagar** (tank) to the west. It is flanked by two smaller pavilions (Sawan and Bhadon—named after the two monsoon months) which purport, in their curved roofs and pillars, to simulate a large pleasure barge, and is fronted by an arch for a swing and two marble thrones with the gardens beyond. Seen from the garden, Gopal Bhawan seems only two stories high while, actually, two lower levels also overlook the water. Many rooms in Gopal Bhawan still have their original furniture and since few tourists visit Deeg, it has been possible to maintain the palace very much as it was when the *maharaja* and his family occasionally stayed here up to the early 1970s. On the northern side of the garden is a large audience hall known as **Nand Bhawan**, while opposite, to the south, is **Krishna Bhawan**. The focal point of the garden is the pillared summer pavilion (**Keshav Bhawan**) with its ingeniously designed waterworks overlooking Roop Sagar to the east. Five hundred fountains, many of which still play during local festivals, used to spout colored water on special occasions against a backdrop of lavish firework displays.

At the southwestern corner is **Suraj Bhawan**, completed by Suraj Mal's son, Jawahar Singh (1764–68). Unlike most of the other buildings which use cream-colored sandstone, Suraj Bhawan is built of white marble, decorated with a mosaic and inlay of semi-precious stones. Much of this marble, including the inlay, was probably looted from Delhi.

Many of the fountains and decorations were also brought to Deeg as booty after Suraj Mal's occupation of Delhi and Agra. The swing in front of Gopal Bhawan was most probably built for Shah Jahan in 1630. A black marble "bed" used for laying out a dead ruler was brought from Delhi and is now in Gopal Bhawan.

One of the original buildings built by Badan Singh, **Purana Mahal**, at the southeastern corner, has a display of Rajput wall paintings, many in-

The Bharatpur family chattris, Govardhan.

KEOLADEO GHANA NATIONAL PARK

In the middle of the 18th century a small reservoir was created three miles (five km) to the southeast of the Bharatpur fort. The building of the Ajan Bund and the subsequent flooding of this natural depression has created during the subsequent 250 years one of the world's most fascinating and spectacular bird reserves. This man-created wilderness was developed and for many years was the shooting preserve of the Maharajas of Bharatpur until the last ruler gifted it to the Rajasthan Government and it became a sanctuary in 1956. It is commonly referred to as the Bharatpur Bird Sanctuary.

Despite its becoming a national park in 1982, human pressures on it are still tremendous. A stone wall built in the late 1970s has helped control grazing by large numbers of domestic buffaloes and cattle, but illegal collection of fodder continues. Of the total area of only 11 square miles (29 square km),

about one-third is, after a satisfactory monsoon, under some one-to-1.5 meters of water.

The range of flora in the park is extraordinary for such a small area. Dozens of grasses provide cover, nest material and food to a range of birds and mammals. Trees range from the thorny acacia or babul which dominates much of the park, to ber, khajur and khejri. Babul and kadam are nesting trees for many bird species. The lakes with their rich range of floating plants, algae, reeds, flowering plants and aquatic grasses provide food and cover to millions of crustaceans, amphibians, insects and fish in such enormous quantities that thousands of birds can depend on the area for raising their young and as a winter home.

From August through November, thousands of indigenous water birds breed and raise their young here. **Painted storks**, **spoonbills**, **cormorants**, three kinds of **egret**, **open-billed storks**, **purple herons**, **night herons** and **sarus cranes** are some of the main breeding species. From the onset of the monsoon, nest-building begins, and by October all eggs will have been laid and young of all sizes demand a constant supply of food.

In early October, the first migrants arrive from the high plateaus of Central Asia, Mongolia, and Siberia. The **ducks**, **geese** and **waders** arrive first. Raptors, including the **steppe eagle**, **golden eagle**, **osprey** and **harrier** follow, and finally, the rare **Siberian Crane**. Some 35 to 40 of this beautiful species feed on sedge tubers till early March when they return to Central Siberia.

The scrub forest and grassland of the park support a range of animals, including **nilgai**, **sambar**, **wild boar**, **feral cattle**, **civet**, **jacket** and the **rhesus macaque**. **Fishing cat**, **jungle cat**, **otter** and **mongoose** are among the smaller species seen.

A metaled road runs through the park from the north gate near the main Agra-Jaipur road. Vehicles are now allowed only as far as the tourist and forest lodges. A good network of raised paths along tree-lined **bunds** give good cover for bird-watching and the visitor can walk through much of the park along the bunds. Visting the park at any time of the year is a rewarding experience.

Spoonbill in breeding plumage.

fluenced by the Mughal schools. This building is now used as a government office and some paintings are now obscured but it is worth visiting as an example of the substantial and simple style of Jat building.

About nine miles (12 km) east of Deeg, en route to Mathura, is the pilgrimage center of **Govardhan**. The town is small and lies along a narrow range of hills which Lord Krishna is fabled to have held aloft on the tip of his finger for seven days and nights to protect the people of Braj from the flood poured down on them by Indra. The focal point of the town is the large stone tank called **Mahasi Ganga** which is surrounded by houses. The **Harideva Temple** nearby was built by Raja Bhagwan Das of Amber (Jaipur) during Akbar's reign. The temple is fairly large and worth visiting. On the opposite side of the tank are the *chhatris* of two rajas of Bharatpur (Ranjit Singh and Balwant Singh) in which colorful paintings on the ceilings of the pavilions depict incidents in the rajas' lives. The series of paintings of unsuccessful assaults by Lord Lake on Bharatpur Fort in Ranjit Singh's *chhatri* is especially vivid.

On the road north of Govardhan to **Radha Kund** (two miles/3 km) is the magnificent *chhatri* erected in honor of Suraj Mal who was killed in 1763 at Shahdara to the east of Delhi. The paintings in the *chhatri* are now in poor condition but, interestingly, show French officers in Suraj Mal's service. Beside the *chhatri* is a tank, **Kusum Sarovar**, and an extensive garden lies behind the buildings.

South to Karauli: Southwest of Bharatpur, Suraj Mal also started to build a fort, palaces and gardens at **Wer** (30 miles/48 km), on lines similar to those of the Deeg complex. Situated between two ranges of the Aravalli hills, 26 miles (41 km) south of Bharatpur on the bank of the Gambir river, is the once-famous but now dusty town of **Bayana**. Babur defeated the Sanga Rana of Chittorgarh nearby on March 16, 1527. Of the numerous Mughal buildings in the town, most are now in a poor state, but there is still a fine gateway to a garden which was laid out by Jahangir's mother when Akbar visited the town in 1601. The now ruined fort was described by Babur in his memoirs as one of the most famous in India. A few miles east, in the Baretha hills, famous for their fine stone, is the man-made lake, **Kishan Sagar**, formed by damming the Kakund river. During the winter months, the lake is often the home of numerous species of migrating birds, in addition to the many resident species who breed here during the post-monsoon months in the network of its picturesque backwaters. On the eastern ridge, a small, attractive palace built during the 1920s overlooks the lake.

Karauli, 38 miles (61 km) further, was once the capital of a small princely state (belonging to the Jadon Rajput clan) that came together with Bharatpur, Dholpur and Alwar in 1948 to form the Matsya Union.

Dholpur: Southeast of Bharatpur, on the National Highway between Agra (36 miles/57 km) and Gwalior (40 miles/64 km) to the south, is the capital of the former princely state of Dholpur. The state was created in 1805 when the British governor-general gave the last Jat Rana of Gohad (a state founded in 1505) three of the defeated Scindia's districts north of the Chambal river and gave Gwalior and Gohad to the Scindia. The ruling family belonged to the clan of Bamrolian Jats who took this name from Bamroli near Alwar which was their adopted home during the 14th century.

Dholpur is today a quiet, agricultural town, famous for its locally-quarried sandstone of which the palace and many of the older buildings are built. This sandstone is finely grained, dark reddish-purple in color and easily worked. It hardens on weathering and is therefore often used for building. The same stone was later used in the building of New Delhi. To connect Delhi with the stone quarries at Barauli, a six-mile (10-km) light railway was specially built by the Imperial Delhi Committee. The High School now uses a building originally built as a mausoleum for one of Akbar's generals, Sadik Muhammad.

Because of the ford and ferry point a few miles south of the town and its proximity to the old Mughal capital at Agra, the area around Dholpur has been the scene of many crucial battles. In 1658, three miles (5 km) east of the town, at Ranka Chabutra, the last great Mughal Emperor, Aurangzeb, defeated his elder brother, Dara Shikoh, during a war of succession. The Chambal river has long been a natural boundary between the territories of the Rajput states and those of the Marathas to the south. For hundreds of miles, a labyrinth of ravines, extending up to four miles from the river banks, the length of the Chambal has been the home and refuge for deposed princes, bandits and thieves. During the 1970s, projects to seed the ravines from the air and redevelop the agricultural potential of the area have brought security and comparative prosperity to the area, with erosion now beginning to be checked. On the north bank, a large, impressive, and now ruined fort, dominates the old ferry point.

Babur's Lost Garden: At the village of **Jhor** 10 miles (16 km) from Dholpur, in 1978, Elizabeth Moynihan, the wife of the then U.S. Ambassador to India, rediscovered the oldest Mughal garden in the subcontinent. In August 1527, on a large outcrop of sandstone above the dry bed of a lake, Babur started building a garden. The ridge stretches north and 60 miles (96 km) away along it, Babur's grandson, Akbar, built his splendid city of Fatehpur Sikri. The lake bed (formed by an ancient dam built by Sikandra Lodi in about 1500) and part of the garden are now farmed by the villagers. Few of Babur's buildings and little of his garden, which must have covered many acres, have survived. The surrounding walls have now gone, but part of the watercourse cut from a single outcrop of sandstone remains unaffected, although damaged. Originally there were three water channels, but the one remaining can be traced: the water flowed from a small, octagonal pool on the edge of the upper terrace, down through a large hexagonal pool on the central terrace, on to a large central pool and the gardens below.

The lotus garden is the first example of Mughal design incorporating Indian skills with Central Asian concepts of garden architecture. A plain rectangular structure now used as a stable by a villager was Babur's hot bath and remains almost as built in 1528. The sunken bath is of white stone. To the west are many abandoned Mughal wells and one pavilion which is now a Hindu shrine. Nearby is a large pre-Mughal tank with three sets of steps,

Flags hoisted during the Kaila Devi Mela, Karauli.

Flags hoisted during the Kaila Devi Mela, Karauli.

each 100 feet (30 m) long.

A mile away is **Mach Kund**, a deep, spring-fed lake surrounded by over a hundred temples, deserted for most of the year but the site of an annual pilgrimage.

Wildlife and Gardens: Eighteen miles (29 km) southwest of Dholpur, over a dry, sparsely-populated ridge of sandstone, is the small town of **Bari**. The local headquarters of the *tahsil* now occupies the fort built in 1286 by the Ghori king, Firoz Shah. Three miles (five km) south is the **Talabe Shahi lake** where duck shoots previously took place and which now forms part of the **Van Vihar Wildlife Sanctuary** together with the adjoining **Ram Sagar Sanctuary**. The Ram Sagar lake forms part of an extensive irrigation system constructed by Maharaja Rana Ram Singh over the years 1901–11.

Beside the Talabe Shahi lake is a long and attractive series of buildings known as **Kanpur Mahal**. Built for Shah Jahan in about 1640, the palace was never occupied. Half of it is now a police post and the other half (fitted with some fascinating Victorian plumbing by a previous *maharaja*) is now a Public Works Department guest house.

These handsome red sandstone buildings along the west shore, between the *bund* (to the north) and a small wood, are reflected in the brilliant blue of the lake which, after a good monsoon, fills and attracts a wide range of waterbirds.

A double row of octagonal sandstone *chhatris* with deep eaves and arches line the *bund*. The pavilions of the gardens are to the north, while at the end opposite the building is a now-deserted, walled garden.

The area covering the old princely states of Bharatpur, Karauli and Dholpur has a fascinating ambience of history. Many small and apparently insignificant villages were once the site of a small hunting lodge or garden and perhaps the scene of a major battle. Because of the area's proximity to the great Mughal capitals of Agra, Delhi and Fatehpur Sikri, many of the influences on the region came from these cities to the north and east rather than from the arid semi-desert of Rajasthan to the west.

271

TRAVEL TIPS

GETTING THERE

BY AIR

Most visitors arriving by air to any part of India – in particular Rajasthan – do so through the international airports at Delhi (**Indira Gandhi International Airport**) or Bombay (**Sahar**). The other international airports at Calcutta, Madras, Trivandrum, Hyderabad and Goa have fewer international flights and no direct connections to Rajasthan. Most tours use Delhi as a gateway while Bombay is a busier airport for business traffic.

Both Delhi and Bombay airports are fairly new and are still being upgraded to create improved passenger facilities and handling.

Customs and immigration formalities are fairly quick although, as with many countries, incoming baggage is often X-rayed by customs before reaching the collection belt. Photographic film and magnetic tape may, as a result, be liable to damage due to this repeated process, and it is therefore advisable to hand-carry film and tape or pack them in lead bags.

Porters are available at most airports and a fixed fee of approximately Rs. 2 per piece of baggage is paid at a desk near the exit. A tip of Rs. 5, or Rs. 1 per piece, is also expected but is not obligatory.

Delhi and Bombay airports have duty-free shops in the arrival hall.

CONNECTING TO RAJASTHAN

Both Indian Airlines and Vayudoot have daily flights to the important centers of Rajasthan. **Indian Airlines** has at least two flights a day from both Delhi and Bombay to Jaipur with stops en route at Udaipur and Jodhpur. Ahmedabad in Gujarat, Aurangabad in Maharashtra and Agra and Varanasi (Banares) in Uttar Pradesh are also

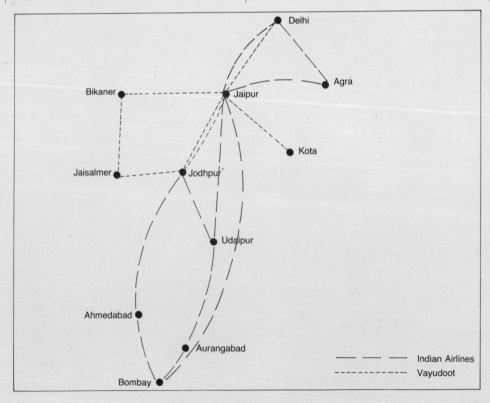

connected to Jaipur by Indian Airlines. **Vayudoot** connects Delhi with Kota, Bikaner and Jaisalmer via Jaipur sometimes enter the airlines' schedule.

BY RAIL

Rajasthan has two railway systems. Many of the old princely states developed a meter-gauge system and this today constitutes most of the network. However, the main Delhi-Bombay line runs through eastern Rajasthan and this is the "broad" or 1.676 meter-gauge. The broad-gauge line links Delhi via Mathura, with Bharatpur, Bayana, Sawai Madhopur and Kota before crossing into Madhya Pradesh and on through Maharashtra to Bombay. The meter-gauge system is extensive throughout the state and provides an interesting way to travel.

MAHARAJA SALOONS

Many of the princely states had their own carriages for officials and maharajas to travel in. Some of these are now available for hire through the railway authorities and can be attached to scheduled trains on certain sectors. To do this, at least two months' notice is required and you need to liaise with the **PRO**, Northern Railway, Baroda House, New Delhi 110001.

The most successful and by far the best organized service uses the Maharaja of Jodhpur's saloons and connects Jodhpur with Jaisalmer. Started in 1978, the service is well established. It is important to remember that these are not luxury saloons, they were locally built in 1942 and are not air-conditioned. However, during the cool winter months from November to March, air-

DISTANCES IN KILOMETERS BETWEEN SELECTED TOWNS

	AGRA	AHMEDABAD	AJMER	ALWAR	BHARATPUR	BIKANER	BOMBAY	BUNDI	CHITTORGARH	DELHI	GANGANAGAR	GWALIOR	INDORE	JAIPUR	JAISALMER	JODHPUR	KOTA	MOUNT ABU	UDAIPUR
AGRA		855	368	172	56	584	1208	438	579	200	612	119	606	230	910	573	446	757	604
AHMEDABAD	855		526	798	658	916	551	485	364	886	1148	852	382	625	590	586	525	221	251
AJMER	368	487		272	313	447	1038	163	191	399	679	487	755	138	535	205	200	375	276
ALWAR	172	798	272		116	462	1343	347	463	163	527	291	941*	141	762	477	383	647	551
BHARATPUR	56	658	313	116		497	1350	366*	523*	251	760*	175	974*	174	854*	537*	403	707	581*
BIKANER	584	916	447	462	497		1379	546*	611	538	232	703	1190	354	326	242	598*	569	577*
BOMBAY	1208	551	1038	1343	1350	1379		1041	928	1408	1611	1089	602	1176	1141	1190	1076	766	802*
BUNDI	438	485	163	347	366	546	1041		121	465	794	364	592	192	653	368	36	418	233
CHITTORGARH	579	364	191	463	523	611	928	121		583	908	485	379	322	657	372	158	297	112
DELHI	200	886	399	163	251	538	1408	465	583		412	319	806	261	864	604	505	767	635
GANGANAGAR	612	1148	679	527	760	232	1611	794	908	412		731	1218	586	558	474	830	994	809
GWALIOR	119	852	487	291	175	703	1089	314	485	319	731		487	349	1002	692	327	786	601
INDORE	606	382	755	941	974	1190	602	593	379	806	1218	487		800	974	960	556	476	441
JAIPUR	230	625	138	141	174	354	1176	192	322	261	586	349	800		680	343	244	565	374
JAISALMER	910	590	535	762	854	326	1141	653	657	864	558	1002	974	680		330	734	552	665
JODHPUR	573	586	205	477	537	242	1190	368	372	604	474	692	960	343	330		362	265	305
KOTA	446	525	200	383	403	598	1076	36	158	505	830	327	556	244	734	362		459	274
MOUNT ABU	737	221	375	647	707	569	766	418	297	767	994	786	476	565	552	265	459		185
UDAIPUR	604	251	276	551	581	577	802	233	112	635	809	601	441	374	665	305	274	185	

* VIA Jaipur

conditioning is not required (in fact, in late December and January, it is often cold).

The saloons have accommodation for a maximum of 20 people: one saloon has seven coupé compartments fitted with individual wash basins and two bathrooms; a second saloon has three larger coupé compartments, one bathroom, a lounge and pantry. These two inter-connecting saloons are attached to the night trains between Jodhpur and Jaisalmer – a 9½ hour journey. A dining saloon is permanently based at Jaisalmer. For further information and costs, write to: The General Manager, Maharaja Saloons, Umaid Bhawan Palace, Jodhpur 342006, Rajasthan (Tel: 22361; Tlx: 0352-202).

PALACE ON WHEELS

Using 13 original saloons built for various maharajas and British viceroys, the palace on wheels operates week-long tours linking Delhi with Jaipur, Chittorgarh, Udaipur, Jaisalmer, Jodhpur, Bharatpur, Fatehpur Sikri and Agra before returning to Delhi. There are departures every Wednesday from Delhi. The tours are organized by **Indian Railways** and **Rajasthan Tourism** and include full catering throughout, sightseeing tours at the places of interest en route, entrance fees etc. Attached to the train are two restaurant cars, and an air-conditioned carriage which serves as a bar and library. For further information contact: Central Reservation Office, Palace on Wheels, Rajasthan Tourism Development Corporation, Chanderlok Building 36, Janpath, New Delhi 110001 (Tel: 332-1820, 332-2332; Tlx: 031-63142).

BY ROAD

The road network throughout the state is extensive and in parts extremely good. Some roads, such as the one between Delhi and Jaipur, are becoming increasingly busy, which sometimes makes driving rather tiring.

Rajasthan Roadways offers an extensive bus service and there are deluxe coaches (many unfortunately showing video films extremely loudly) linking major towns. In Delhi, buses leave every few hours for Jaipur from Bikaner House, near India Gate, New Delhi. The journey takes about 4½ hours.

Self-drive car hire has been introduced in some Indian cities in mid-1990 but it is not yet available in Rajasthan. The hiring of a range of vehicles, with drivers, can be arranged through travel agencies and hotels. **Hertz** and **BudgetCar** have recently begun operations in India but neither have a office in Rajasthan at present. The Hertz office in Delhi (Tel: 331-8695, 331-0190; Tlx: 031-61153) is one of many through whom bookings can be made. Due to the nature of traffic on the roads, the average speed rarely exceeds 50 mph (80 kmph).

Journeys by bus can be booked in advance but there are times when passengers booked on an air-conditioned coach find themselves on a deluxe non air-conditioned bus. The difference in fare is compensated but not the inconvenience.

GETTING ACQUAINTED

THE INDO-PAKISTAN BORDER

There is no official cross-over point along the India-Pakistan border in Rajasthan. Foreign nationals are prohibited from going closer than 32 miles (50 km) to the border. If there is a particular area or village you wish to visit, obtain written permission from the local collector (civil head of a district) or police.

FAIRS & FESTIVALS

In addition to the many Hindu, Muslim, Christian and Sikh festivals celebrated throughout India, Rajasthan has many local variations which combine with traditional fairs. There are also recently established festivals with a range of activities including camel polo, music, dance and races which are organized by the Department of Tourism. Information can be obtained from the **Department of Tourism**, Government of Rajasthan, 100 Jawaharlal Nehru Marg,

Jaipur 302004, Tel: 74857, 73873, 69713.

There is a festival somewhere in Rajasthan every month. The projected dates for 1990 to 1995, location etc., are given below.

Desert Festival: At **Jaisalmer**. A new festival started by Rajasthan Tourism in 1979 to promote local folk arts. It also includes acrobatics, camel races, tug-of-war competitions and turban tying displays.

December 28, 1990; January 1, 1991; January 15-19, 1992; January 4-8, 1993; January 23-27, 1994; January 12-16, 1995.

Nagaur Fair: At **Nagaur** (70 miles/110 km from Bikaner; 85 miles/135 km from Jodhpur). This is a traditional cattle fair where villagers also trade in camels, horses and bullocks.

January 23-25, 1991; February 11-13, 1992; January 30 - February 2, 1993; February 18-21 1994; February 6-10 1995.

Baneshwar Festival: At **Baneshwar** (Dungarpur Dist.). Situated at the confluence of the Mali and Som rivers about 37 miles (60 km) southeast of Dungarpur, this festival offers one of the few opportunities to see a large gathering of Bhil tribes.

January 26-30, 1991; February 14-18, 1992; February 3-6, 1993; February 22-26, 1994; February 11-15, 1995.

Hadoti Festival: At **Kota**. Local music, dance and folk culture from Bundi, Jalawar and Kota.

Brij Festival: At **Bharatpur**. For a few days prior to Holi, this traditional festival includes performances of Raslila, enacting the love story of Krishna and Radha.

February 24-26, 1991; March 14-16, 1992; March 4-6, 1993; March 22-24, 1994; March 12-14, 1995.

Elephant Festival: At **Jaipur**, during Holi. A recently created festival with elephant parades, polo and races.

February 28, 1991; March 18, 1992; March 8, 1993; March 26, 1994; March 16, 1995.

Gangaur Festival: At **Jaipur**. A traditional spring festival celebrated throughout Rajasthan. Mainly celebrated by women who commemorate the love between Lord Shiva and Parvati.

March 29-30, 1991; April 6-7, 1992; March 26-27, 1993; April 14-15, 1994; April 3-4, 1995.

Mewar Festival: At **Udaipur**. Also celebrated at Gangaur and dedicated to Parvati. The women of Udaipur gather to dress the idols of Ishar and Gangaur (Shiva and Parvati) that are then carried in procession through the city to Gangaur Ghat at Lake Pichola, and then in boats along the shore.

March 19-20, 1991; April 6-7, 1992; March 26-27, 1993, April 14-15, 1994; April 3-4, 1995.

Summer Festival: At **Mount Abu**. A three day festival of Rajasthani and Gujarati folk music and dance.

June 1-3, every year.

Teej Festival: At **Jaipur**. A traditional festival welcoming the monsoon with excitement and color. Particularly important for women when they apply henna, buy new bangles and new clothes.

August 12-13, 1991; August 1-2, 1992; July 22-23, 1993; August 10-11, 1994; July 30-31, 1995.

Kajli Teej: At **Bundi**. Celebrates Teej on the third day of the month of Bhadra and continues for eight days till **Janamasthami**, which celebrates Lord Krishna's birthday.

August 27-28, 1991; August 16-17, 1992; August 5-6, 1993; August 23-24, 1994; August 12-13, 1995.

Marwar Festival: At **Jodhpur**. Music and local dance performed on the night of the full moon.

October 3-4, 1990; October 22-23, 1991; October 10-11, 1992; October 29-30, 1993; October 18-19, 1994; October 7-8, 1995.

Pushkar Festival: At **Pushkar**, 7 miles (11 km) from **Ajmer**. At the full moon during the month of Kartika, thousands of pilgrims flock to the small town of Pushkar for a ritual bath in the lake. The nearby cattle, horse and camel fair takes place during the preceding four days.

October 30-November 3, 1990; November 18-21, 1991; November 7-10, 1992;

November 26-29, 1993; November 15-18, 1994; November 6-8, 1995.

Bikaner Festival: At **Bikaner.** The **Kolagat** mela and cattle fair is an important annual festival for the desert people, held on the banks of the holy lake, about 28 miles (45 km) from Bikaner.

November 1-3, 1990; November 20-22, 1992; November 9-11, 1992; November 28-30, 1993; November 17-19, 1994; November 6-8, 1995.

Candrabhaga Kartik Fair: At **Jhalrapatan,** 19 miles (30 km) from Jhalawar. A large cattle fair, next in size to that of Pushkar, is held over the period of Kartik Purnima. Pilgrims from Hadoti and parts of the neighbouring state of Madhya Pradesh come and bathe in the holy waters of the Chandrabhaga river.

November 1-3, 1990; November 20-22, 1991; November 9-11, 1992; November 28-30, 1993; November 17-19, 1994; November 6-8, 1995.

At all these above festivals, the RTDC establishes tented villages with functioning bathing facilities and catering tents.

COMMUNICATIONS

MEDIA

The main language throughout Rajasthan is **Hindi** although in many areas, **Marwari** is also spoken. In larger towns or places of tourist interest, **English** is widely spoken. Most local newspapers are in Hindi. In Jaipur, a local edition of the daily national newspaper, *The Times of India,* is published along with the local English language daily, *Rajasthan Patrika.* The Hindi newspapers include *Rajasthan Patrika* and *Navjyoti.*

Both the radio and television stations are government-run. Both have national networks with programs in Hindi and English as well as local programs in regional languages. Jaipur has a few local television broadcasts but mostly relays the national program broadcast from New Delhi. The local radio relay stations carry local news on the Hindi service, in addition to national and international coverage.

On television, the English language news programs are broadcasted at 7.50 a.m. and 9.30 p.m. every day.

POSTAL SERVICES

The international mail service is in most cases, good. The rates (at the time of press) for inland letters is 60 paise for the first 10 grams and 40 paise for every additional 10 grams. Picture postcards and postcards with printed matter require 40 paise stamps.

For foreign destinations, airmail letters require Rs. 6.50 for the first 10 grams. Aerograms cost Rs. 5.

It is advisable to personally affix stamps to letters or postcards and hand them over the post office counter for immediate franking rather than to slot them in a letter box. Sending a registered parcel overseas is a complicated and time consuming process. Most parcels should be stitched into cheap cotton cloth and then sealed (there are often people sitting outside major post offices offering this service). Two customs forms also need to be completed. Once the parcel has been weighed and stamps affixed, make sure they are franked and a receipt of registration issued to you. All important or valuable material should be registered.

Many shops offer to despatch goods but not all of them are reliable. It is usually only safe when handled by one of the government-run emporia.

Air freighting purchases is possible but can be equally time-consuming. However you send your package, you will need the cash memo or bill and receipt, encashment certificate (showing that the item was purchased with foreign exchange), your passport and return airline ticket. There are many air freight agents in Jaipur and in most other towns in Rajasthan, major travel agencies such as Rajasthan Tours will also be able to provide assistance.

Reasonably efficient and reliable courier services operate domestically and internationally. The Indian agents of DHL, Skypak, UPS, Federal Express (Blue Dart in India), all have offices in Jaipur.

Poste Restante: In most towns this works well but make sure your name is clearly written. Most towns have only one main post office although in Delhi/New Delhi there are two. "New Delhi" is near Connaught Circus while "Delhi" is between the Red Fort and Kashmere Gate in Old Delhi.

TELEPHONE, TELEX & FAX

Overloaded exchanges can make calls a frustrating business. Long-distance calls can in many cases be dialed direct, or booked through the domestic trunk operation. Demand services, available to certain places, are faster but more expensive. Lightning calls are the quickest but cost eight times as much as regular calls. International calls can be dialed direct in some cases, or booked. Both systems are unpredictable. Sometimes, it is possible to get through immediately, at others it can take 24 hours. Book through your hotel operator, if possible, to avoid frayed nerves.

Telex services, both domestic and international are good and reasonably priced. Fax services are becoming more popular and most hotels and many companies now use them.

PARKS & RESERVES

Bhensrodgarh Sanctuary: Established in 1983 over 88 sq. miles (229 sq. km) of scrub and dry deciduous forest. The area has been increasingly threatened by illegal grazing and collection of fuel wood. Despite these threats, **leopards** are still seen in the area along with **chinkara**, **sloth bear** etc.
Best time to visit: October-May
Accommodation: Rest houses
Contact: Range Forest Officer, Rawatbhuta, Dist. Chittor

Nearest town: Rawatbhuta
Rail & Air: Kota (33 miles/53 km)

Darrah Sanctuary: Established in 1955, but previously the hunting reserve of Kota State. The former Maharao kept an interesting photographic record of the tigers in the area, part of which is still on display. The sanctuary covers 102 sq. miles (266 sq. km) of dry deciduous forest (mostly *Anogeissus penduai*). The animals include **wolf**, **sloth bear**, **chinkara** and **leopard**. Despite the disturbance from local villages, it is still worth visiting.
Best time to visit: February-May
Accommodation: 1 rest house
Contact: Range Officer, Darrah Wildlife Sanctuary, via Kamalpura, Dist. Kota
Nearest town & Air: Kota (31 miles/ 50 km)
Rail: Darrah (5 miles/8 km)

Desert National Park: Established in 1980, this large park of 1,220 sq. miles (3,172 sq. km) is only 20 miles (32 km) from Jaisalmer. Although known as a park, much of the area in fact has only sanctuary status, but the area as a whole has its own distinct wildlife. Very little of the area is a Sahara type of desert with rolling sand dunes; in fact, much of the area is covered with patchy scrub and even trees and flowers. The scrubs have adapted themselves to the harsh climate and although many are leafless, they provide shelter and shade for many animals. There are many Bishnoi villages in the sanctuary area and environs, and **blackbuck** and **chinkara** are usually seen nearby. Other animals seen include the **wolf**, **desert fox**, **hare** and **desert cat**. Many birds of prey such as the **tawny eagle**, **short-toed eagle**, **spotted eagle**, **kestrel** and **laggar falcon** are seen. Other birds often seen are flights of **sandgrouse** in the early morning, **gray partridge** and approximatly 350 **great Indian bustard**.
Best time to visit: September-March (Summer temperature exceeds 122°F/50°C)
Accommodation: 6 small rest houses; some villages have rooms to let
Contact: Dy. Director, Desert National Park, Jaisalmer
Nearest town & Rail: Jaisalmer (20 miles/32 km)
Air: Jodhpur

Jaisammand Sanctuary: Established in 1957, this sanctuary is beside the large man-made (62 sq. mile/160 sq. km) lake from which it takes its name. The lake was built by Maharana Jai Singh in the 16th century and the surrounding hills are dotted with *chhatris*, a marble palace and other buildings. Some of the islands are inhabited by Bhils – a tribe of southern Rajasthan. The sanctuary is small (20 sq. miles/52 sq. km) but ranges from the lake shore to the open dry deciduous forests on the adjoining hills. A large range of birds is to be seen and the forest holds **chital**, **chinkara**, **wild boar** and a few **leopard**. Many **crocodiles** feed on a large population of fish. A boat is available from the Irrigation Department.

Best time to visit: November-January

Accommodation: Jaisammand Tourist Bungalow (RTDC) on Udaipur-Banswara Road

Contact: Wildlife Warden (Jaisammand Dist.), Udaipur

Nearest town, Rail & Air: Udaipur (30 miles/48 km)

Keoladeo Ghana National Park: Previously known as the Bharatpur Bird Sanctuary, this magnificent park is one of the world's greatest and most important heronries. Originally protected for the occasional duck shoot, the area became a sanctuary in the mid-1950s and a national park in 1983. About a third of its 11 sq. miles (29 sq. km) is a shallow, fresh-water marsh formed by retaining water after the monsoons. The dry areas are mostly scrub, thorn and mixed deciduous forest. Over 12,000 nests produce over 30,000 chicks. Although mainly famous for its water birds, many other species including many raptors, can also be seen. Mammals include **sambar**, **blackbuck**, **chital**, **nilgai**, **fishing cat**, **jungle cat**, **otter** and **mongoose**.

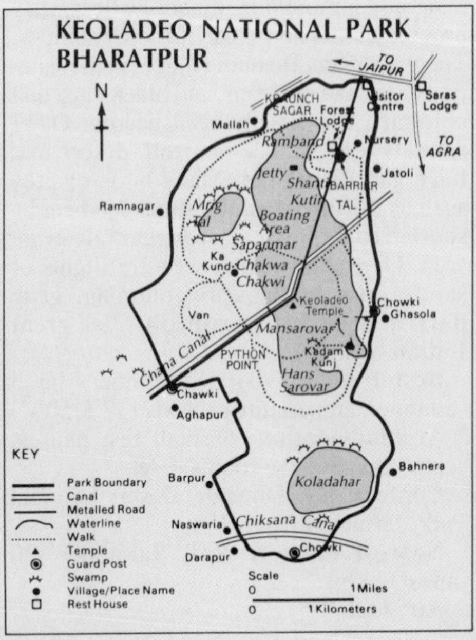

Best time to visit: Open throughout the year. Breeding season: August-October; migrants: October to late February

Accommodation: In the sanctuary: Shanti Kuti Forest Rest House; ITDC Forest Lodge (Tel: 2322, 2864, 2260) with restaurant, bar, air-conditioned and non air-conditioned rooms. Outside the sanctuary: Saras Tourist Bungalow (RTDC), Fatehpur Sikri Road, has both air-conditioned and non air-conditioned rooms (Tel: 2169); Golbargh Palace Hotel, Agra Road (Tel: 3349)

Contact: Dy. Chief Wildlife Warden, Keoladeo national park, Bharatpur

Nearest town & Rail: Bharatpur (1 mile/2 km)

Air: Agra (3 miles/55 km)

Kumbalgarh Sanctuary: This large sanctuary (222 sq. miles/578 sq. km) in the rugged Aravalli Hills is perhaps the only area in India where the highly endangered **wolf** is successfully breeding. Other animals seen here include **leopard**, **sloth bear**, **chinkara**, **chousingha**, **ratel** and **flying squirrel**. The Kumbalgarh fort to the east is one of the most impressive in Rajasthan, with 365 temples within its walls. The sanctuary is dry and apparently barren for much of the year but comes alive during the monsoon and in October when the deciduous trees change color before shedding their leaves.

Best time to visit: March-May (hot days), September-November

Accommodation: Gokul Tourist Bungalow (RTDC) at Nathwara; Shilpi Tourist Bungalow (RTDC) at Ranakpur; and Ghanerao Royal Castle at Ghanerao (Tel: 35), only 3 miles (5 km) from the sanctuary. Aoudhi with 9 double rooms is 1 mile (1.5 km) from the entrance

Contact: Wildlife Warden, Kumbalgarh

KEOLADEO NATIONAL PARK
BHARATPUR

N

TO JAIPUR
Saras Lodge
KRUNCH SAGAR Forest Lodge
Mallah
Visitor Centre
Rambagd
Nursery
TO AGRA
Jetty
Shanti
Jatoli
Kutir
BARRIER
Ramnagar
Mor
Tal
Boating Area
TAL
Sapanmar
Ka Kund
Chakwa
Chakwi
Keoladeo Temple
Chowki
Ghasola
Van
Mansarovar
Chha Canal
PYTHON POINT
Kadam Kunj
Hans Sarovar
Chawki
Aghapur
Barpur
Koladahar
Bahnera
Naswaria
Chiksana Canal
Darapur
Chowki

KEY
Park Boundary
Canal
Metalled Road
Waterline
Walk
Temple
Guard Post
Swamp
Village/Place Name
Rest House

Scale
0   1 Miles
0   1 Kilometers

. Sanctuary, Dist. Udaipur
 Nearest town: Sadri (5 miles/7 km)
 Rail: Falna (15 miles/25 km)
 Air: Udaipur (75 miles/120 km)

Mount Abu Sanctuary: A small sanctuary established in 1960 consisting of 110 sq. miles (289 sq. km) of forested hills to the northeast of Mount Abu. Includes **Guru Shikhar** which at 4,895 feet (1,772 meters) is the highest point in the Aravalli Hills. Animals include **leopard**, **chinkara** and, in the lower areas, **sloth bear**, **sambar** and **wild boar**. Among the interesting birds is the **gray jungle fowl**.
 Best time to visit: March-June
 Accommodation: Shikhar Tourist Bungalow (RTDC) in Mount Abu; also many hotels, PWD bungalows and Circuit Houses.
 Contact: Wildlife Warden, Mount Abu
 Nearest town: Mount Abu (5 miles/8 km)
 Rail: Abu Road (17 miles/28 km)
 Air: Udaipur (115 miles/185 km)

National Chambal Sanctuary: Established in 1983 along the Chambal river from Rana Pratap Sagar to the southwest of Kota to its confluence with the Jamuna. It has an area of 211 sq. miles (549 sq. km) and has sanctuary status to protect the **garial crocodilian**. Southeast of Sawai Madhopur, the Chambal joins the Parbati river which forms the border with Madhya Pradesh. The Madhya Pradesh bank is also a sanctuary. **Blackbuck**, **caracal**, **chinkara** and **wolf** are among the many animals that enjoy protection here. Boats can be taken upstream from Kota and in the winter, **garials** are often seen basking on the sand banks.
 Best time to visit: October-March
 Accommodation: Chambal Tourist Bungalow (RTDC), Kota; forest rest houses at other places
 Contact: Warden, National Chambal Sanctuary, Kota
 Nearest town, Rail & Air: Kota

Ranthambore National Park: Established as a sanctuary in 1955 and one of the original areas under Project Tiger. Although the smallest of the Project Tiger reserves, Ranthambore has an impressive range of animal species including **sambar**, **chital**, **nilgai**, **chinkara**, **wild boar**, **sloth bear**, **hyena**, **jackal**, **leopard** and **tiger** within its

150 sq. miles (392 sq. km). Since coming under Project Tiger management, these arid hills at the junction of the Aravalli and Vindhya ranges have been restored to their full dynamism. Artificial lakes now blend with the forest hills and form the integral part of the park. Excellent birdlife, including the **crested serpent eagle**, are among the many birds of prey to be seen. Many water birds are seen on the lakes. A thousand-year-old fort rises 700 feet (214 meters) above the park.
 A private trust, The Ranthambore Foundation, carries out a variety of projects in the villages and buffer areas of the park. These projects are among the first of their kind in India and involve the restoration of degraded land, alternative fuel and energy projects, rural health and creation of fuel wood and grazing areas outside the park so villagers will not need to gain illegal entry into the nearby park. For further information and offers of support write to: The Ranthambore Foundation, 19 Kautilya Marg, New Delhi 110021 (Tel: 301-6261).
 Best time to visit: October-April
 Accommodation: Jogi Mahal in the park, bookings can be made through the Field Director's Office; Castle Jhoomer Baori Forest Lodge (RTDC) at Ranthambore Road, Sawai Madhopur (Tel: 620), will arrange vehicles; Sawai Madhopur Lodge,

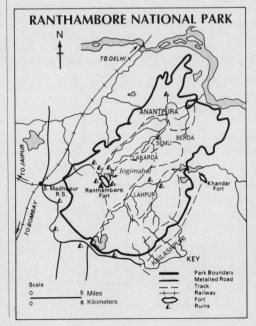

RANTHAMBORE NATIONAL PARK

Ranthambore Road, Sawai Madhopur 322001 (Tel: 2541). The former hunting lodge of the royal family of Jaipur is now part of the Taj Group of Hotels and can be booked through any travel agent or Taj Central reservations, Chandralok, Janpath, New Delhi 110001 (Tel: 332-2333, 332-2256; Tlx: 031-65196 TAJ IN). "Tiger Moon" cottages at the edge of the park. Book through Indian Adventures, 257 S. V. Road, Bandra, Bombay 400050, Tel: 642-2925, 640-6399; Fax: (91) 22-640-2309; Tlx: 011-78180 CBS IN

Contact: The Field Director, Ranthambore National Park, Sawai Madhopur

Nearest town & Rail: Sawai Madhopur (9 miles/14 km).

Air: Jaipur (108 miles/175 km)

Sariska National Park, Tiger Reserve and Sanctuary: Originally the shooting area of the Alwar ruling family, Sariska became a sanctuary in 1958. The sanctuary came under Project Tiger in 1979 and the core area of 191 sq. miles (498 sq. km) became a national park in 1982. The park also has 9th- and 10th-century ruins of Shiva temples and the Kankwari fort. Most of Sariska is hilly with a wide valley from the gate to Thana Gazi. It has a good network of roads. Animals seen include **leopard**, **wild dog** (first sighted in 1986), **nilgai**, **chital**, **chousingha**, **chinkara**, **ratel** and **tiger**.

Best time to visit: November-June. Very dry summers make June good for game-viewing, although hot

Accommodation: Forest rest house; Tiger Den Tourist Bungalow (RTDC) has air-conditioned and non air-conditioned rooms (Tel: 42); Hotel Sariska Palace, opposite the park entrance, is a converted Royal Palace – has jeep for hire

Contact: The Field Director, Sariska Tiger Reserve, Dist. Alwar

Nearest town & Rail: Alwar (22 miles/ 36 km)

Air: Jaipur (68 miles/110 km)

Sitamata Sanctuary: Established in 1979 in the southern forests of Rajasthan over 163 sq. miles (423 sq. km) of dry deciduous forest and bamboo. The **flying squirrel** is more often seen here than in most other sanctuaries. Other species seen include **leopard**, **caracal**, **chousingha**, **pangolin**, **sambar**, **wild boar** and **chinkara**.

Best time to visit: April-July

Accommodation: Forest rest house

Contact: Wildlife Warden, Sitamata Wildlife Sanctuary, Dhariawad, Dist. Udaipur

Nearest town: Dhariawad

Rail: Bansi (19 miles/31 km)

Air: Udaipur (65 miles/108 km)

Tal Chapper Sanctuary: This small sanctuary covering 27 sq. miles (71 sq. km) has a large **blackbuck** population. **Chinkara**, **partridge** and **sandgrouse** are the other animals and bird species usually seen, including the occasional **desert fox** and **cat**. Mostly thorn scrub with high summer temperatures and low rainfall.

Best time to visit: April and October

Accommodation: 1 rest house

Contact: Dy. Conservator of Forest, Churu

Nearest town: Chapper, Bikaner (63 miles/100 km)

Air: Jaipur (130 miles/210 km)

Other sanctuaries in Rajasthan include **Jamia Ramgarh** (Jaipur Dist.), **Jawahar Sagar** (Kota, Bundi Dist.), **Kaila Devi** (Sawai Madhopur Dist.), **Nahargarh** (Jaipur Dist.), **Phulwari** (Udaipur Dist.), **Ramgarh** (Bundi Dist.), **Shergarh** (Kota

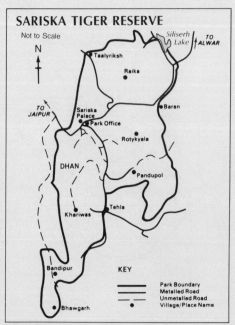

SARISKA TIGER RESERVE

Not to Scale

N

Siliserh Lake

TO ALWAR

Taalyriksh

Raika

TO JAIPUR

Sariska Palace

Park Office

Baran

Rotykyala

DHAN

Pandupol

Khariwas

Tehla

Bandipur

Bhawgarh

KEY

Park Boundary
Metalled Road
Unmetalled Road
Village/Place Name

Dist.), **Sonkhaliya Closed Area** - Bustard Sanctuary (Ajmer Dist.), **Sorson Closed Area** - Bustard Sanctuary (Kota Dist.), **Todgarh-Rad**, (Ajmer, Udaipur and Pali Dists.) and **Vanvihar** (Dholpur Dist.). Information on all these areas can be obtained from: **The Chief Wildlife Warden's Office**, Van Bhawan, Bhagwan Das Road, Jaipur.

SHOPPING

The bazaars in most towns reflect the rich culture of Rajasthan with a range of bright, colorful fabrics, handicrafts and cloths. Using local materials, these craftsmen manage to meet the everyday needs of the local people, producing simple utensils of great beauty. The same facilities that built and decorated the splendid forts, palaces and memorials throughout the state today keep alive these traditions and skills by adapting them to changing needs.

The traditional tie-and-dye textiles made by knotting the material and dipping it in color to form the delicate *bandhani* patterns are found throughout the state. The block prints of Sanganer, many with *khari* (overprinting with gold); the *ajrah* prints from Barmer; the *jaajam* prints of Chittor and the floral prints from Bagru are found not only where they are made, but also in the old city bazaars of Jaipur and other large towns. In many large towns, Rajasthan Government Emporia sell fabric from throughout the state by the yard, as made-up clothes or as wall hangings at fixed prices.

Jaipur and Sanganer are famous for their "blue pottery". These hand-painted vessels, plates, dishes, pots and other utensils are decorated with floral motifs or geometrical patterns in combinations of blue, white and, occasionally, other colors. All are hand-molded and well-glazed.

Leather workers using camel and other hides provide a variety of local traditional footwear. In Jaipur, the cobblers make *mojadis* which are soft slippers embroidered in bright colors. Combinations of camel leather, cloth and velvet are now also used to make a range of other items, including purses, cases, handbags, and even garments.

In Jaipur and a few small villages, carpets and *durries* are made for both the local and export markets. Orders can be placed for both traditional and contemporary designs in any color combination and many manufacturers keep a range for ready sale.

Throughout Rajasthan, local jewelers make splendid jewelry for the princes, and the same tradition of finely cut precious and semi-precious stones set in gold with enamel inlay work has continued.

In many village bazaars or *melas* (fairs), the traditional silver jewelry belts, chains, bangles etc. can still be found where it is sold by weight.

The **Johari Bazaar** of Jaipur (and bazaars in other towns) also presents a full range of bangles, beads and rings. In addition, ear studs made of ivory, bone, lac and glass are available.

Among the many other items available throughout the state are *pichwais* or cloth paintings. The best selection of both traditional and modern design is probably available in Jaipur. Engraved brassware, enamel work using cobalt and sulphate of copper mined in the hills near Khetri, and inlay work are made throughout the state and are available in most towns.

Warning: The export of ivory in any form and items made with wild animal products is banned.

FURTHER READING

Agarwala, R.A. *Marwar Murals*. New Delhi: Agam Prakashan, 1977.

Agarwal, R.C. *Temples of Rajasthan*. Acts Asiatiques Vol. XI, 1965.

Anand, Uma. *Guide To Rajasthan*. New Delhi: I.T.D.C., 1975.

Archer, William. *Rajasthan Painting*. Kotah: Marg Vol. XI, 1958.

Beny, Roloff. *Rajasthan*. London: Muller, 1984.

Brooke, Col. J.C. *A Political History of Jaipur*.

Coomaraswamy, Ananda. *Rajput Painting*. Oxford: OUP, 1916. An Indian reprint is available.

Crewe, Quentin. *The Last Maharaja*. London: Michael Joseph, 1985.

Davenport, Hugh. *The Trials and Triumphs of the Mewar Kingdom*. Udaipur: Maharana Mewar Charitable Foundation, 1975.

Devi, Gayatri. *A Princess Remembers*. London: Weidenfeld & Nicolson, 1976.

Devenish, J.A. *The Bhawans and Garden Palaces of Deeg*. Allahabad, 1903.

Ferguson, James. *History of Indian and Eastern Architecture*. London: John Murray.

Gascoigne, Bambar. *The Great Mughals*. London: Cape, 1971. New Delhi: Dass Media, 1985.

Goetz, Hermann. *The Art and Architecture of Bikaner*. Oxford: Bruno Cassirer, 1950.

Gupta, Mohan Lal. *Frescoes and Wall Paintings of Rajasthan*. Jaipur, 1965.

Gupta, Om Prakash. *Mount Abu*. Ajmer, 1960.

Hendley, E.B. *Rulers of India and The Chiefs of Rajputana*. London, 1897.

Joshi, M.C. *Deeg*. New Delhi: ASI, 1968.

Mehta, Rama. *Inside the Haveli*. New Delhi, 1977.

Menon, V.P. *Story of the Integration of the Indian States*. Hyderabad, 1956.

Roy, A.K. *History of the Jaipur City*. New Delhi: Manohar, 1978.

Sigh, Harnath (of Dundlod). *The Shekhavats and Their Lands*. Jaipur, 1970.

Singh, K. Natwar. *Maharaja Suraj Mal 1707-63*. London, 1980.

Singh, Raghubir. *Rajasthan, India's Enchanted Land*. London, 1981.

Skelton, Robert. *Rajasthan Temple Hangings of the Krishna Cult*. New York, 1973.

Sarkar, Judamati. *A History of Jaipur*. Hyderabad: Longman, 1984.

Timberg, Thomas. *The Marwaris: From Traders to Industralists*. New Delhi, 1978.

Tod, Col James. *Annuals and Antiquities of Rajasthan*. Many editions still in print.

JAIPUR & ENVIRONS

Capital of Rajasthan since 1949, this city of over one million was built in the early 18th century as a planned entity according to traditional Hindu concepts of the cosmos. Wide streets divide the walled city east-west and north-south. Since the 19th century, the city has grown and developed outside the old city walls and, although bounded by hills to the north and east, the modern city has spread south and west, incorporating old villages previously set in an arid landscape. This city of Jai Singh II (1699-1744) has retained much of the original architecture.

Tourist Information: Foreigners Regional Registration Office, behind Hawa Mahal at the Rajasthan Police Head Office (Tel: 49391). Government of India Tourist Office, Hotel Khasa Kothi, M.I. Road, Jaipur (Tel: 72200).

GETTING THERE

By Air: Jaipur Airport is near the town at Sanganer 10 miles (15 km) to the south on the Tonk Road. There are (at the time of press) Indian Airlines flights to Delhi (twice daily), Bombay (twice daily), Agra, Udaipur (twice daily), Jodhpur (twice daily), Ahmedabad, Aurangabad and Varanasi (Banares). Vayudoot connects Jaipur with Kota, Indore, Bhopal, Jodhpur, Jaisalmer, Bikaner and Delhi.

The Indian Airlines city office is at Mundra Bhawan, on the Ajmer Road (Tel: 72940, 74500). The airport numbers are 822222, 822519 and 822718.

Vayudoot also has an office at Jaipur (Tel: 61269, 62782). The airport number is 822603.

Many international airlines have offices in Jaipur, including Air India at Rattan Mansion (opp. All India Radio), M.I. Road (Tel: 65559).

By Rail: There are regular trains connecting Jaipur with most of Rajasthan. The old meter-gauge track covers most of the state and links Jaipur with Delhi (via Alwar), Agra (via Bharatpur), Sawai Madhpur, Ajmer, Jodhpur, Udaipur, Abu Road and Ahmedabad, Bikaner (via Sikar and Fatepur) among other cities.

The station is located toward the west of the city. There is a Government of Rajasthan Tourist Information Center near the station. Advance reservations can be made between 9 a.m. and 4.30 p.m. For train enquiries, call 72121; reservations: 72122, 68372.

By Road: The main bus station at Sindhi Camp has regular services to all major towns in Rajasthan and neighboring states. Rajasthan Roadways offer a comprehensive but basic service. Haryana Roadways have regular buses linking Jaipur with Delhi, Chandigarh and other towns in Haryana (Tel: 75834, 66579).

GETTING AROUND

As with most towns, the most flexible way of traveling in an Indian town is by cycle-rickshaw (or by foot). Auto-rickshaws and taxis are available but not metered, so it is best to agree on a price before starting your journey. Some routes have fixed fares such as for going to or from the airport, from or to The Rambagh Palace, Raj Mahal and Jai Mahal hotels. This fare at the time of press was Rs. 90 one way.

ACCOMMODATIONS

Jaipur is an exception to the general rule that India has only luxury hotels or rough budget accommodation. At the top end, Jaipur has two excellent hotels in the Taj Group's **Rambagh Palace** and **Jai Mahal,** with a promise of a third with **Raj Mahal Palace**.

Clark's Amer
Jawaharlal Nehru Marg, Jaipur
Tel: 822616, 822701; Tlx: 0365-276;
Cable: CLARKS AMER
Situated near the airport. Transport to/from the city can be a problem.

Jai Mahal Palace Hotel
Jacob Road, Civil Lines, Jaipur
Tel: 68381; Tlx: 0365-2250, 2716;
Fax: 0141-68337; Cable: JAIMAHAL
Can be booked through any Taj Group Hotel or Utell Worldwide.

Jaipur Ashok
Jaisingh Circle, Bani Park, Jaipur
Tel: 75121, 75171; Tlx: 0356-2262;
Cable: ASHOKOTEL
Can be booked through any ITDC hotel or Ashok Travels

Mansingh Hotel
Sansar Chandra Road, Jaipur 302001
Tel: 78771; Tlx: 0365-2344 WICO IN;
Cable: WELCOMOTEL
Centrally located but uninspiring hotel.

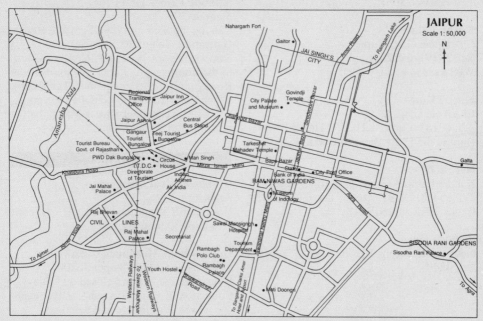

Meru Palace
Sawai Ram Singh Road, Jaipur
Tel: 61212, 77841; Tlx: 0365-2259;
Cable: HOTEL MERU
A new 4-star hotel close to M.I. Road.

Raj Mahal Palace
Sardar Patel Marg, Jaipur 302001
Tel: 61257/8/9; Tlx: 0365-313 JAI IN;
Cable: RESIDENCY
A small hotel of 11 rooms adapted from the
old British residency. Can be booked
through the Taj Group.

Rambagh Palace
Bhawani Singh Road, Jaipur 302005
Tel: 75142; Tlx: 0365-2254, 2147;
Fax: 0141-73798; Cable: RAMBAGH
Apart from 110 air-conditioned rooms, this
hotel has an excellent health club with
squash court and swimming pool. Can be
booked through any Taj Group Hotel or
Utell Worldwide.

Mid-Range Hotels: In many old towns in
Rajasthan, some of the most interesting
places to stay in are converted family houses
now run as guest houses or small hotels. In
Jaipur these include:

Achrol Lodge
Civil Lines, Jaipur
Tel: 72254, 75067.

Bissau Palace
Chandpole Gate, Jaipur
Tel: 74191, 67728; Cable: HOBI
Well located in the walled city.

Khetri House
Chadpole Gate, Jaipur
Tel: 69183; Cable: KHETRI HOUSE
Built in the 1930s, next to Bissau Palace.

Narain Niwas
Kanota Bagh, Narain Singh Road, Jaipur
Tel: 65448, 72291, 74666; Tlx: 0365-2482;
Cable: NARAINNIWAS.

Samode Haveli
Gamgapole, Jaipur 302002
Tel: 42407

Other hotels include:

Gangaur Tourist Hotel
(Rajasthan Tourist Dev. Corp. – RTDC)
M.I. Road
Tel: 60231/9.

LMB
Johari Bazaar, Jaipur
Tel: 48844
A vegetarian hotel located in the old city.

Teej Tourist Bungalow (RTDC)
Collectorate Road, Bani Park,
Jaipur 302006
Tel: 74206, 69072.

Accommodations around Jaipur

Circuit House
Tonk.
South of Jaipur, Tonk, a small predominantly Muslim town, has a magnificent
museum and library.

The Ramgarh Lodge
Jamuva Ramgarh, Jaipur 303109
Situated overlooking the Ramgarh Lake
(Jaipur's resevoir), the 9-bedroom lodge is
managed and booked through the Rambagh
Palace Hotel in Jaipur.

Samode Palace Hotel
Samode 303806
Can be booked through Samode House,
Gangapole, Jaipur 302002 (Tel: 42407)
Samode is a small village 26 miles (42 km)
to the northwest of Jaipur, off the Bikaner
Road (turn right after Chomu). The Palace,
which has 20 rooms, is itself the main attrac-
tion with an excellent Sheesh Mahal (hall of
mirrors) and public rooms.

MUSEUMS

Archaeological Museums
Amber
Hours: 7-10.30 a.m. and 3-6 p.m. (Summer);
10 a.m.-4.30 p.m. (Winter).

Government Museum (Albert Hall)
Ram Niwas Garden, Jaipur 302004
Hours: 10 a.m.-5 p.m.; closed on Fridays.
Collection of Rajasthan handicrafts, weap-
ons, jewelry, sculpture and paintings.

Jaigarh Fort
Jaigarh, Amber, Jaipur
Tel: 44848
Hours: 10 a.m.-4 p.m.
Situated above the Amber palace complex, the Jaigarh Fort and its extensive buildings are open throughout the year. The collection includes an armory, a cannon foundry, maps and artifacts. A temple to Ram Hari Har and Kal Bhairava is open to worship.

Maharaja Sawai Man Singh II Museum
City Palace, Jaipur 302002
Tel: 74146
Hours: 9.30 a.m.-4.45 p.m.; closed on public holidays.
Excellent collection of manuscripts, paintings, textiles, arms and weapons.

SHOPPING

The old walled city, often referred to as "the pink city", still has traditional areas or zones for the various crafts or trades. Johari Bazaar is the area for jewelry and now saris. **Tripolia Bazaar** is for brassware, carvings and lacquerwork. **Bapu Bazaar** has textiles and perfumes (attar) and **Chandpol Bazaar,** bangles and trinkets. The main shopping area outside the city wall is Mirza Ismail Road (commonly referred to as M.I. Road).

City GUIDE
ALWAR & ENVIRONS

Alwar is 103 miles (164 km) from Delhi and 90 miles (143 km) from Jaipur on National Highway No. 8. (The more direct road from Delhi to Jaipur lies to the west.) Set amid the Aravalli hills, the area around Alwar is very attractive, in parts still forested (see Sariska Tiger Reserve) and has numerous man-made lakes.
Tourist Information: Tourist Information Center, near Purjan Vihar Garden, Alwar (Tel: 21868).

GETTING THERE

By Rail: The meter-gauge line between Delhi and Jaipur runs through Alwar and there are numerous trains, both during the day and at night.
By Road: There are regular bus services

to/from Jaipur, Delhi, Sariska and Bharatpur (70 miles/117 km).

GETTING AROUND

Local transport in Alwar is by *tonga* (horse-drawn buggies), cycle-rickshaws or auto-rickshaws. There are a few metered cars available as taxis at the railway station.

ACCOMMODATIONS

Circuit House
Tel: 28350.

Forest Rest House
Sariska
May be booked through the Field Director, Sariska Tiger Reserve. Sariska is 23 miles (37 km) south of Alwar.

Kota Rao Guest House
31 Moti Doonagri
Tel: 3787.

Lake Palace Hotel (RTDC)
Siliserh, Dist. Alwar
Tel: 3764
10 rooms in a small palace overlooking the man-made Siliserh Lake (5 miles/8 km south of Alwar).

Phool Bagh Palace
Opp. New Stadium, Alwar 301001
Tel: 2274
A small family hotel with air-conditioned and air-cooled rooms. About a mile (2 km) from the railway station and 2 miles (3½ km) from the bus stand.

PWD Rest House
Near Railway Station
Tel: 2886.

Rajasthan Motel (RTDC)
Midway Behror
Tel: 49
Midway between Delhi and Jaipur on the main highway.

Sariska Palace Hotel
Dist. Alwar 301022
Tel: Sariska 22
12 air-conditioned rooms and 15 non air-conditioned rooms in one of the largest

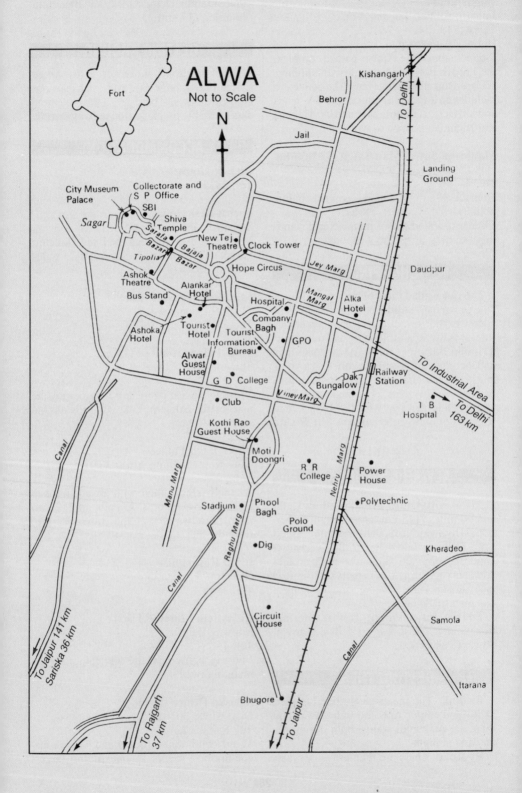

"hunting lodges" in India. Jeeps are available to visit the National Park. Bookings can be made in Delhi (Tel: 732365) and Jaipur (Tel: 66804).

Tiger Den Tourist Bungalow (RTDC)
Dist. Alwar 301022
Tel: Sariska 42
17 rooms, restaurant and bar near the park entrance.

MUSEUMS

Government Museum
(located in Vinay Vilas Mahal or City Palace), Alwar 301001
Hours: 10 a.m.-5 p.m.; closed on Fridays and government holidays.
Extensive collection of manuscripts, paintings, arms and armor. Permission to visit the fort above the City Palace must be obtained from the Superintendent of Police.

City GUIDE

AJMER & PUSHKAR

Located in the center of Rajasthan on the main highway between Jaipur, 86 miles (138 km) to the north, and Jodhpur and Udaipur, respectively 130 miles (205 km) and 150 miles (236 km) to the south, Ajmer has long been a town of importance. An important Muslim shrine (the Dargah of Khwaja

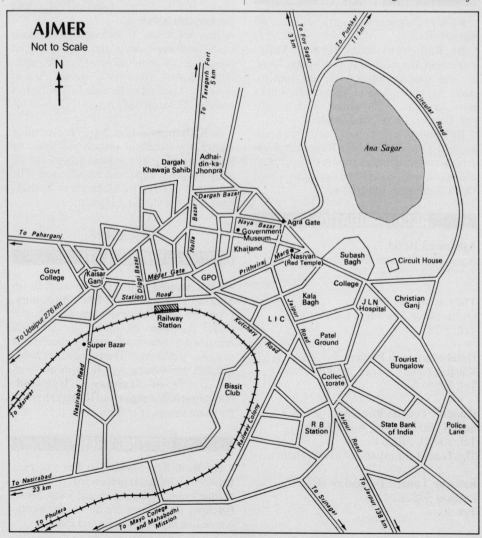

AJMER
Not to Scale
N

Moinuddin Chisti), it attracts tens of thousands of pilgrims throughout the year, although festivities reach a peak during the *urs* (death anniversary ceremonies). Seven miles (11 km) to the west, the temples of Pushkar are a focal point for Hindu pilgrims from throughout the area. From 1818, Ajmer was the only part of modern Rajasthan which was part of British India.

Festival: The Pushkar Fair is held every year at **Kartik Poornima** (the November full moon). This pilgrimage is now better known for the large camel and horse fair that takes place at the same time. See page 277 for dates from 1990 to 1995.

GETTING THERE

By Air: The nearest airport is at Jaipur (86 miles/138 km).

By Rail: Most trains between Delhi, Jaipur and Ahmedabad stop at Ajmer. There are also train connections to and from Indore, Secunderabad (Hyderabad), Lucknow, Agra and, in Rajasthan, to/from Jodhpur, Barmer, Chittor and Udaipur.

By Road: The road from Jaipur (via Kishangarh) is one of the best in Rajasthan. Both private and state buses connect Ajmer with all the major towns in Rajasthan as well as in Delhi, Agra and Ahmedabad.

ACCOMMODATIONS

Ajaymeru Hotel
Annasagar Circular Road, Ajmer
Tel: 20089.

The Circuit House
Overlooking Ana Sagar Lake
Tel: 20795.

Hotel Mansingh Palace
Vaishali Nagar, Ajmer 305001
Tel: 30855/6.

Khadim Tourist Bungalow (RTDC)
Savitri Girls College Road, Ajmer
Tel: 20490, 21626
The Tourist Information Office is here.

Sarovar Tourist Bungalow (RTDC)
Pushkar 305022
Tel: 40.

During the annual fair at Pushkar, a large well-organized tented village with clean bathrooms is erected by the Rajasthan Tourism Development Corporation (RTDC). There are communal dining tents but no alcohol is available locally. Best to book the tents well in advance through one of the Jaipur travel agents such as: **Rajasthan Tours Pvt. Ltd.**, Rambagh Palace Hotel, Bhavani Singh Road, Jaipur 302005 (Tel: 76041, 69885; Tlx: 288 RAJI IN).

MUSEUMS

Government Museum
(Rajputana Museum)
Near Naya Bazaar, Ajmer
Hours: 10 a.m.-5 p.m.; closed on Fridays and government holidays.
A fine collection of archaeological items, coins, sculpture, arms and armor, Rajput paintings, and items collected from throughout Rajasthan since 1902 by the British Resident. Located in the main hall of the fort built by Akbar in 1572.

At **Kishangarh**, 17 miles (27 km) north of Ajmer, the excellent private collection of Rajput painting of the local school can be seen by prior appointment. Contact: The Secretary to HH The Maharaja of Kishangarh, The Palace, Kishangarh.

City GUIDE

SHEKHAVATI

The painted walls of the *havelis* in Shekhavati are a product of the 19th century. From the 15th century, when Rao Shekha defied the rulers of Amber, the area has remained a semi-independent collection of *thikanas* (fifedoms). The two district headquarters are **Churu** and **Jhunjhunu**, with the towns of **Mandawa**, **Dundlod**, **Nawalgarh**, **Fatehpur** and **Ramgarh** being the main places of interest.

GETTING THERE

By Rail: The Shekhavati Express runs between Delhi and Jaipur each day, stopping at Jhunjhunu, Mukundgarh and Sikar. Sikar, Fatehpur and Churu are all on the metergauge line between Jaipur and Bikaner.

By Road: The most convenient way to travel through Shekhavati is by private car but there are regular bus services linking most of the towns with Sikar and Jaipur.

ACCOMMODATIONS

Birla Institute Guest House
Pilani, Dist. Jhunjhunu 333031.

Desert Camp
Mandawa, Dist. Jhunjhunu 333704
Village-like atmosphere created by an intriguing complex of deluxe rooms (with attached bathrooms) located a mile (2 km) from Mandawa Castle. Can be booked through: Old Mandawa House, Sansar Chandra Road, Jaipur 302001 (Tel: 75358, 65901).

Dundlod
Fort
Fort has retained much of its original character. It is located 94 miles (150 km) from Jaipur, 22 miles (35 km) from Sikar. Can be booked through: Dundlod House, Hawa Sarak, Civil Lines, Jaipur 302006 (Tel: 66276).

Hotel Shiv Shekhavati
Muni Ashram, Jhunjhunu 333001
Tel: 51
Good clean lodgings. Vegetarian food.

Mandawa Castle
Mandawa, Dist. Jhunjhunu 333704
Tel: 24
Located 100 miles (168 km) from Jaipur, 15 miles (25 km) from Jhunjhunu, 9 miles (14 km) from Mukundgarh. Excellent service. 35 rooms, all with attached bathrooms. Created out of an old family fort. Can be booked through: Old Mandawa, Sansar Chandra Road, Jaipur 302001 (Tel: 75358, 65901).

Roop Niwas Haveli
Nawalgarh, Dist Sikar 333042
Tel: 8
Located 17½ miles (28 km) from Sikar, Nawalgarh has numerous *havelis*, many are worth visiting along with the frescoed telephone exchange.

There are PWD rest houses and/or dak bungalows at Sikar, Churu, Jhunjhunu, Khetri, Pilani and Loharu.

MUSEUMS

Birla Museum
Pilani, Dist Jhunjhunu 333031
Tel: Pilani 58
Hours: 9 a.m.-5 p.m.; closed on Mondays. Largely industrial and technological, in keeping with the Birla Institute. Small collection of western paintings and sculptures.

Private Museum
Castle Mandawa, Dist Jhunjhunu.

Sikar Museum
Sikar
Hours: 7-11 a.m. & 4-7 p.m. (Summer); 8-11 a.m. & 4-6 p.m. (Winter)
A small private collection covering the arts and crafts of Shekhavati, local archaeology and some sculpture.

City GUIDE

BIKANER & ENVIRONS

Five centuries old (it was founded in 1488), Bikaner, with its large fort, commanded the great caravan routes from the west and was an important staging post. A remote stronghold, Bikaner is surrounded by a scrub desert of thorn, gorse and short acacia trees.

GETTING THERE

By Air: Vayudoot have an occasional flight to and from Delhi via Jaipur. On some days, the flight also links Bikaner with Jaisalmer. The Vayudoot Office is at 148 Sadul Ganj (Tel: 5445).

By Rail: There are regular trains linking Bikaner with Delhi (Via Hanumangarh), Jodhpur and Jaipur. For enquiries, call 4600; reservations: 3294, 4887. Open: 8 a.m.-noon, 12.30-3 p.m.

By Road: Delhi is 286 miles (458 km) from Bikaner via Ratangarh, Churu, Jhunjhunu and Pilani; 333 miles (538 km) via Hissar and Rohtak. Jaipur is 220 miles (354 km) away via Ratangarh, Fatehpur and Sikar; Jodhpur is 150 miles (242 km) via

Deshnok and Nagar; while Jaisalmer is 200 miles (326 km) away via Phalodi and Pokran. Regular bus services ply on all these routes. Between Jaipur and Bikaner there is an occasional air-conditioned coach service.

The Central Bus Stand is on KEM Road, Tel: 6688.

GETTING AROUND

There are a few unmetered taxis (negotiate the fare at the start of the journey – ask your hotel for the local rate per kilometer); also auto-rickshaws and *tongas*. In the outlying areas, the local form of transport is a camel. A transfer from the Cayudoot office in the city to the airport by coach costs about Rs. 25 at the time of press.

ACCOMMODATIONS

Circuit House
Tel: 3142.

Dak Bungalow
Near Railway Station

Tel: 3018.

Dak Bungalow
Kalibangan (125 miles/200 km north of Bikaner)
Tel: 151.

Dholamaru Tourist Bungalow (RTDC)
Near Major Puran Singh Circle, Bikaner 334001
Tel: 5002
A mile (1.6 km) from the bus stand, 2 miles (3.2 km) from the railway station. Local tourist office (Tel: 5445) is located here.

Hotel Gajner Palace
Gajner
Tel: 39
15 rooms in the Maharaja's old hunting lodge, 20 miles (32 km) west of Bikaner. Book through the Lalgarh Palace.

Hotel Karni Bhawan Palace
Tel: 3308.

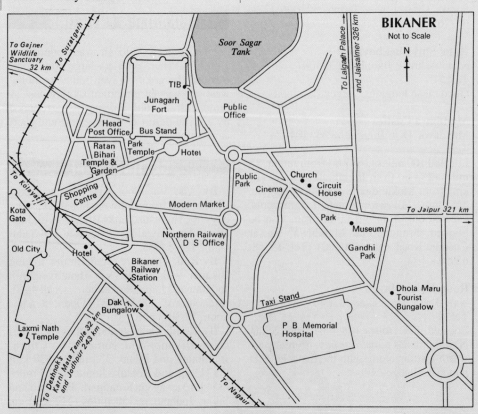

Lalgadh Palace Hotel

Bikaner
Tel: 3263, 5963
Has 34 rooms, many with original furnishings and carpets made in the local prison. Part of the palace houses a museum, another part is still a private residence. Has a private golf course, squash court etc.

Thar Hotel

Hospital Road, Dr. Ambedkar Circle, Bikaner
Tel: 6480.

MUSEUMS

ASI (Archaeological Survey of India) Site Museum

Kalibangan, 125 miles (200 km) north of Bikaner
Mostly photographs of the recent excavations of this important site (Indus civilization, 2500 B.C.).

Government Museum

Near Gandhi Park, Bikaner
Hours: 10 a.m.-5 p.m.; closed on Fridays and government holidays.
Previously, and locally still, known as the Ganga Golden Jubilee museum. Has good collection of Harappan items, Gupta sculpture and Bikaner school miniature paintings.

Lalgarh Palace Museum

Lalgarh Palace
Hours: From 10 a.m.-5 p.m.; closed on Wednesdays.
Interesting collection of photographs, some Bikaner school miniatures, numerous shikar trophies.

City GUIDE

JAISALMER

The sandstone citadel of Jaisalmer rises out of the Thar, the Great Indian Desert, welcoming visitors as it did travelers on the ancient trade routes. The city retains much of its medieval charm and is often referred to as a living museum.

Tourist Information: The Tourist Office is at the Moomal Tourist Bungalow, Amar Sagar Road (Tel: 2392, 2406).

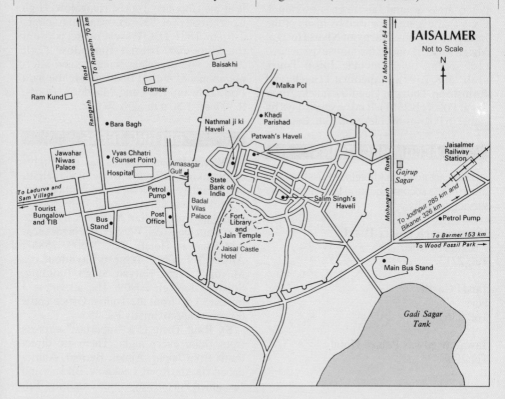

GETTING THERE

By Air: Vayudoot operates a regular service during the winter from Delhi via Jaipur and either Bikaner or Jodhpur. The Vayudoot Office is at Moomal Tourist Bungalow, Amar Sagar Road (Tel: 2392, 2406). The airport is 4 miles (7 km) from the town and the transfer coach to and from the Tourist Bungalow costs Rs. 20 at press time.

By Rail: There are day and night trains from Jodhpur via Pokran. The Maharaja of Jodhpur's private saloons can be hired through the Umaid Bhawan Palace, Jodhpur, and connected to the above trains. Station enquiries at 2354.

By Road: There are regular bus services from and to Jodhpur via Pokran, Deehu and Balesar; from and to Bikaner via Phalodi and Pokran. There are also local buses to Barmer (96 miles/153 km) to the southeast.

GETTING AROUND

Unmetered taxis and jeeps are available. Bicycles can be hired.

By Camel: The best way of exploring the desert areas around Jaisalmer is by camel. Camel safaris are organized by many of the local travel agents. **Narayan Nivas Hotel** at Malka Road, is one of the more experienced (Tel: 2408); others include **Jaisal Tours** (Tel: 2408, 2397), **Mahendra Travels,** and **Rajasthan Tours** at Gandhi Chowk, Amar Sagar Pol (Tel: 2561). It takes seven days by camel to Pokran and eleven days to Bikaner.

ACCOMMODATIONS

There are no luxury hotels in Jaisalmer but much of the accommodation is clean and the service friendly.

Himmatgarh Palace Hotel
1 Ramgarh Road
Tel: 2213.

Jaisal Castle
Fort
Tel: 2362.

Jawahar Niwas Palace Hotel
Tel:2208.

Moonal Tourist Bungalow
Amar Sagar Road
Tel: 92, 192.

Narayan Niwas Hotel
Malka Road
Tel: 2408.

MUSEUMS

Two of the five Patwa Havelis are now owned by the government and open daily from 10.30 a.m. to 5 p.m.

Government Museum
Near the Moomal Tourist Bungalow
Hours: 9 a.m.-4 p.m.; closed on Fridays.

Jaisalmer Folklore Museum
Garhsisar
A private collection; open most days.

City GUIDE

JODHPUR & ENVIRONS

Tourist Information: The Tourist Office is at the Ghoomar Tourist Bungalow, High Court Road (Tel: 25183), open 8 a.m.-noon, 3-6 p.m. The RTDC Travel Counter is also at the Ghoomar Tourist Bungalow (Tel: 21900), and organizes morning and afternoon tours of Umaid Bhawan, Mehrangarh Fort, Jaswant Tada and Mandore (Hours: 9.30 a.m.-1.30 p.m., 2-6.30 p.m.).

GETTING THERE

By Air: Indian Airlines has two flights daily linking Jodhpur with Delhi via Jaipur, and Bombay via Udaipur or Ahmedabad. Vayudoot has an occasional flight to and from Jaisalmer. **Indian Airlines** City Office is at Ratnada Road, West Patel Nagar (near Ajit Bhawan Hotel), Tel: 28600, 25867; Airport Tel: 30617. Write to **Vayudoot**, c/o Mayur Travels, Kalyan Singh Building, Sojati Gate, Tel: 20909. The airport is 3 miles (5 km) from the Tourist Office and a taxi costs approximatly Rs. 35.

By Rail: There is a "superfast" express from Delhi every night. There are direct trains from Jaipur, Ajmer, Barmer, Ahmedabad via Abu Road, Lucknow, Bikaner and Jaisalmer. For railway station enquiries, Tel:

32535; for reservations, Tel: 20842.

By Road: There are regular bus services between Jodhpur and Jaipur (215 miles/343 km), Ajmer (128 miles/205 km), Udaipur (190 miles/305 km), Kota (226 miles/362 km) and Ranakpur (109 miles/175 km). The bus station (Tel: 22986) is near the Raikabagh Railway Station.

GETTING AROUND

There are unmetered taxis, auto-rickshaws and *tongas*. There are buses to Mandore (6 miles/9 km), Mahamandir and Balsamand Lake.

ACCOMMODATIONS

Ajit Bhawan
Near Circuit House, Jodhpur 342006
Tel: 20409.

Ghoomer Tourist Bungalow (RTDC)
High Court Road
Tel: 21900.

Hotel Karni Bhawan
Defence Laboratory Road, Ratanada, Jodhpur 342006
Tel: 20517, 22220.

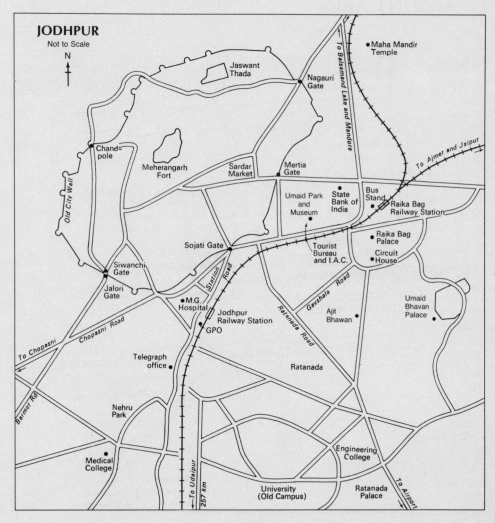

295

Hotel Ratanada International
Residency Road, Jodhpur 342001
Tel: 31910/4; Tlx: 0552-233.

Royal Castle Hotel
Khimsar (62 miles/100 km north of
Jodhpur)
Tel: 28.
Book through Umaid Bhawan or any Wel-
comGroup Hotel.

Umaid Bhawan Palace
Jodhpur 342006
Tel: 22316, 22366, 22516; Tlx: 0552-202
UBP IN.

Can be booked through any Welcomgroup
Hotel or reservation office.

MUSEUMS & THEATERS

Government Museum
Umaid Public Garden
Hours: 10 a.m.-4.30 p.m.; closed on Fridays.

Mehrangarh Fort Museum
Hours: 8 a.m.-1 p.m. (Summer); 9 a.m.-5
p.m. (Winter).

Rajasthan Sanget Natak Akademi
B-Road, Padta Area

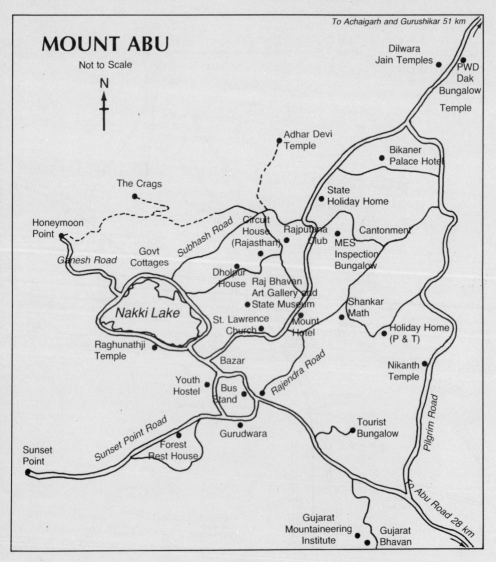

MOUNT ABU

Not to Scale

N

To Achaigarh and Gurushikar 51 km

Dilwara
Jain Temples

PWD
Dak
Bungalow
Temple

Adhar Devi
Temple

Bikaner
Palace Hotel

The Crags

State
Holiday Home

Honeymoon
Point

Subhash Road

Circuit
House
(Rajasthan)

Rajputana
Club

Cantonment

MES
Inspection
Bungalow

Govt
Cottages

Ganesh Road

Dholpur
House

Raj Bhavan
Art Gallery and
State Museum

Shankar
Math

Nakki Lake

St. Lawrence
Church

Mount
Hotel

Holiday Home
(P & T)

Raghunathji
Temple

Bazar

Rajendra Road

Nikanth
Temple

Youth
Hostel

Bus
Stand

Pilgrim Road

Sunset Point Road

Gurudwara

Tourist
Bungalow

Sunset
Point

Forest
Rest House

To Abu Road 28 km

Gujarat
Mountaineering
Institute

Gujarat
Bhavan

Hours: 10 a.m.-5 p.m.; closed on Sundays. An academy with regular performances of traditional music and dance.

Umaid Bhawan Palace Museum
Hours: 9 a.m.-5 p.m.

City GUIDE
MOUNT ABU & ENVIRONS

The only hill resort in Rajasthan, Mount Abu is located at the highest point between the Himalayas and the Nilgiri Hills of South India. Guru Shikhar (10 miles/15 km) from Mount Abu is 5,596 feet (1,722 meters) high. Though rarely visited by overseas tourists, Mount Abu is popular with domestic tourists, especially those from Gujarat and the south.

March-June and September-November are popular months. Morning and afternoon tours are operated by the RTDC (5 hours) and can be booked at the Tourist Office, near the bus station (Tel: 51).

The 11th-13th century Dilwara Jain Temples are open from noon-6 p.m. for non-Jains. There is a camera fee. No leather articles (shoes, belts, bags, camera cases etc.) are allowed in the temple complex.

GETTING THERE

By Air: The nearest airport is at Udaipur (116 miles/185 km).

By Rail: The railway station is at Abu Road, 17 miles (27 km) away. Trains between Ahmedabad (117 miles/187 km) and Delhi via Jaipur and Ajmer stop at Abu Road. Regular buses connect Mount Abu with Abu Road.

By Road: There are regular buses linking Mount Abu with Ahmedabad and Udaipur (116 miles/185 km).

GETTING AROUND

Unmetered taxis, *tongas* and auto-rickshaws are available. Most routes in and around Mount Abu follow fixed fares. There are regular buses to and from both Dilwara and Achalgarh (7 miles/11 km). Guides are available from the Tourist Information Bureau, opposite the Bus Stand (Tel: 51).

ACCOMMODATIONS

There are numerous hotels of various standards in Mount Abu. Among the better ones are:

Abu International
Opp. Polo Ground, Mount Abu 307501
Tel: 177.

Hotel Hilltone
P.O. Box 18, Mount Abu 307501
Tel: 137, 237.

Mount Hotel
Dilwara Road, Mount Abu 307501
Tel: 55.

Palace Hotel
Bikaner House, Dilwara Road, Mount Abu 307501
Tel: 21, 33.

Shikkar Tourist Bungalow (RTDC)
Opp. Polo Ground
Tel: 29, 69.

MUSEUM & ART GALLERY

Museum and Art Gallery
Opp. Post Office, Raj Bhawan Road.
Hours: 8.30-10.30 a.m., 3.30-6 p.m. (Summer); 10 a.m.-5 p.m. (Winter); closed on Fridays and government holidays.

City GUIDE
UDAIPUR & ENVIRONS

Set in a green valley surrounded by the undulating Aravallis, Udaipur is a welcoming, romantic and still largely unspoilt city. The area of Mewar extends to the borders of Gujarat to the south and north to include the ancient fort of Kumbhalgarh and temple complex at Ranakpur.

Tourist Information: The Tourist Office is at the Kajri Tourist Hotel, Shastri Circle, Tel: 23605.

GETTING THERE

By Air: There are daily flights linking Udaipur with Delhi via Jodhpur and Jaipur, and with Bombay direct and via Aurangabad. Dabok Airport is 15 miles (25 km) from the city. Occasionally, there is a connecting bus, otherwise cars are available. The charges are Rs. 80 at the time of press but the rate should be confirmed before embarking. **Indian Airlines** is at LIC Building, Delhi Gate, Tel: 24433; Airport Tel: 23011; Tlx: 033-239.

By Rail: The Chetak Express between Delhi and Udaipur via Jaipur and Ajmer operates daily. There is a daily express to and from Ahmedabad. Railway enquiries and reservations (Tel: 23535) are open 8.30 a.m.-12.30 p.m. and 2.30-4.30 p.m.

By Road: There are numerous daily buses linking Udaipur with Ahmedabad (157 miles/251 km), Mount Abu (115 miles/185 km), Jodhpur (190 miles/305 km), Ajmer (172 miles/374 km), Kota via Bundi (171 miles/274 km) and Jaipur (239 miles/374 km). There are hourly buses to and from Chittorgarh (70 miles/112 km). There are also buses linking Udaipur with Delhi and Bombay. The State Transport Bus Stand is at City Station Road, Udiyapol, Tel: 27191.

GETTING AROUND

There are unmetered taxis and auto-rickshaws. At the time of press, the taxi rate was Rs. 1.75 to Rs. 2 per kilometer for trips outside the town and Rs. 35 per hour for trips within the city. It is always advisable to confirm the rate **before** starting your journey. Bicycles can be hired near the Tourist Bungalow for a few rupees per day.

There are regular bus services to nearby places of interest such as Eklingi (14 miles/ 22 km) where you can **occasionally** hire bicycles; Nathdwara (30 miles/48 km); Kumbalgarh (52 miles/84 km); and Ranakpur (61 miles/98 km). There are also buses to towns in the south, including Dungarpur (60 miles/95 km), Banswara (120 miles/192 km) and Pratapgarh. Dungapur is also on the Udaipur-Ahmedabad railway line. A sightseeing coach leaves the Kajri Tourist Bungalow each morning and, taking only 4 hours, is a convenient and inexpensive way of seeing the major attractions.

Cars can be hired from **Rajasthan Tours**, Garden Hotel (Tel: 230300, 2577; Tlx: 033-209 RAJT IN) and other travel agents.

ACCOMMODATIONS

Udaipur has some of the most splendid hotels in India. The Lake Palace is an image of romance and luxury now known around the world.

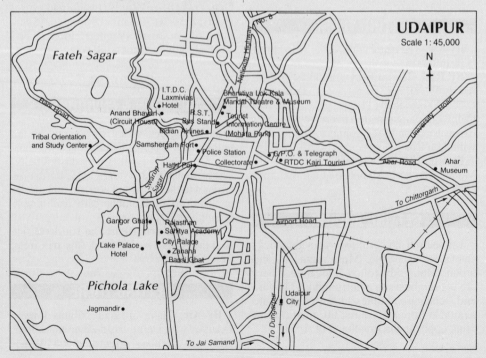

Anand Bhawan Circuit House
Fatehsagar Road, Udaipur
Tel: 23256/7.

Kajri Tourist Bungalow
Shastri Circle, Udaipur
Tel: 23509, 25122.

The Lake Palace Hotel
Pichola Lake, Udaipur 313001
Tel: (0294) 23241/5; Tlx: 033-203 L PAL
IN
Can be booked through any Taj Hotel in
India or through Utell International Sales
and Reservations offices worldwide.

Laxmi Vilas Palace Hotel
Fateh Sagar Road, Udaipur
Tel: 24411/2/3.

Shikarbadi Hotel
(a mile or two south on the Ahmedabad
Road) Govardhan Vilas, off NH 8, Udaipur
Tel: 83201/5; Tlx: 033-227.

Shiv Niwas Palace
Udaipur 313001
Tel: 28239/41; Tlx: 033-226
The magnificent guest apartments of the
City Palace have now been converted into
India's most exclusive hotel with prices to
match.

Outside Udaipur

Ghanerao Royal Castle
(11 miles/18 km northeast of Ranakpur)
P.O. Ghanerao, Dist. Pali
Tel: 35.

Gokul Tourist Bungalow (RTDC)
Lal Bagh, Nathdwara
Tel: 85.

Haldighati Rest House (RTDC)
Haldighati.

Maharani Bagh Orchard Retreat
(2½ miles/4 km north of Ranakpur)
Tel: Sadri (Via Falna) 51, 55
Set amidst a 19th-century mango orchard,
midway between Udaipur and Jodhpur. Has
a swimming pool. Book through Umaid
Bhawan Palace, Jodhpur (Tel: 20941).

Midway (RTDC)
Ratnapur, Udaipur-Ahmedabad Highway.

Shipli Tourist Bungalow (RTDC)
Ranakpur, Dist. Pali 306709.

Tourist Bungalow (RTDC)
(30 miles/48 km south of Udaipur) Jaisa-
mand, Udaipur-Banaswara Road.

Udai Bilas Palace
Dungarpur.

MUSEUMS

Archaeological Museum
Ahar, Udaipur
Hours: 10 a.m.-5 p.m.
A small collection of material from the Ahar
mound and sculpture from the nearby vil-
lage. The maharanas' *chhatris* are here.

Bhartiya Lok Kala Mandal
Near City Palace, on Pichola Lake
Hours: 9 a.m.-6 p.m.
A new museum of Rajasthan folk arts, cos-
tumes, masks, instruments and local crafts.
Has regular puppet shows.

City Palace Museum
Enter via the Ganesh Deori to the Royal
Courtyard (Rai Angan)
Hours: 9.30 a.m.-4.30 p.m.
A fine collection of miniatures, royal arti-
facts and stuffed Siamese twin deer.

Government Museum
Victoria Hall, Udaipur 313001
Hours: 10 a.m.-5 p.m.; closed on Fridays.

City GUIDE

CHITTORGARH

To many people, the fort at Chittor sym-
bolizes the Rajput heroism of history and
legend. The fort covers about 700 acres and,
despite periodic sackings, many buildings,
palaces, and temples remain standing within
it. The Rajasthan Tourism Development
Corporation (RTDC) operates half-day
tours every morning (8 a.m.-1 p.m.) and
afternoon (2.30-5.30 p.m.). These can be
booked at the Panna Tourist Bungalow (Tel:
273).

GETTING THERE

By Air: The nearest airport is at Udaipur (61 miles/112 km) to the west.

By Rail: Chittor is on the line from Delhi via Ajmer to Ratlam in Madhya Pradesh. There is a branch line to Udaipur and through to Ahmedabad. The railway station is 4 miles (6 km) from the fort.

By Road: Regular bus services connect Chittor with Ajmer, Bundi, Kota, Udaipur and Jaipur.

GETTING AROUND

Tongas and unmetered auto-rickshaws are available. Bicycles can also be hired.

ACCOMMODATIONS

Janta Avas Grah (RTDC)
(budget accommodation) Near Railway Station, Chittorgarh
Tel: 2009.
The Tourist Office is here.

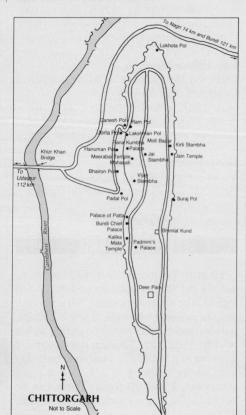

CHITTORGARH
Not to Scale

Panna Tourist Bungalow (RTDC)
Udaipur road, Chittorgarh
Tel: 273.

MUSEUMS

Government Museum
Fateh Prakash Palace, Chittorgarh
Tel: 14
The Archaeological Survey of India Office at the museum has approved guides and sells ASI publications.

City GUIDE

KOTA, BUNDI & ENVIRONS

The area of Haroti is comparatively unknown and presents a range of fascinating towns, majestic forts, ruined temples and areas of scrub jungle still to be explored. Kota is today an industrial town with chemical and engineering factories. The nearby Rajasthan Atomic Power Station contracts with Kota's traditional *doria* saris.

GETTING THERE

By Air: Vayudoot operates a thrice weekly service from Delhi via Jaipur.

By Rail: Kota is on the main broad-gauge line between Delhi and Bombay via Bharatpur and Sawai Madhopur. The meter-gauge line from Jaipur to Sawai Madhopur connects with trains to Kota. There are also services to/from Kota from/to Agra, Lucknow and Ahmedabad.

By Road: Regular bus services connect Kota with Delhi, Agra, Gwalior and all major towns in Rajasthan. Bundi is connected by road to Kota (32 miles/36 km) and Ajmer (100 miles/163 km). There are also buses to/from Jaipur, Chittorgarh and Udaipur.

GETTING AROUND

In the towns there are rickshaws, auto-rickshaws, "tempos" and unmetered taxis. In Bundi, the best way to explore is on foot. *Tongas* are available.

Brijraj Bhawan Palace Hotel
Civil Lines, Kota
Tel: 23071.

The Chambal Tourist Bungalow (RTDC)
Nayapura, Kota
Tel: 26527.

Circuit House
Bundi
Tel: 19, 6.

Dak Bungalow
Jhalawar, 40 miles southeast of Kota.

Navrang Hotel
Civil Lines
Tel: 23294, 26862/3.

Payal Hotel
Nayapura
Tel: 25401.

MUSEUMS

The Government Museum
Kota 324006
Hours: 10 a.m.-5 p.m.; closed on Fridays and gazetted holidays.
Good collection of manuscripts, coins and sculpture from Baroli, 25 miles to the west.

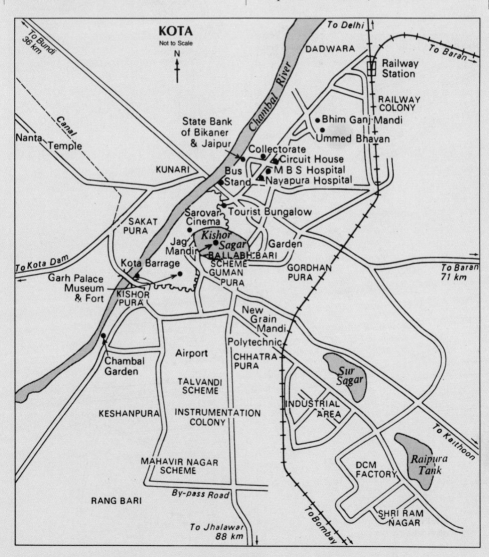

The Government Museum

Jhalawar

Hours: 10 a.m.-5 p.m.; closed on gazetted holidays.

Founded in 1915 by a previous maharaja, the museum has some interesting sculptures, paintings and costumes.

The Maharaja Madho Singh Museum

Kota Palace

Hours: 10 a.m.-5 p.m.; closed on Fridays and government holidays.

Extensive collection of miniature paintings of the Kotah School.

BHARATPUR & ENVIRONS

The Keoladeo National Park 4 miles (7 km) from Bharatpur is certainly the focal point in the area, but the forts and palaces at Deeg and Bharatpur are also well worth visiting.

GETTING THERE

By Air: The nearest airport is at Agra, 34 miles (54 km) from Bharatpur and 35 miles

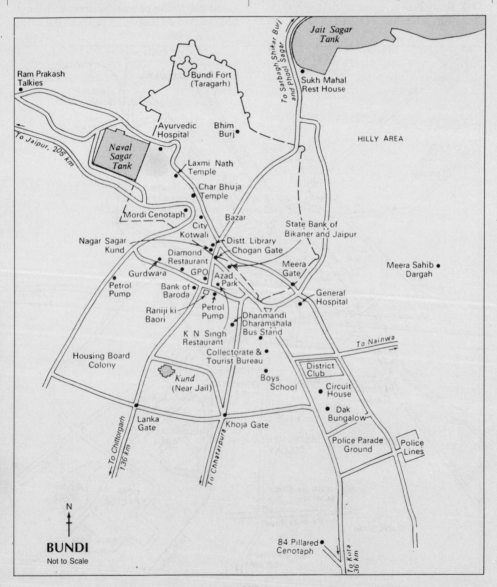

BUNDI
Not to Scale

(57 km) from Dholpur. Agra has daily flights from Delhi, Jaipur, Bombay, Varanasi (via Khajuraho) and Lucknow.

By Rail: Bharatpur is on the main Delhi to Bombay line with regular connections to Mathura, Sawai Madhopur and Kota on the same line. A meter-gauge line from Agra to Jaipur also runs through Bharatpur. Dholpur is on the main line between Agra and Delhi to the north, and Gwalior and Jhansai to the south.

By Road: National Highway No. 11 runs between Jaipur and Agra and buses run through Bharatpur. Many deluxe buses stop at the ITDC Forest Lodge in the bird sanctuary. There are regular buses from Delhi and Mathura. Dholpur is on a National Highway, with regular buses from/to Agra (36 miles/57 km) and Gwalior (40 miles/64 km). There are buses from Bharatpur to Deeg and on to Alwar (72 miles/116 km).

GETTING AROUND

Cycle rickshaws are available in the town and within the national park. Bicycles can also be hired.

ACCOMMODATIONS

Circuit House
Agra Road (near bus station), Bharatpur
Tel: 2366.

Golbagh Palace Hotel
Agra Road, Bharatpur
Tel: 3349.

ITDC Forest Lodge
Keoladeo National Park, Bharatpur
Tel: 2322, 2260, 2864
Situated inside the bird sanctuary. Both air-conditioned and non air-conditioned rooms are available, plus bar and restaurant. Naturalists available. Book through any ITDC Hotel or travel agent.

Jagan Bhawan
Dholpur.

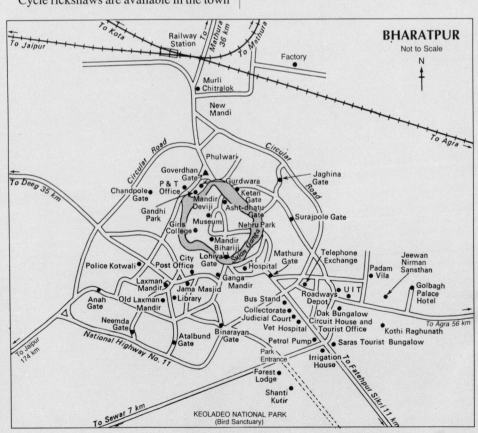

BHARATPUR
Not to Scale

KEOLADEO NATIONAL PARK
(Bird Sanctuary)

303

Midway Restaurant
Mahuwa (midway between Agra and
Jaipur), Dist. Sawai Madhopur
Tel: 60.

PWD Dak Bungalow
Deeg
Tel: 18.

Saras Tourist Bungalow (RTDC)
Fatehpur Sikri Road, Bharatpur 321001
Tel: 2169.

Government Museum
Fort, Bharatpur
Hours: 10 a.m.-5 p.m.; closed on Fridays and
government holidays.
Excellent sculpture from nearby excava-
tions. Usual collection of arms and armor.

The Palace
Deeg
This museum is administered by the Archaeological Survey of India and is open
everyday from 8 a.m.-noon and 1-7 p.m.

CREDITS

119R, 178	**Ping Amranand**
59L&R, 61L&R, 66, 72, 169	**Vivek Anand**
185	**David Beatty/APA**
48, 84, 109, 110, 126L	**Bodo Bondzio**
214/215, 216	**Bodo Bondzio/APA**
206/207, 208	**Vivian Bose**
38	**Marcus Brooke**
49	**A. Cassio**
190, 221R	**A. Cassio/APA**
108	**From the Collection of Toby Sinclair**
116	**K. Debnicki**
70, 86, 182R, 192, 205	**Gen. R. K. Gaur**
195	**Joanna Van Gruisen**
18/19, 20/21, 87, 96/97, 104/105, 113, *114, 127, 162/163, 164, 167, 176/177,* *188/189, 194, 197, 199, 203*	**Hans Höfer**
40, 106, 161	**Luca Invernizzi**
111, 121	**Thomas Kelly**
14/15, 16/17, 25, 52/53, 62, 117, 182L, *209, 219, 223, 226, 230, 232, 254*	**Wilhelm Klein**
233	**Jean Kuglar**
56, 57	**Lyle Lawson**
225, 260/261	**Lyle Lawson/APA**
124	**D. Messent**
224	**D. Messent/APA**
184, 193	**Francesco Milaneso**
115, 175	**Pramod Mistry**
22, 28/29, 80, 82, 125, 129, 138, 147, *150, 152/153, 155, 156, 158, 172, 224*	**Aman Nath**
102, 118, 119L, 122, 160, 168, 198, *211, 212/213, 220, 221L, 222, 228*	**Kim Naylor**
46, 65, 74, 245, 251	**Avinash Pasricha**
3, 30, 32L&R, 35, 36, 37, 41, 42, 43, *47, 50, 54/55, 64, 67, 68/69, 73L&R,* *76, 77, 100/101, 112, 120, 130/131,* *132, 135, 137, 139, 140, 149, 154,* *170, 171, 173, 200, 201, 204, 210,* *229, 231, 235, 238, 240, 241, 242/243,* *248, 249, 252, 253, 256, 257L&R,* *258, 262, 264, 266, 267, 270, 271, 272*	**Aditya Patankar**
44/45, 142/143, 181	**Günter Pfannmuller**
159, 187	**Kailash Sankhala**
58L&R, 60L&R, 78/79, 98/99, 144, *148, 151*	**Shalini Saran**
88/89, 90, 92L&R, 93, 94, 95	**Geeti Sen**
63	**M. D. Sharma**
26/27, 126R, 128, 141, 202, 227, *236/237, 259, 268*	**Toby Sinclair**
13	**Tony Stone**

INDEX

H

I

J

Prithviraj, 145, 167
Priyatama Villas, in Udaipur, 219
Public Park, in Bikaner, 172
Public Works Department, in Jaipur, 117
Pubuji, (warrior), 202
puppeteers, in Jodhpur, 192
Purana Mahal, in Deeg, 267
purple herons, 268
Pushkar, 25, 148-149
Pushkar Fair, 149
Pushpavati, (Queen of Vallabhi), 217

Q – R

quails, 187
quartzites, 24
Queen Victoria, 41
Radha Kund, 269
raga, (coloring), 93
Ragamala paintings, 92, 93, 198
Raghunathgarh, in Shekhavati, 159
Ragini Ahiri, (painting), 93
Ragini Bhairavi, (painting), 92
Ragini Todi (painting), 93
Raikabagh Palace, in Jodhpur, 200
Raikas, (camel-drovers), 186
rainfall, 245
Rainmal, (Rao Chanda's son), 191
Raj Angan, (Royal Courtyard), in Udaipur, 218
Raj Mahal, 121, 247, 248
Raja Jai Singh, 34
Raja Satwant Singh, 150
Rajasthan,
  creation of a state, 47-48
  Indira Gandhi Nahar, 51
  influence of the Jaghirdans, 48
  present day, 50
  industrial development, 51
  princely influence, 48
  since 1949, 47-51
Rajasthan Academy of Music, in Jodhpur, 192
Rajasthan Canal project, *see* Indira Gandhi Nahar
Rajasthanis, 57-66
  conservationists, 66
  farmers, 65-66
  Muslims, 62-63
  pastoral people, 64-65
  population, 57-59
  priest and scholars, 61-62
  scheduled castes, 64-65
  scheduled tribes, 63-64
  warrior-caste, 59-61
Rajasthan school of painting, 43
Rajasthan State Archives, in Bikaner, 171
Rajasthan Union, (1948), 47
Rajgarh, (fort), in Alwar, 136
Rajputs, *(rajputras)*, in early history, 31-35, 38, 39, 58-64
Rajput Hinduism, 61
Rajput painting, 92
Rajput states, history of, 33-34, 35
Rama, (hero of Aryan epic), 71
Ramantras, (instrument for reading altitudes and azimuths), 111-112
Ramayana, (epic), 71, 91
Ram Bagh, (Garden of Ram), in Jaipur, 119-120
Rambagh Palace, in Jaipur, 119

Rambagh Palace Hotel, in Jaipur, 49
Ramdeo Baba, 74
Ramdeoji, 61
Ramdeoji Fair, 204
Ramdevra Fair, 186
Ramgarh, 127, 160, 253
Ram Niwas Public Gardens, in Jaipur, 117
Ram Pol, 240
Ram Sagar Sanctuary, 271
Ram Singh, (Maharaja), *see* Maharaja Ram Singh
Rana Kumbha, 36, 211, 240
Rana Pratap Singh, 34-35, 36, 37, 38, 218-219
  statue of, 225
Ranakpur, 232
Rana Sanga, 36, 37, 194
Rang Bhawan, in Udaipur, 220
Rangwalon-ki-Gali, in Jaipur, 116-117
Rani-ki-Baodi, (Rajput architecture), 255
Rani Sati Temple, in Shekhavati, 160
Rann of Kutch, 25
Ranthambhore, 122, 128, 258, 259
Ranthambhore fort, in Sawai Madhopur, 122, 128, 259
Ranthambhore National Park, 259
Rao, Chandra, 191
Rao Jodha, 191, 193
Rao Jodhaji's Falsa, in Jodhpur, 194
Rao Kandhal, 165
Rao Madho Singh Museum Trust, 247
Rao Madho Singh, 245, 247
Rao Maldeo, 191, 194
raptors, 268
Ras-Leela, 263
Rashivilayas, (instrument for calculating latitudes), 112
Rasikapriya, (song), 93
Ratan Bihari Temple, in Bikaner, 168
Rathi, 25
Rathors, 60, 165, 191
rats, 187
Rattan Daulat, (public audience chamber), 254
Rattan Mahal, 255
Rattan Singh, 239
Ravana Devra, 134-135
Ravindra Rangmanch, in Jaipur, 117
Rawal Lunakaran, 180
Rawals, 179
Rawal, Bappa, *see* Bappa Rawal
Rawat Bhatta Dam, 250
rebellion of 1857, 40-41
religion, 34, 71-75 *see also* individual listings
Residents, 40-41
rhesus macaque, 141
Rig Veda, 72
Rishabdeoji, 233
Rishabdevji Temple, in Jaisalmer, 183
Ritusamhara, (poem), 93
rivers, 24-25, *see also* individual listings
rock, 24, 25, *see also* individual listings
Roe, (Sir) Thomas, 145
Roop Niwas, (structure), in Shekhavati, 158
Royal Cenotaphs, 186
rulers, *see* individual listing
Rupbas, 266

S

Z